I0464740

CYBARIS®
AN INTELLECTUAL PROPERTY
LAW REVIEW

Volume 7   2015   Issue 1

2015

Cybaris®, an Intellectual Property Law Review, is published two times per year by the students of the Intellectual Property Institute of Mitchell Hamline School of Law at 875 Summit Avenue, Saint Paul, Minnesota, 55105.   Telephone: 651-290-6425.   E-mail: eic.cybaris@mitchellhamline.edu

---

Manuscripts: Cybaris®, an Intellectual Property Law Review, welcomes unsolicited manuscripts. All manuscripts submitted for consideration should be double spaced, with citations placed in footnotes that conform to THE BLUEBOOK: A UNIFORM SYSTEM OF CITATION (20th ed. 2015). Please forward all submissions to the Cybaris® Editorial Office at the address listed above.

Opinions expressed in Cybaris®, an Intellectual Property Law Review, do not necessarily represent the views of the publication, its editors, the Mitchell Hamline School of Law, or any person connected therewith.

CYBARIS®
AN INTELLECTUAL PROPERTY
LAW REVIEW

Volume 7   2015   Issue 1

Articles

THE USPTO PATENT PRO BONO PROGRAM

Jennifer M. McDowell & Saurabh Vishnubhakat†

† Jennifer M. McDowell is the Pro Bono Coordinator of the United States Patent and Trademark Office. She was previously an Associate Counsel in the USPTO's Office of General Counsel. Saurabh Vishnubhakat is an Expert Advisor in the USPTO's Office of Chief Economist. Sincere thanks to Grant Corboy and Jeffrey Siew for their tireless efforts in support of the Patent Pro Bono Program, to Janet Gongola for helpful comments, and to Alan Marco and Charles DeGrazia for valuable data assistance.

I.   INTRODUCTION

Pro bono service is an important contribution of the legal profession to civil society. Not only does it promote greater access to justice in the traditional sense of legal representation,[1] but it also increasingly reflects an investment in the social capital of communities who lack adequate economic resources—though this investment is often difficult to quantify.[2] Put another way, pro bono service is important to those who have had their rights violated and cannot afford their own lawyers. Yet pro bono can be an invaluable benefit to anyone who is developing an invention or launching a startup and cannot afford his or her own lawyer. This prospective vision of pro bono as social investment is more ambitious. It is a vision particularly well suited for the U.S. innovation system, which reflects a similar balance of future investment with present benefit.

It is now somewhat rote in innovation economics and law that property rights, such as patents, are a temporary way to constrain competition and tolerate higher prices today as a way of rewarding innovators who create and disseminate valuable knowledge that will be freely available to society tomorrow.[3] Patent rights are particularly important to entrepreneurs and startups, as raising venture capital and securing a competitive advantage against established incumbents is

---

[1] *See* Deborah L. Rhode, *Cultures of Commitment: Pro Bono for Lawyers and Law Students*, 67 FORDHAM L. REV. 2415, 2418 (1999) (identifying the fundamental quality of legal representation as a widely needed, and scarce, resource in the pro bono context).
[2] *See, e.g.,* Scott L. Cummings & Rebecca L. Sandefur, *Beyond the Numbers: What We Know—And Should Know—About American Pro Bono*, 7 HARV. L. & POL'Y REV. 83, 107 (2013) (characterizing pro bono as a "social investment"). *See generally* Deborah L. Rhode, Symposium, *Rethinking the Public in Lawyers' Public Service: Pro Bono, Strategic Philanthropy, and the Bottom Line*, 77 FORDHAM L. REV. 1435, 1451 (2009).
[3] *See generally* David J. Kappos, *Investing in America's Future Through Innovation: How the Debate over the Smart Phone Patent Wars (Re)Raises Issues at the Foundation of Long-Term Incentive Systems*, 16 STAN. TECH. L. REV. 485 (2013). Former USPTO Director Kappos framed the question this way:

> [A]s regards our national innovation system, do we want today's innovations now on the cheap, or are we prepared to moderate what we take today with in-vestment [sic] so that we and our children will have even more, and better, innovations to enjoy 5, 10, and 20 years from now?

Id. at 487.

difficult and complex.[4] In these unforgiving economic conditions, patents can be a valuable quality signal to attract both funding and talent.[5] But by the same token, innovators often are constrained by a lack of resources to pay for patent counsel necessary to protect the full scope of their invention.[6]

To help fill that need, the United States Patent and Trademark Office (USPTO) has systematically been engaging the legal community with inventor assistance beyond the agency's usual business of examining applications for patents and trademarks. This Article describes the brief history, flexible structure, and ongoing growth of that effort, embodied in the USPTO Patent Pro Bono Program.

The Patent Pro Bono Program is a national network coordinated by the USPTO to connect inventors and small businesses with registered patent attorneys and agents to assist in the filing and prosecution of patent applications for free. At the regional level, a broad array of non-profit organizations, bar associations, community economic development organizations, and institutions of higher education support

---

[4] *See generally* Stuart J.H. Graham et al., *High Technology Entrepreneurs and the Patent System: Results of the 2008 Berkeley Patent Survey*, 24 BERKELEY TECH. L.J. 1255, 1288–90 (2009).

[5] *Id.* at 1303–04. *See generally* David H. Hsu & Rosemarie H. Ziedonis, Paper presented at the DRUID Summer Conference in Copenhagen, CBS, Denmark: *Patents as Quality Signals for Entrepreneurial Ventures* (2007), *available at* http://www2.druid.dk/conferences/viewpaper.php?id=1717&cf=9.

[6] *See* Ted Sichelman & Stuart J.H. Graham, *Patenting By Entrepreneurs: An Empirical Study*, 17 MICH. TELECOMM. & TECH. L. REV. 111, 115 (2010) (finding that "young technology companies are especially sensitive to the costs of acquiring and enforcing patents, which . . . are roughly double the reported average for all patentees."); *see also* USPTO, INTERNATIONAL PATENT PROTECTIONS FOR SMALL BUSINESSES 16–22 (2012), *available at* http://www.uspto.gov/sites/default/files/aia_implementation/20120113-ippr_report.pdf (finding that patenting costs are also substantial in international markets and that patenting expenses occur early in the life of small firms and are difficult to fund).

the USPTO in matching low-income inventors with experienced patent professionals. At the individual level, volunteer patent attorneys and their inventor clients engage in the usual back-and-forth of the USPTO examination process, seeking patent protection as a way to enter or advance in the marketplace. In short, the program is a structural effort to bring independent inventors and startups the same opportunity of investment and economic competition that large and established incumbents enjoy.

The Article proceeds in three parts. Part I explains the origins of the program from a local pilot initiative within Minnesota's patent law community to a national endeavor codified in the landmark Leahy-Smith America Invents Act of 2011 (AIA). Part II describes the contours of the program as it has been adopted and implemented throughout the entire country. Part III offers empirical insights into the Minnesota pilot program, for which initial data is now available. The Article concludes with a discussion of pro bono's benefits and of the program's outlook for the future.

II.   FROM FIRST STEPS IN MINNESOTA TO THE AIA

Prior to 2011, no systematic client-side patent pro bono assistance existed in the United States. Thus, the USPTO's Inventors Assistance Center was, and still is, a valuable source of general information about patent examining policy and procedure.[7] Notably, the Inventors Assistance Center also connects the public with appropriate USPTO personnel, just as the related Patent Ombudsman Program does later during the patent application process.[8] By its nature, however, the USPTO is not permitted to provide legal advice or answer questions about particular inventions or patent applications.[9] That support previously came only from individual lawyers who, on an informal basis, performed prosecution work at reduced rates and sometimes for free.

As a first step to strengthening the support available to financially-needy independent inventors and small businesses, the USPTO, together with the non-profit LegalCORPS,[10] announced a pilot pro

---

[7] *See Inventors Assistance Center (IAC)*, USPTO, http://www.uspto.gov/learning-and-resources/support-centers/inventors-assistance-center-iac (last visited Aug. 10, 2015).
[8] *See id.*
[9] *See id.*
[10] "LegalCORPS provides free assistance in non-litigation business law matters to low-income owners of small businesses, small nonprofit organizations and low-income

bono legal assistance program for Minnesota in June 2011.[11] The Minnesota pilot was the first of its kind in the United States and was, from its creation, intended to serve as a model for more ambitious inventor assistance nationally.[12] With support from the Minneapolis legal and business communities, the program matched qualifying inventors with registered patent attorneys who were prepared to guide them through the patent application process.[13]

In addition to income qualifications, the Minnesota pilot program also had a risk-sharing feature that is common to many kinds of market support systems ranging from corporate governance[14] to legal services:[15] It required a committed investment from the beneficiary inventors themselves. Candidate inventors were required to have completed an online USPTO training program on intellectual property and to have conducted a patent search to explore as an initial matter that their inventions were, indeed, inventive.[16] They also were required to have filed either a provisional or non-provisional patent application,

---

innovators in Minnesota—through the services of volunteer lawyers . . . ." *What is LegalCORPS?*, LEGALCORPS, http://legalcorps.org (last visited Aug. 18, 2015) .

[11] *See* David Kappos, *Director's Forum: A Blog from USPTO's Leadership*, USPTO (June   20,   2011), http://www.uspto.gov/blog/director/entry/new_pilot_program_to_provide.

[12] *See id.*

[13] *See id.*

[14] *E.g.*, Alan O. Sykes, *The Economics Of Vicarious Liability*, 93 YALE L.J. 1231, 1246–47 (1984) (explaining how the vicarious liability doctrine encourages more socially optimal investment in a principal's oversight of its agent through risk-sharing between them).

[15] *E.g.*, Lester Brickman, *Contingent Fees Without Contingencies: Hamlet Without the Prince of Denmark?*, 37 UCLA L. REV. 29, 43 (1989) (framing contingent-fee representation as a means of risk sharing to hedge against exposure to loss in the provision of legal services).

[16] *See* Kappos, *supra* note 11.

and to have paid a modest administrative fee to signal the seriousness of their intent to pursue patent protection further.[17]

At the same time that the USPTO's Minnesota pilot program was being established, Congress was considering a comprehensive patent reform bill that would conclude years of legislative effort.[18] In June 2011, the House Committee on the Judiciary issued a favorable report on H.R. 1249, which provided that the Director of the USPTO would "work with and support intellectual property law associations across the country in the establishment of pro bono programs designed to assist financially under-resourced independent inventors and small businesses."[19] In endorsing a national programmatic expansion of pro bono assistance for patent applicants, the committee report identified "the importance of individuals and small businesses to the patent system and our national culture of innovation" as the motivation of Congress.[20] By September 2011, H.R. 1249 had passed both chambers by large bipartisan margins[21] and was enacted as the America Invents Act (AIA).[22]

Implementing the AIA's pro bono program requirement[23] would require an evaluation of the Minnesota pilot program. Establishing the pilot took over a year, during which time LegalCORPS had determined

---

[17] *See id.*

[18] *See* Patent Lawsuit Reform Act of 2010, H.R. 6352, 111th Cong. (2010); Patent Reform Act of 2009, S. 610, 111th Cong. (2009); Patent Reform Act of 2009, S. 515, 111th Cong. (2009); Patent Reform Act of 2009, H.R. 1260, 111th Cong. (2009); Patent Reform Act of 2008, S. 3600, 110th Cong. (2008); Patent Reform Act of 2007, S. 1145, 110th Cong. (2007); Patent Reform Act of 2007, H.R. 1908, 110th Cong. (2007); Patent Reform Act of 2006, S. 3818, 109th Cong. (2006); Patents Depend on Quality Act of 2006, H.R. 5096, 109th Cong. (2006); U.S. Patent & Trademark Fee Modernization Act of 2005, H.R. 2791, 109th Cong. (2005); Patent Reform Act of 2005, H.R. 2795, 109th Cong. (2005).

[19] H.R. REP. NO. 112-98, at 38 (2011) (reproducing § 29 of the Act, later enacted as § 32).

[20] *Id.* at 56.

[21] First introduced in the Senate as S. 23, the AIA passed the Senate on March 8, 2011, by a vote of 95-5. *Senate Vote 35 – Approves Patent System Overhaul*, N.Y. TIMES http://politics.nytimes.com/congress/votes/112/senate/1/35 (last visited Aug. 18, 2015). The bill passed the House with amendment on June 23, 2011, by a vote of 304-117 as H.R. 1249. *House Vote 491 – H.R.1249: On Passage*, N.Y. TIMES, http://politics.nytimes.com/congress/votes/112/house/1/491 (last visited Aug. 18, 2015). The amended bill passed the Senate on September 8, 2011, by a vote of 89-9 and was signed into law on September 16, 2011. *Senate Vote 129 - Passes Patent Reform Bill*, N.Y. TIMES, http://politics.nytimes.com/congress/votes/112/senate/1/129 (last visited Aug. 18, 2015).

[22] Pub. L. No. 112-29, 125 Stat. 284 (2011).

[23] *Id.* at 340.

what best practices Minnesota would try to model for other programs in the future. Of particular importance were the intake, screening, and referral services by which potential clients would be properly identified and vetted to manage the liability and conflict concerns that law firms routinely confront and that pro bono programs are particularly concerned with resolving.[24] These best practices would later inform the establishment of similar programs around the country,[25] as other programs were already emerging, including efforts in Colorado, northern and southern California, and the DC metropolitan area, with expressions of interest from a dozen others.[26]

To build on this momentum under the AIA's mandate, the USPTO convened a Pro Bono Task Force of practitioners and leaders in the IP community, including members of the American Intellectual Property Law Association, the IP Section of the American Bar Association, and the Federal Circuit Bar Association.[27] By October 2012, the task force

---

[24] The best practices were subsequently compiled and published. *See* Amy M. Salmela and Mark R. Privratsky, *Patent Law Pro Bono: A Best Practices Handbook*, 4 CYBARIS. AN INTELL. PROP. L. REV. 1, 3 (2012), *available at* http://web.wmitchell.edu/cybaris/wp-content/uploads/2012/09/Salmela-Privratsky-Pro-Bono-Best-Practices-Handbook.pdf.

[25] *Id.* at 286.

[26] *See* Salmela & Privratsky, *supra* at 24.

[27] As of August 2012, the Pro Bono Task Force included the following members outside the USPTO:

- James Brookshire, Federal Circuit Bar Association
- Jay Erstling, William Mitchell College of Law
- Candee Goodman, Lindquist & Vennum
- Georgann Grunebach, Fox Group
- Harry Gwinnell, Greenblum & Bernstein
- James Patterson, Patterson Thuente IP
- Mark Privratsky, Lindquist & Vennum
- The Hon. Randall Rader, U.S. Court of Appeals for the Federal Circuit
- Kevin Rhodes, 3M Innovative Properties Company

had begun considering potential governing structures to offer ongoing support and guidance to the regional programs in existence at the time, and to encourage the establishment of additional programs.[28] As a result of these efforts, the task force concluded its work with the establishment of an initial governance body, the Pro Bono Advisory Council in October 2013.[29] The advisory council replaced the earlier task force, and the council's charter was itself limited to two years, when it would have to be renewed or replaced.[30] Notably, under the charter, the USPTO would participate in the pro bono program only indirectly as an advisor and convener rather than directly as a member.[31]

By early 2014, the patent pro bono efforts had substantial support in all three branches of the federal government. Congress had already clearly spoken in the AIA about the need for a national commitment to serving resource-constrained inventors and startups;[32] then-Chief Judge Rader of the Federal Circuit had been an early leader of the task force and had signed the advisory council's first charter at a ceremony in his own judicial chambers;[33] and in February 2014, President Obama issued an executive action to "dedicate educational and practical resources to assist inventors who lack legal representation, appoint a full-time Pro Bono Coordinator, and help expand the existing America Invents Act Pro Bono Program to cover all fifty states."[34] The

---

- Paul Roberts, Foley & Lardner
- Amy Salmela, Patterson Thuente IP
- Warren Tuttle, United Inventors Association
- Laura Zeman-Mullen, Zeman-Mullen & Ford

[28] See generally REPORT OF THE PRO BONO TASK FORCE, LEGAL SERVS. CORP. (Oct. 2012), http://www.lsc.gov/sites/default/files/LSC/lscgov4/PBTF_%20Report_FINAL.pdf

[29] See USPTO Applauds Pro Bono Programs and Newly Formed Advisory Council, USPTO (Nov. 12, 2013), http://www.uspto.gov/news/pr/2013/13-32.jsp.

[30] CHARTER OF THE PRO BONO ADVISORY COUNCIL (on file with the USPTO).

[31] Id.

[32] H.R. REP. NO. 112-98, at 56 (2011) ("The Committee acknowledges the importance of individuals and small businesses to the patent system and our national culture of innovation. Consistent with this sentiment, the Act requires the USPTO Director to support intellectual property law associations across the United States to establish pro bono programs to assist under-resourced independent inventors and businesses.").

[33] See Sections Signs Charter for AIA Pro Bono Advisory Council, ABA, http://www.americanbar.org/publications/section_enews_home/intelprop_eNews_novem ber2013.html (last visited Aug. 18, 2015).

[34] Answering the President's Call to Strengthen Our Patent System and Foster Innovation, THE WHITE HOUSE (Feb. 20, 2014), http://www.whitehouse.gov/the-press-

executive action cited the Pro Bono Advisory Council's leadership in coordinating the program and urged the patent bar to participate.[35]

III.   A NATIONAL PATENT PRO BONO COMMITMENT[36]

For all the support it received and momentum it generated, the patent pro bono program has had a strikingly simple design: independent groups match qualifying clients into a network of patent lawyers willing to volunteer their services. These groups may be bar associations, non-profits, universities, or others. The USPTO, being a federal agency, does not control the pro bono activities of these referral networks, but rather, it provides resources and expertise to help establish them in the first place and help them expand their reach.

In general, most regional programs have three basic requirements for an inventor to qualify for assistance: (1) income below a specified level, (2) some sort of knowledge of the patent system, and (3) an invention (not merely an idea). Each of these concepts is implemented in slightly different ways by various programs across the United States.[37]

A.   First Movers: 2011–2012

1.   Minnesota

Minnesota's Inventor Assistance Program was established by LegalCORPS, a non-profit organization created by the Minnesota State Bar Association that, at the time the Inventor Assistance Program was created, had already proven successful in matching low-income

---

office/2014/02/20/fact-sheet-executive-actions-answering-president-s-call-strengthen-our-p.

[35] *See id.*

[36] This Article does not purport to outline the policies and procedures of every Patent Pro Bono Program, but rather surveys practices across the regional programs. Additional information is available directly from each regional program.

[37] *See infra* Parts III.A–C.

entrepreneurs with attorneys in transactional business matters.[38] As
Minnesota's only statewide business pro bono legal program,
LegalCORPS was best positioned to add patent prosecution to the
existing portfolio of services available to entrepreneurs.[39] The program
opened its doors to Minnesota residents on June 8, 2011.[40]

The program's requirements are straightforward. Inventors must be
at or below an income limit of 300% of the federal poverty guidelines
in order to qualify.[41] The income threshold helps to ensure that pro
bono assistance does not crowd out the work of private attorneys whose
services are, in fact, affordable to their clients.[42] In addition to
individual inventors, the program also accepts small businesses where
each owner's income falls below the 300% threshold.[43] Inventors must
pay a $50 administrative fee when completing an application for the
program.[44] Inventors must already have filed a provisional patent
application prior to acceptance into the program.[45] This requirement
ensures that inventors have a sufficient interest in their invention and
that they are willing to take initial steps to protect their potential
rights.[46] Additionally, applicants must have a strong connection to

---

[38] See *History*, LegalCORPS, http://www.legalcorps.org/about-legalcorps/history (last
visited Aug. 10, 2015) [hereinafter *LegalCORPS History*].

[39] *Id.*

[40] See John Calvert, *Pushing Ahead with Pro Bono Assistance*, Inventorseye,
http://www.uspto.gov/custom-page/inventors-eye-pushing-ahead-pro-bono-assistance
(last visited Aug. 18, 2015).

[41] See Salmela & Privratsky, *supra* note 24, at *18.

[42] See *id.*

[43] See *300% of Federal Poverty Level Guidelines—2015*, LegalCORPS,
http://legalcorps.org/wp-content/uploads/2015/03/2015-200-300-Percent.pdf (last visited
Aug. 18, 2015).

[44] See *Frequently Asked Questions*, LegalCORPS, http://www.legalcorps.org/small-
businesses/frequently-asked-questions (last visited Aug. 10, 2015) [hereinafter *Small
Business FAQ*].

[45] *Id.*

[46] See *Frequently Asked Questions*, LegalCORPS,
http://legalcorps.org/inventors/frequently-asked-questions (Aug. 18, 2015) [hereinafter
Inventors FAQ] ("[A] requirement that an applicant already have an application helps
ensure that the inventor has developed the innovation beyond the 'I've got an idea'
stage—and does not expect an attorney to provide a viable framework for a patentable
(and marketable) invention that the inventor cannot."). If an inventor requesting
assistance has not yet filed a provisional application, LegalCORPS refers her to the
nearby William Mitchell College of Law, where students at a USPTO-certified IP clinic
can draft and file provisional applications for clients, enabling them to participate in the
LegalCORPS program. LegalCORPS, Inventor Assistance Program, MIPLA
(2012), *available at* http://www.mipla.net/ricofiles/pdf/LegalCORPSIAPforMIPLA.pdf.

Minnesota.[47] Lastly, applicants must pass a subject-matter screening as to their inventive ideas in order to be eligible.[48]

Significantly, the Minnesota program provides professional liability insurance for volunteer attorneys taking on a patent matter that LegalCORPS has referred to them.[49] This allows in-house counsel, who may not be covered by a portable malpractice insurance policy, to volunteer in the program. Attorneys who volunteer for the program must have a minimum of three years' experience or, otherwise, must partner with a more senior attorney.[50]

As the oldest of the patent pro bono initiatives, the Minnesota program and its volunteer attorneys have refined the intake process over time to screen applicants, educate inventors, and solicit volunteer lawyers more effectively.[51] The Minnesota program has not only led the way in the establishment of patent pro bono programs across the country, but has also modeled an approach for existing programs to offer services in nearby states. Implicit in its approach is that individual inventors and startups have individual needs that require flexible and adaptive ways to deliver legal services to them. These particularities may include the geographic clustering of certain technology fields, the economic and industrial needs of local pools of engineers and scientists, and even financial concerns such as access to local capital and credit. The result has been a fundamentally regional approach to a broadly national effort.

---

[47] *Id.*

[48] *See* Salmela & Privratsky, *supra* note 24, at *23, *33. The screening committee does not conduct a formal assessment but rather evaluates basic patentability for purposes of further review and engagement with the inventor. *See id.* at *33.

[49] *LegalCORPs History, supra* note 38

[50] *See* William Mitchell Coll. of Law, *4-20-15 Patent Pro Bono Attorney Orientation*, VIMEO (Apr. 20, 2015), http://www.vimeo.com/125519060.

[51] *See generally* Salmela & Privratsky, *supra* note 24.

2. *Colorado*

After Minnesota's initial success, Colorado followed suit with ProBoPat, administered by the Mi Casa Resource Center, a non-profit organization dedicated to advancing family prosperity and entrepreneurial training for low-income residents of Colorado.[52] Mi Casa and the Intellectual Property Section of the Colorado Bar Association established ProBoPat in April 2012, as the state's patent pro bono program.[53]

Like LegalCORPS in Minnesota,[54] ProBoPat has set an income limit of 300% of the federal poverty guidelines.[55] Also, at least initially, ProBoPat limited its program to Colorado residents.[56] Unlike LegalCORPS, however, ProBoPat does not charge candidate inventors an administrative fee nor require the prior filing of a provisional patent application.[57] Moreover, ProBoPat does not accept requests from small businesses or non-profits, only individuals.[58] In the ProBoPat program, inventors who successfully complete the screening process join a list

---

[52] *See Vision & Impact*, MI CASA, http://www.micasaresourcecenter.org/about-us/vision/ (last visited Aug. 10, 2015). Mi Casa was established in the 1970s to help women educate themselves and acquire employment skills, and evolved over the years to help all Latino families have realistic opportunities to pursue professional, educational, and entrepreneurial advancement. *See History*, MI CASA, http://www.micasaresourcecenter.org/about-us/history/ (last visited Aug. 10, 2015).

[53] *See Pro Bono Patent Program*, MI CASA, http://www.micasaresourcecenter.org/business-development/pro-bono-patent-program/ (last visited Aug. 10, 2015); Heather Draper, *Denver Launches Pro Bono Patent Law Initiative for Low-Income Inventors*, DENVER BUS. J. (Apr. 25, 2012), http://www.bizjournals.com/denver/news/2012/04/25/denver-launches-pro-bono-patent.html.

[54] *See supra* Part III.A.1.

[55] *See Pro Bono Patent Program*, MI CASA, http://www.micasaresourcecenter.org/business-development/pro-bono-patent-program/ (last visited Aug. 18, 2015) ("Eligible applicants include individual Colorado residents who have a target annual income of three times the federal poverty guidelines or less . . . .").

[56] Press Release, Senator Michael Bennett, Bennett: Pro Bono Patent Program Will Help Colorado's Entrepreneurs, Inventors (Apr. 25, 2012), http://www.bennet.senate.gov/?p=release&id=1315. The program is now open to residents of Colorado, New Mexico, Utah, and Wyoming. *See ProBoPat Frequently Ask Questions*, MI CASA RESOURCE CENTER (last updated Feb. 3, 2015), http://www.micasaresourcecenter.org/wp-content/uploads/2013/04/ProBoPat-FAQ-Document.pdf.

[57] *See ProBoPat Frequently Ask Questions*, MI CASA RESOURCE CENTER, http://www.ipsectioncolorado.org/content/20130201_ProBoPat_FAQ.pdf (last updated Feb. 1, 2013).

[58] *See id.*

from which any patent lawyer registered with ProBoPat may volunteer to accept a particular client.[59] ProBoPat also provides some clients with "low bono" patent services—services at reduced fees rather than for free.[60]

When ProBoPat began, no patentability search was required at all,[61] but now program attorneys perform a basic search of the invention prior to the inventor's placement on the list of qualified inventors seeking assistance.[62] The decision to proceed, notwithstanding any search results, remains with the inventor rather than ProBoPat.[63]

On the attorney side, ProBoPat accepts volunteer patent attorneys and agents who are registered in good standing to practice before the USPTO and who reside in Colorado.[64] The program also welcomes participation from interested students from local law schools.[65] Volunteer attorneys must provide their own professional liability insurance for work referred through the program.[66]

---

[59] *See The ProBoPat Program*, COLO. B. ASSOC. INTELL. PROP. SEC., http://www.ipsectioncolorado.org/probopat/ (last visited Aug. 18, 2015).

[60] *Id.*

[61] *Compare ProBoPat Frequently Ask Questions*, MI CASA RESOURCE CENTER, http://www.ipsectioncolorado.org/content/20120706_ProBoPat_FAQ.pdf (last updated July 6, 2012) (detailing request of a one-sentence summary of the basic subject matter).

[62] *See The ProBoPat Program, supra* note 59 ("More recently, ProBoPat has implemented a required patent search prior to putting an applicant onto the main referral list."(last visited Aug. 18, 2015).

[63] *Id.*

[64] *Id.* ("[T]he applicant first goes to a volunteer searcher to perform a patent search, after which the representation ends and the *applicant* is to decide whether to proceed through the ProBoPat process to file a patent application.") (emphasis added).

[65] *Id.*

[66] *ProBoPat Colorado Volunteer Interest Form G1*, COLO. B. ASS'N IP SEC., http://www.ipsectioncolorado.org/content/20120712_ProBoPat_Form_G1.pdf (last updated July 12, 2012). The ProBoPat steering committee is currently searching for ways to offer "easy, inexpensive malpractice insurance for volunteers." *See Spotlight on*

3. *California*

The Patent Pro Bono Program reached California in October 2012.[67] Unlike the state-specific programs in Minnesota and Colorado, the California initiative served as a regional hub for residents in nine western states: California, Washington, Oregon, Montana, Idaho, Nevada, Arizona, Alaska, and Hawaii.[68] The program, styled the California Inventors Assistance Program, is administered by the California Lawyers for the Arts, a lawyer referral service certified by the California state bar.[69] Reflecting the patent pro bono initiative more generally, the California Lawyers for the Arts takes as its mission the empowerment of the creative community by education, legal representation, and dispute resolution.[70]

The California program's intake process requires a $125 fee that is refunded to applicants if they do not complete the screening process.[71] The program also sets an income threshold of 300% of the federal poverty guidelines and does not require any patent search or provisional filing in order to be accepted into the program.[72] Small businesses are also accepted into the program provided that each of the owners meets the program's income threshold. The program requires independent inventors to review the USPTO's training video prior to requesting assistance.[73] Rather than a rule-based approach, the California program's financial screening process works to take a holistic view of each applicant's financial situation.[74] To date,

---

Upcoming Events, COLO. B. ASSOC. INTELL. PROP. SEC., http://www.cobar.org/index.cfm/ID/22952/subID/29304/PATENT// (last visited Aug. 18, 2015).

[67] *USPTO Launches New California Inventors Assistance Program*, FENWICK & WEST LLP (Oct. 8, 2012), http://www.fenwick.com/Media/Pages/USPTO-Launches-New-California-Inventors-Assistance-Program.aspx.

[68] *See* Jenny McDowell, Pro Bono Coordinator, USPTO, Remarks at the Patent Public Advisory Committee Quarterly Meeting (Aug. 20, 2015).

[69] *California Inventors Assistance Program*, CAL. LAWS. FOR ARTS, http://www.calawyersforthearts.org/CIAP (last visited Aug. 18, 2015)..

[70] *CLA Home*, CAL. LAWS. FOR ARTS, http://www.calawyersforthearts.org/ (last visited July 26, 2015).

[71] *USPTO Launches New California Inventors Assistance Program*, *supra* note 67.

[72] *Inventors*, USPTO, http://www.uspto.gov/patents-getting-started/using-legal-services/pro-bono/inventors (last modified Jun. 12, 2015, 9:36 AM).

[73] *California Inventors Assistance Program*, *supra* note 69.

[74] Press Release, Fish & Richardson, Fish & Richardson and California Lawyers for the Arts Hosted Protecting Little Guys' Big Ideas: The California Inventors Assistance Program (Mar. 6, 2015), *available at* http://www.fr.com/news/fish-richardson-and-california-lawyers-for-the-arts-hosted-protecting-little-guys-big-ideas-the-california-

California has served the most inventors of all the regional patent pro bono programs due to the large number of states for which it provides coverage, including California itself, from which a disproportionately high share of patent application filings originate.[75] From the program's inception through March 2015, 835 applicants have sought patent pro bono services from the California hub, and 131 applicant-attorney matches have emerged.[76] The total value of patent pro bono services by California's volunteer lawyers is estimated at over $1 million and growing.[77]

A notable feature of the California program is that it provides legal malpractice insurance for its volunteer lawyers, as the professional liability policy of the California Lawyers for the Arts extends to lawyers participating in the patent pro bono program.[78] This is significant because it encourages attorneys from organizations that do not have independent malpractice coverage to volunteer for the program and also broadens the pool of legal talent that is available to the inventor community.

4. Washington, DC

Like California, the Washington, DC-area program opened its doors in 2012.[79] Also like California, the DC program was a regional

---

[75] Document on file with author.

[76] Id.

[77] Id.

[78] BAR ASS'N OF SAN FRANCISCO, PRO BONO RESOURCE GUIDE 14 (2015), *available at* http://www.sfbar.org/forms/barristers/pro-bono-resource-guide.pdf.

[79] *Programs*, USPTO (Sept. 15, 2011, 11:02 AM), http://www.uspto.gov/patent/laws-and-regulations/america-invents-act-aia/programs (last modified Jun. 24, 2015, 7:38 PM); *see also PTO Pro Bono Program*, FED. CIR. B. ASS'N, http://www.fedcirbar.org/olc/pub/LVFC/cpages/misc/pto.jsp (last visited July 26, 2015).

inventors-assistance-program/ ("CLA's financial screening process takes a holistic approach to make sure CLA sees the complete financial picture of each applicant, rather than a simple formulaic approach used by many pro bono services.").

hub from the start, serving residents of the District of Columbia, Maryland, and Virginia.[80] The program has been administered by the Federal Circuit Bar Association (FCBA), and draws from the large group of patent lawyers who are also members of the FCBA.[81]

The DC program requires inventors to have an income below 300% of the federal poverty guidelines, to complete a training video on the USPTO's website, and an invention that is more developed than merely an idea.[82] The program also accepts small businesses subject to certain conditions. First, there must be no more than four inventors.[83] Second, those inventors must not be under an obligation to assign the rights to the invention to another entity.[84] Third, all inventors must have current household incomes below 300% of the federal poverty guidelines.[85] Fourth, the small business as a whole must have a gross income of less than $150,000 in the preceding calendar year and an expected gross income of less than $150,000 in the current calendar year.[86]

Attorneys who wish to volunteer in the DC program must be members of the FCBA.[87] The FCBA may pair an attorney with less than three years of experience with an attorney mentor.[88] Additionally, all volunteer attorneys must carry their own professional liability insurance, as the FCBA does not provide malpractice coverage.[89]

---

[80] *Frequently Asked Questions for Attorneys*, FED. CIR. B. ASS'N, http://www.fedcirbar.org/olc/filelib/LVFC/cpages/9005/Library/FAQ%20for%20Attorne ys.pdf (last visited July 26, 2015).

[81] *Id.* Since 1982, the Federal Circuit has been the exclusive federal appellate forum for patent cases, leading to considerable specialization of its bar in patent and related intellectual property issues. *See* 17 CHARLES ALAN WRIGHT, ET AL., FEDERAL PRACTICE AND PROCEDURE JURISDICTION AND RELATED MATTERS § 4104 (3d ed. 2015).

[82] *See PTO Pro Bono Program, supra* note 79; *Inventors, supra* note 72.

[83] *Frequently Asked Questions for Inventors*, FED. CIR. B. ASS'N, http://www.fedcirbar.org/olc/filelib/LVFC/cpages/9005/Library/FAQ%20for%20Invento rs.pdf (last visited Aug. 18, 2015).

[84] *Id.*

[85] *Id.*

[86] *Id.*

[87] *PTO Pro Bono Regional Volunteer Attorney Information Submission,* FED. CIR. B. ASS'N, https://secure.www.fedcirbar.org/olc/pub/LVFC/event/showEventForm.jsp?form_id=132 084 (last visited Aug. 18, 2015).

[88] *Frequently Asked Questions for Attorneys*, FED. CIR. B. ASS'N, http://www.fedcirbar.org/olc/filelib/LVFC/cpages/9005/Library/FAQ%20for%20Attorne ys.pdf (last visited Aug. 18, 2015).

[89] *Id.*

In addition to operating the DC regional program, the FCBA also administers a national information clearinghouse for the Patent Pro Bono Program.[90] In this capacity, the FCBA has served as a single intake source for regional programs. Thus, an inventor may apply directly to the regional program of the state in which he or she lives (or works, depending upon the relevant program's criteria).[91] Alternatively, an inventor could apply through the clearinghouse, which would pass the request on to the appropriate program.[92] The clearinghouse does not screen applicants other than to verify U.S. citizenship or legal residency status.[93]

In the early days of the national program, the clearinghouse was quite active in pointing inventors to the correct place to obtain help, though initially there was often nowhere to refer an inventor because so few states were covered by a regional pro bono assistance program. Today, as regional programs have arisen across the United States, the clearinghouse is a less prominent, though still important source of referrals as many inventors apply directly to their respective regional programs.

B.   *National Reach: 2013–2014*

1.   *Texas*

Nine months after the inception of the California and DC programs, the Texas regional program came online in July 2013, serving residents of Texas and Louisiana.[94] The program was

---

[90] *PTO Pro Bono Program, supra* note 79.

[91] *Id.*

[92] *Id.*

[93] *Id.*

[94] *Texas AIA-USPTO Pro Bono Patent Assistance Program*, CENTER FOR INNOVATION, http://www.thecenterforinnovation.org/texas-aia-uspto-pro-bono-patent-assistance-

administered by the Arlington County Chamber of Commerce's Texas Center for Innovation (CFI).[95] CFI, in turn, is a non-profit association affiliated with TechComm, a federal technology transfer intermediary.[96] TechComm brought two sets of skills to the newly developed program: (1) commercializing federally funded research through patent license agreements and cooperative research and development agreements between businesses and federal laboratories, and (2) identifying technology from the market that is of interest to federal agencies and laboratories.[97] As a result, the CFI partnership came to the patent pro bono world with considerable expertise in the downstream uses of the patents that inventors would seek through the program. It also marked Texas as the first patent pro bono program associated with a technology transfer office. The program started up with grant funding from the Texas Bar Foundation for advancing invention-based economic development and job creation in Texas.[98]

Although the Texas program did not initially disclose its applicant criteria, it has recently published those criteria on its website.[99] An applicant's earnings are reviewed, using submitted tax records.[100] The Texas program has differing eligibility requirements depending on the type of applicant. Solo inventors must have a total household income of less than 300% of the federal poverty guidelines and must not currently be under an obligation to assign rights to the invention.[101]

Non-profits must have four or fewer inventors who are under an obligation to assign rights to another organization, have 501(c)(3)

---

program (last visited Aug. 18, 2015). The USPTO provides a link to the Texas Pro Bono Patent Assistance Program for those residents of Louisiana. *See Louisiana*, USPTO, http://www.uspto.gov/learning-and-resources/inventors-entrepreneurs/louisiana   (last modified May 29, 2015, 9:24 AM).

[95] *The Center for Innovation Receives Grant from Texas Bar Foundation for Office for Inventor Assistance Pro Bono Program*, CENTER FOR INNOVATION, https://thecenterforinnovation.org/center-innovation-receives-grant-texas-bar-foundation-office-inventor-assistance-pro-bono-program (May 21, 2014).

[96] *Texas AIA-USPTO Pro Bono Patent Assistance Program*, *supra* note 94.

[97] *Id.*

[98] *The Center for Innovation Receives Grant from Texas Bar Foundation for Office for Inventor Assistance Pro Bono Program*, *supra* note 95.

[99] *Texas AIA-USPTO Pro Bono Patent Assistance Program*, *supra* note 94. The newly updated website can be found at: https://thecenterforinnovation.org/texas-aia-uspto-pro-bono-patent-assistance-program

[100] *See Application for Free Legal Assistance*, CENTER FOR INNOVATION, https://thecenterforinnovation.org/uploads/Application_for_Free_Legal_Assistance.pdf (last visited Aug. 18, 2015).

[101] *Texas AIA-USPTO Pro Bono Patent Assistance Program*, *supra* note 94.

status, and have a budget of less than $1 million per year.[102] Additionally, the non-profits must not be a research institution or an institution of higher learning, and must not be under any obligation to assign the rights to the invention to another entity.[103]

Small businesses must have four or fewer inventors who are under an obligation to assign the rights to another organization, where all inventors have a current household income of less than 300% of the federal poverty guidelines, had a total gross income of less than $150,000 in the preceding calendar year, expect a total gross income of less than $150,000 in the current calendar year, and are not currently under an obligation to assign the rights to the invention to another entity.[104]

Importantly, the program may disqualify an applicant whose inventor has been listed on more than four previous USPTO applications or U.S. patents.[105]

The program requires applicants to perform an initial patent search of their respective inventions, as well as to complete a training video on the USPTO's website.[106] The program charges an administrative fee for entry into the program.[107]

2. Ohio

Soon after the Texas program expanded the scope of patent pro bono to include commercialization-oriented technology transfer

---

[102] *Id.*

[103] *Id.*

[104] *Id.*

[105] *Id.*

[106] *See id.*; SHEKAR RAO, AMERICA INVENTS ACT PRO BONO ASSISTANCE PROGRAM: STATE BAR OF TEXAS ADVANCED IP LAW COURSE 13 (2014), *available at* http://www.texasbarcle.com/Materials/Events/12716/161828_01.pdf.

[107] $50 for solo inventors, $100 for non-profits, and $150 for small businesses. *Texas AIA-USPTO Pro Bono Patent Assistance Program, supra* note 94.

partners, a new program in Ohio expanded it to include the law school community. In 2013, the IP Venture Clinic of the Case Western Reserve University School of Law began offering patent pro bono assistance to underserved Ohio inventors.[108] Per the national norm, the Ohio program sets its income threshold at 300% of the federal poverty guidelines.[109] The program also requires applicants to complete a training video on the USPTO's website and charges no fee for participation in the clinic.[110] The program also screens "new ventures" (small businesses) using a revenue, investment, and income basis.[111]

Because it is based in a legal clinic setting, the Ohio program has also added a natural second step to its pro bono operations. Initially, the clinic itself performs administrative functions including all the intake, screening, and referral of applicants.[112] Yet while the IP Venture clinic retains much of the patent prosecution work for itself, it does refer some matters to outside volunteer attorneys for filing and prosecution.[113] Notably, law students have assisted many "new ventures" in pre-engagement counseling to assist the founders in reaching agreements on key issues prior to formally launching a business.

The Case Western clinic model for Ohio also benefits from a related USPTO program that has gained increasing prominence in the

---

[108] *IP Venture Clinic is a 'New Economic Force'*, CASE W. RES. U. SCH. OF L., (Nov. 14, 2014), http://law.case.edu/Home/Trending/tabid/820/vw/1/ItemID/325/Default.aspx.
[109] *IP Venture Clinic*, CASE W. RES. U. SCH. OF L., http://www.law.case.edu/Academics/AcademicCenters/LTA/IPVentureClinic.aspx (last visited Aug. 18, 2015) ("The IPVC works with a limited number of early stage entrepreneurs that do not have the financial resources to cover the cost of obtaining legal counsel."). Ohio applies the standards of the Federal Circuit Bar Association. *See Pro Bono Service Request Form*, FED. CIR. B. ASS'N, https://secure.www.fedcirbar.org/olc/pub/LVFC/event/showEventForm.jsp?form_id=131881 (last visited Aug. 18, 2015).
[110] *IP Venture Clinic*, *supra* note 109; *see also CWRU's new Venture Clinic puts patents in reach of rookie inventors*, PLAIN DEALER (Nov. 14, 2015), http://www.cleveland.com/business/index.ssf/2014/11/cwru_venture_clinic_puts_paten.html .
[111] *See* Email from Case Western Clinic Coordinator, Case Western Law University School of Law, to Jennifer McDowell, Pro Bono Coordinator, USPTO (on file with author).
[112] *FAQ*, CASE W. RES. U. SCH. OF L., http://law.case.edu/Academics/AcademicCenters/LTA/IPVentureClinic/FAQ.aspx (last visited Aug. 18, 2015) [*hereinafter Case Western Clinic FAQ*].
[113] *See IP Venture Clinic*, *supra* note 109 (stating that "students will prepare . . . materials necessary to support investor discussions").

last two years: the Law School Clinic Certification Program.[114] Clinic certification allows law students at participating schools to practice before the USPTO under clinical faculty supervision and to gain direct experience in drafting and filing applications for patents, trademarks, or both.[115] Of the forty-two schools currently participating, six are certified for patent prosecution alone, nineteen are certified for trademark prosecution alone, and seventeen are certified for both.[116]

The Clinic Certification Program's benefits to law students are a strong complement to the Pro Bono Program's benefits to low-income inventors, particularly as it not only offers students IP practice experience, but also cultivates their broader acumen in business counseling and instills a professional commitment to pro bono service. As a result, other law schools have followed Case Western's lead in combining USPTO clinical certification with patent pro bono initiatives, including Indiana[117] as well as the original program in Minnesota.[118]

3. Massachusetts

Also in the fall of 2013, Massachusetts joined the pro bono circuit with a program launched by Volunteer Lawyers for the Arts in partnership with the Boston Patent Lawyers Association.[119] The program was supported locally by the Arts and Business Council of

---

[114] *See Case Western Clinic FAQ, supra* note 112; Law *School Clinic Certification Program,* USPTO, http://www.uspto.gov/learning-and-resources/ip-policy/public-information-about-practitioners/law-school-clinic-1 (last visited Aug. 18, 2015).

[115] *Id.*

[116] *See Id.*

[117] *See infra* Part III.C.2.

[118] *See infra* Part III.D.

[119] *Patent Pro Bono Program of New England,* ARTS & BUS. COUNCIL GREATER BOS., http://www.artsandbusinesscouncil.org/programs/patent-program.html (last visited Aug. 18, 2015).

Greater Boston,[120] a non-profit organization that provides legal and
business services, as well as ongoing educational programs to creative
communities in Massachusetts.[121] The program uses an income
threshold, though it is not publicly disclosed, and applicants must
demonstrate financial eligibility by submitting tax documents or
equivalent financial information.[122] The program charges a $55
application fee, and applicants who complete the screening process are
placed on a list that is sent to volunteer patent attorneys roughly once a
month to initiate a pro bono client relationship.[123] Attorneys and agents
in good standing who are licensed to practice before the USPTO may
volunteer for the program.[124]

4.   Greater Philadelphia

The last pro bono program to come online in 2013 was in Greater
Philadelphia. Created by the Philadelphia Volunteer Lawyers for the
Arts, an initiative of the Arts and Business Council of Greater
Philadelphia, the program began serving residents of eleven counties in
and around Philadelphia and the Delaware Valley.[125] Unlike previous
regional programs, this has served a limited geographic area across
multiple states centered around Philadelphia. The program charges a
nonrefundable $50 administrative fee, though a hardship waiver is
available for applicants earning less than 187.5% of the federal poverty
guidelines or have other extenuating circumstances.[126]

Unlike other programs that utilize the federal poverty guidelines,
the Philadelphia criteria are only based loosely on the 300% level.
Specifically, the program accepts requests for assistance both from
individuals whose gross income is $35,000 or less per year (or $55,000

---

[120] *Pro Bono*, BUS. PAT. L. ASS'N, http://www.bpla.org/?27 (last visited Aug. 18, 2015).
[121]   *About   Us*,   ARTS   &   BUS.   COUNCIL   GREATER   BOS.,
http://www.artsandbusinesscouncil.org/about-us.html (Aug. 18, 2015).
[122] *Patent Pro Bono Program of New England, supra* note 119.
[123] *Id.*
[124] *Id.*
[125] *Arts + Business: The successful Philadelphia story*, PHILA. BUS. J., (May 7, 2015),
http://www.bizjournals.com/philadelphia/blog/guest-comment/2015/05/arts-business-the-
successful-philadelphia-story.html ("[T]he Arts + Business Council has done this [pro
bono] work under the umbrella of the Greater Philadelphia Chamber of Commerce . . .
[which] represents over 600,000 employees in eleven counties of Pennsylvania, New
Jersey, and Delaware that make up the Greater Philadelphia region.").
[126]   *PVLA Application Fee Hardship Policy*, ARTS & BUS. COUNCIL PHILA.,
http://www.artsandbusinessphila.org/pvla/documents/PVLAHardshipPolicyandWaiverF
Y12.pdf (last visited Aug. 18, 2015).

for a married couple or cohabitating couple), with a $3,000 credit per dependent.[127] Groups of individuals are also accepted, provided each member's individual gross income falls below the threshold standard.[128] Nonprofits with an annual operating budget of less than $1 million per year may also apply.[129] Inventors must complete a training video on the USPTO's website.[130] Volunteer patent attorneys in the program are required to take a three-hour course of continuing legal education (CLE) covering best practices for pro bono attorneys.[131]

5. The Carolinas

The Carolinas brought a pro bono program online in May 2014, organized by the North Carolina Bar Association as the North Carolina Lawyers for Entrepreneurs Assistance Program, or NC LEAP.[132] Serving residents of North and South Carolina, the program provides free legal services to low-wealth entrepreneurs, small businesses, and established non-profits that are in the process of starting or expanding their businesses.[133] The NC LEAP program screens clients without charging an administrative fee and requires that volunteer attorneys have at least three years of experience practicing patent law before the

---

[127] *Frequently Asked* Questions, ARTS & BUS. COUNCIL PHILA., http://www.artsandbusinessphila.org/pvla/pvlafaq.asp (last visited Aug. 18, 2015).
[128] *Id.*
[129] *Id.*
[130] *Patent Pro Bono Program*, ARTS & BUS. COUNCIL GREATER PHILA., http://www.artsandbusinessphila.org/pvla/patentprobono.asp (last visited Aug. 18, 2015) [*hereinafter Philadelphia Patent Pro Bono Program*].
[131] *Id.*
[132] *Inventor Assistance Program Expands Into Tennessee*, N.C. BAR. ASS'N, http://www.ncbar.org/news/patent-pro-bono-program-expands-into-tennessee/   (last visited Aug. 18, 2015) ("The Inventor Assistance Program was launched in North Carolina on May 5, 2014.").
[133] *Frequently Asked Questions*, N.C. BAR ASS'N, http://www.ncbar.org/public-resources/nc-leap/faqs/ (last visited Aug. 18, 2015) [*hereinafter N.C. Bar FAQ*]

USPTO.[134] Initially, the program set its income limit at 80% of the state-established poverty guidelines, which varied by the county in which the inventor resided.[135] More recently, however, the program has increased the threshold—to allow more inventors to qualify for assistance—by raising the limit to 300% of the federal poverty guidelines.[136]

A unique aspect of the NC LEAP program is that volunteer attorneys often do not file the patent application for the client. Instead, the client is directly responsible for making all USPTO filings and responses to Office Actions and does so with the attorney's assistance.[137] To encourage wider participation by the state bar, the NC LEAP program also provides professional liability insurance coverage to volunteer lawyers.[138]

6. New York

In 2014, New York created its pro bono assistance program, run by the New York Volunteer Lawyers for the Arts.[139] In line with the predominant approach, the New York program serves primarily "those innovators who believe they have a novel invention but have not yet filed for a patent."[140] Yet on a case-by-case basis, the program also assists patent applicants who have filed a patent application and have received an Office Action.[141] The New York program financially screens applicants by requiring them to provide an affidavit of income and bank statements from their primary checking account for the previous twelve months.[142]

Four types of applicants may request assistance in the NY Pro Bono Patent Program: individuals, for-profit entities and partnerships, non-profit unincorporated entities, and non-profit incorporated

---

[134] N.C. INVENTORS ASSISTANCE PROGRAM GUIDE (on file with the USPTO).
[135] Id.
[136] N.C. Bar FAQ, supra note 133.
[137] N.C. INVENTORS ASSISTANCE PROGRAM GUIDE (on file with USPTO), supra note 134.
[138] Id.
[139] VLA Patent Pro Bono Program, N.Y. VOLUNTEER LAWS. FOR ARTS, http://www.vlany.org/legalservices/patent_program.php (last visited Aug. 18, 2015).
[140] Id.
[141] Id.
[142] VLA Frequent Asked Questions, N.Y. VOLUNTEER LAWS. FOR ARTS, http://www.vlany.org/aboutus/vla_faq.php (Aug. 18, 2015).

entities.[143] The program charges an administrative fee that depends upon the status of the entity filing the request.[144] Applicants who qualify for the program consult with a program staff attorney and are placed on a case list for referral to a volunteer patent attorney.[145] Over 90% of the applicants on the case list are matched with patent counsel.[146]

The New York program accepts volunteer attorneys who have completed a short orientation course on the program, its requirements, and its procedures.[147] Volunteer lawyers must be covered by their own legal malpractice insurance policy or that of their employers.[148] Moreover, attorneys who have been admitted to practice for less than three years must find their own supervising attorney.[149] Interestingly, the New York program is approved to provide CLE credit to attorneys who provide pro bono legal services through the program.[150] With few exceptions, eligible pro bono activity is limited to legal services that are performed within New York to clients who are otherwise unable to afford counsel.[151]

---

[143] *VLA Online Intake Forms*, N.Y. VOLUNTEER LAWS. FOR ARTS, http://www.vlany.org/legalservices/online_intake_form.php (last visited Aug. 18, 2015).
[144] *Individual, Artist and Attorney Membership*, N.Y. VOLUNTEER LAWS. FOR ARTS, http://www.vlany.org/supportvla/indmem.php (last visited Aug. 18, 2015).
[145] *VLA Patent Pro Bono Program, supra* note 139.
[146] *Id.*
[147] *New Attorney Orientations*, N.Y. VOLUNTEER LAWS. FOR ARTS, http://www.vlany.org/legalservices/orientations.php (last visited Aug. 18, 2015).
[148] *Id.*
[149] *Id.*
[150] *See CLE Credit for Pro Bono Work*, N.Y. VOLUNTEER LAWS. FOR ARTS, http://www.vlany.org/legalservices/clecredit.php (last visited Aug. 18, 2015).
[151] *Id.*

7.   Michigan

In late 2014, Michigan began receiving patent pro bono services through a program established by two groups within the State Bar of Michigan: the Pro Bono Initiative and the IP Law Section.[152] The program requires that applicants earn a gross income of 200% or less of the federal poverty guidelines and have less than $5,000 in liquid assets.[153] This income threshold is, by mandate, the same as other pro bono programs operated by the state bar.[154] The program also requires applicants to file a provisional application with the USPTO prior to entry into the program.[155]

The intake, screening, and referral process itself is administered by the State Bar of Michigan.[156] The program is funded entirely by bar dues paid by attorneys licensed to practice law in Michigan.[157] Unlike many other programs that accept volunteer services from USPTO-registered practitioners—whether attorneys or agents—the Michigan program does not allow patent agents to volunteer.[158]

8.   Georgia

Around the same time in late 2014, the Georgia program also began accepting inventor requests for pro bono assistance. Run by the Georgia Lawyers for the Arts, the program is styled the Pro Bono Assistance and Training for Entrepreneurs and New, Talented, Solo inventors (PATENTS) program.[159] Applicants are required to pay an administrative fee—$50 for solo inventors, $100 for non-profits, and

---

[152]   *Michigan   Pro   Bono   Patent   Project*,   STATE   BAR   OF   MICH., http://www.connect.michbar.org/iplaw/patent (last visited Aug. 18, 2015).

[153]   *Id.*

[154]   *E.g.*, Memorandum from Robert Mathis to Michigan Litigation Assistance Partnership Project   (May   20,   2014),   *available   at* http://www.michbar.org/file/programs/pdfs/TaxReferralProcess.pdf.

[155]   *Michigan Pro Bono Patent Project, supra* note 152.

[156]   *See id.*

[157]   *See* AN ASSESSMENT OF PRO BONO IN MICHIGAN, 1–2 (Feb. 2013) *available at* http://www.michbar.org/file/programs/pdfs/probonoreport2013.pdf (stating that "[l]egal aid organizations funded by the [Michigan State Bar Foundation] or affiliated with the Access to Justice Fund are expected to engage pro bono lawyers and their work.").

[158]   *Patent   Pro   Bono   Attorney   Registration*,   ST.   B.   MICH., https://michbar.wufoo.com/forms/patent-pro-bono-attorney-registration/   (last   visited Aug. 18, 2015).

[159]   *Inventor Information*, GA. LAWS. FOR ARTS, http://www.glarts.org/patents/ (last visited Aug. 18, 2015).

$150 for small businesses—after the intake appointment and prior to placement with an attorney.[160]

The Georgia PATENTS program has differing eligibility requirements depending on the type of applicant. Solo inventors must have a total household income of less than 300% of the federal poverty guidelines and must not currently be under an obligation to assign rights to the invention.[161]

Non-profits must have four or fewer inventors who are under an obligation to assign right to another organization, have 501(c)(3) status, have a budget of less than $1 million per year, must not be a research institution or an institution or higher learning, and must not be under any obligation to assign the rights to the invention to another entity.[162]

Small businesses must have four or fewer inventors who are under an obligation to assign the rights to an organization, where all inventors have a current household income of less than 300% of the federal poverty guidelines, had a total gross income of less than $150,000 in the preceding calendar year, expect a total gross income of less than $150,000 in the current calendar year, and are not currently under an obligation to assign the rights to the invention to another entity.[163] Importantly, the program may disqualify an applicant whose inventor has been listed on more than four previous USPTO applications or U.S. patents.[164] Acceptance into the Georgia program also requires a good-faith belief that the relevant invention constitutes

---

[160] *Georgia Patents Program Qualifications*, GA. LAWS. FOR ARTS, http://www.glarts.org/patents/inventors/ (last visited Aug. 18, 2015).
[161] *Id.*
[162] *Id.*
[163] *Id.*
[164] *Id.* (citing 37 C.F.R. § 1.29 (2014)).

novel and non-obvious subject matter that has been reduced to practice.[165]

Additionally, applicants must have completed an approved patent training seminar.[166] Moreover, prior to acceptance into the program, applicants must complete a prior art search and provide the program with between three and ten prior art references identified through the search.[167] In this regard, the Georgia program reflects a more well-developed view of patent pro bono infrastructure that builds on the approaches of other regional programs, particularly with the refined intake and screening process suited to local needs.

As for providing services, the program accepts volunteer patent attorneys as well as patent agents.[168] It also provides malpractice coverage for in-house counsel representing a case referred through the program, though it requires attorneys in law firms to use their firms' respective professional liability policies.[169]

C. Latest Additions: 2015

Before 2015, patent pro bono programs were coming online at a rate of about four new programs per year. The first part of 2015, however, has already exceeded that trend with five new programs and startup efforts in several more. As the number of states with access to a patent pro bono program more than doubled in the last half of 2014, the first half of 2015 rounds out the USPTO's efforts to provide every state with access to a patent pro bono program. On August 6, 2015, the President announced that the Patent Pro Bono Program now extends to all 50 states.[170]

---

[165] *Id.*

[166] *Id.* Although the USPTO video training is the only approved course for this purpose as of this writing, the Georgia Lawyers for the Arts program anticipates additional approved courses will be coming soon. *See Upcoming Seminars*, GA. LAWS. FOR ARTS, http://glarts.org/upcomingevents/seminars/ (last visited Aug. 18, 2015).

[167] *Georgia Patents Program Qualifications, supra* note 160.

[168] *Id.*

[169] *Legal Volunteer Registration*, GA. LAWS. FOR ARTS, https://glarts.formstack.com/forms/legalvolunteer (last visited Aug. 18, 2015).

[170] Fact Sheet, President Obama Announces New Commitments from Investors, Companies, Universities, and Cities to Advance Inclusive Entrepreneurship at First-Ever White House Demo Day (Aug. 4, 2014), *available at* https://www.whitehouse.gov/the-press-office/2015/08/04/fact-sheet-president-obama-announces-new-commitments-investors-companies.

1.   The Midwest

Similar to the Greater Philadelphia program's coverage of multiple neighboring states, the Midwest regional program began operating in February 2015 to serve its home base of Missouri, as well as Nebraska, Kansas, Oklahoma, and Arkansas.[171] The program is administered by Gateway VMS, an entrepreneur support organization in St. Louis that offers business-mentoring services to early-stage innovators.[172] In this regard, the Midwest program is the first patent pro bono initiative focused specifically on the start-up community.

The program requires an income equal to or less than 300% of the federal poverty guidelines and a basic knowledge of the patent process, which can be demonstrated through evidence of the prior filing of a provisional or nonprovisional application or by completing the USPTO's online training course.[173] The program charges no administrative fee.[174] An initial patentability screening is available through the Entrepreneurship and Intellectual Property Clinic at Washington University in St. Louis School of Law.[175]

2.   Indiana

More availability in the Midwest region also came in early 2015 to Indiana, when the Patent Connect program began offering patent pro

---

[171] *See About Patent Pro Bono*, PAT. PRO BONO, http://patentprobono.com/about/ (last visited Aug. 18, 2015).

[172] *See GVMS*, GATEWAYVMS, http://gvms.ite-stl.org/wordpress/?page_id=7G (last visited Aug. 18, 2015).

[173] *See Guidelines*, PAT. PRO BONO, http://www.patentprobono.com/guidelines/ (last visited Aug. 20, 2015).

[174] *See id.*

[175] *See id.*; *see also Entrepreneurship and Intellectual Property Clinic*, WASH. U. L., http://law.wustl.edu/clinicaled/pages.aspx?id=6835 (last visited Aug. 20, 2015).

bono services to that state's residents.[176] The program is administered
by the Indiana University Maurer School of Law and the Center for
Intellectual Property Research.[177] The Center for Intellectual Property
Research was itself established in 2010 to oversee all aspects of
intellectual property law education at IU's law school[178] and is certified
for both patents and trademarks under the USPTO's Law School Clinic
Certification Program.[179]

Indiana's requirements are similar to those in Texas and
Georgia.[180] Inventors applying to the program must have an income of
less than 300% of the federal poverty guidelines and must not be
obligated to assign the rights to the invention.[181] Non-profit firms must
have four or fewer inventors who are under an obligation to assign
rights to the organization, have 501(c)(3) status, have a budget of less
than $1 million per year, not be a research institution or an institution
of higher learning, and not be under any obligation to assign the rights
to the invention to another entity.[182]

Small businesses, for their part, must have four or fewer inventors
who are under an obligation to assign the rights to the organization,
where all inventors have a current household income of less than 300%
of the federal poverty guidelines, had a total gross income of less than
$150,000 in the preceding calendar year and expect a total gross
income of less than $150,000 in the current calendar year, and must not
currently be under an obligation to assign the rights to the invention to
another entity.[183]

---

[176] *See Launch Event Date Set for the IP Clinic and Patent Connect for Hoosiers*,
CENTER FOR INTELL. PROP. RES. MAURER SCH. L., (July 27, 2015),
http://ip.indiana.edu/launch-event-date-set-for-the-ip-clinic-and-patent-connect-for-
hoosiers/.
[177] *See Maurer School of Law IP Clinical Program Certified for Pro Bono Practice
Before U.S. Patent Office*, IND. U. BLOOMINGTON (July 31, 2014),
http://news.indiana.edu/releases/iu/2014/07/iu-maurer-ip-program-certified-by-
uspto.shtml
[178] *See Our Mission*, IND. U. BLOOMINGTON, http://www.ip.indiana.edu/our-mission/ (last
visited Aug. 19, 2015).
[179] *See infra* Table 1.
[180] *See supra* Parts III.B.I, 8
[181] *Patent Connect for Hoosiers*, IND. U., http://www.indiana.edu/~patconn/ (Aug. 19,
2015).
[182] *Id.*
[183] *Id.*

There is no application fee for the program, but inventors must have either taken the USPTO online training course or have previously filed a provisional or nonprovisional application with the USPTO.[184]

3. Florida

Closely following Indiana's example of administering a patent pro bono program through a well-established public institution, Florida brought its program online in May 2015.[185] The program administrator[186] is the Institute for the Commercialization of Public Research (ICPR), a non-profit organization formed by the Florida Legislature in 2007 to support the creation of new companies and jobs based on publicly-funded research across the state.[187] The ICPR's business model is to collaborate with licensing officers at universities and private research institutions in Florida to help identify commercially viable startup company opportunities and to provide company-building support and seed funding.[188] To this existing portfolio of services regarding management, growth, capitalization, and general intellectual property strategy, in 2015, ICPR added patent referrals for inventors and businesses.[189]

The Florida program, nicknamed "Flobono," reflects similar income and ownership thresholds for inventors and small businesses as

---

[184] Id.

[185] Nancy Dahlberg, *Patent Pro Bono Program Launches for Florida Inventors*, MIAMI HERALD (May 4, 2015), http://www.miamiherald.com/news/business/technology/article20216364.html .

[186] Id.

[187] *See Background*, FLA. INST. FOR COMMERCIALIZATION PUB. RES., http://www.florida-institute.com/about/background (last visited Aug. 19, 2015).

[188] *See Frequently Asked Questions*, FL. INST. FOR COMMERCIALIZATION PUB. RES., http://www.florida-institute.com/about/faq (last visited Aug. 19, 2015).

[189] *See The Florida Patent Pro Bono Program*, FL. INST. FOR COMMERCIALIZATION PUB. RES. http://www.florida-institute.com/FloBono (last visited Aug. 19, 2015).

the Texas, Georgia, and Indiana programs.[190] Flobono requires that applicants complete the USPTO online training course.[191] In addition, applicants must demonstrate viability in their inventions by providing a detailed description or graphical representation of its use.[192] Individual inventors must be Florida residents and businesses must be Florida-based in order to qualify for the program.[193]

The program has benefited in particular from the Washington DC-based national information clearinghouse.[194] Even before its official May 2015 launch in Miami, Flobono received a large number of requests from inventors for assistance through the program. The pro bono element of the program has since grown quickly and efficiently to serve a significant population of low-income inventors in Florida.

4. Alabama and Mississippi

In May 2015, patent pro bono in the Gulf Coast region also came to Alabama and Mississippi, where the Birmingham Bar Association's Volunteer Lawyers Program began serving the inventor communities of those states.[195] The Volunteer Lawyers Program had already been providing free legal services to low-income clients on general civil matters.[196] A formal launch event is slated for the fall of 2015, but eligible inventors are already able to receive assistance through the program.

To be eligible, an inventor must have an income below 200% of the federal poverty guidelines.[197] This is a notable departure from most other programs, which set a higher threshold at 300% of the federal poverty guidelines.[198] The reason for this policy choice is that the average income in Alabama and Mississippi is often lower than

---

[190] *See Inventor Information*, FLA. INST. FOR COMMERCIALIZATION PUB. RES., http://www.florida-institute.com/programs/inventor-information (last visited Aug. 19, 2015) [*hereinafter FLA Inventor Information*].

[191] *See id.*

[192] *See FLA Inventor Information, supra* note 190.

[193] *Id.*

[194] *See supra* Part III.A.4.

[195] *See BBVLP Patent Program*, BIRMINGHAM B. VOLUNTEER LAWS. PROGRAM, http://www.vlpbirmingham.org/patent-program/ (last visited Aug. 6, 2015).

[196] *See Welcome to the Birmingham Bar Volunteer Lawyers Program*, BIRMINGHAM B. VOLUNTEER LAWS. PROGRAM, http://www.vlpbirmingham.org/about/ (last visited Aug. 6, 2015).

[197] *See BBVLP Patent Program, supra* note 195

[198] *See supra* Parts III.A–C.

national averages.[199] Put another way, an Alabama or Mississippi inventor earning 300% of the federal poverty guidelines is relatively better off than the same inventor in many other states and, therefore, less in need of pro bono assistance.

Small businesses are not currently accepted into the program, though groups of individual inventors may be eligible, provided they each meet the criteria.[200] The program requires inventors to have completed the USPTO's online training course or to have participated in an approved training seminar.[201] There is no fee for applying to the Alabama and Mississippi program.[202]

5.   Illinois

In June 2015, Illinois joined the ranks of patent pro bono programs, thanks to the Illinois Institute of Technology (IIT), Chicago-Kent College of Law, which serves as the administrator for the program.[203] As a leader in IP-related research and programming of events, this program is well suited to capitalize on its established relationships with IP firms and corporate law departments throughout the state. Akin to the Texas, Georgia, Indiana, and Florida programs, individual inventors must earn less than 300% of the federal poverty

---

[199] *State and Country Quick Facts: Alabama*, U.S. CENSUS BUREAU, http://quickfacts.census.gov/qfd/states/01000.html (last revised May 28, 2015) ($23,680 compared to $28,155); *State and County Quick Facts: Mississippi*, U.S. CENSUS BUREAU, http://quickfacts.census.gov/qfd/states/28000.html (last revised May 28, 2015) ($20,618 compared to $28,155).

[200] *BBVLP Patent Program, supra* note 195.

[201] *See id.*

[202] *Welcome to the Birmingham Bar Volunteer Lawyers Program, supra* note 196.

[203] *Chicago-Kent Patent Hub*, IIT CHI.-KENT C. LAW, http://www.kentlaw.iit.edu/seeking-legal-help/illinois-patent-pro-bono (last visited Aug. 19, 2015).

guidelines, and must be Illinois residents.[204] The ownership and income criteria for small businesses are also like the Texas, Georgia, Indiana, and Florida programs.[205]

Applicants are required to provide financial information to demonstrate that they have a total household income of less than 300% of the federal poverty guidelines.[206] Inventors must also show that they understand the patent process and what they can do with a patent, if granted, by filing a provisional or nonprovionsal application or by successfully completing the USPTO training module.[207] Lastly, the inventor must be able to describe the invention.[208]

Unlike most other programs, the Illinois program sets forth the general scope of representation on its website.[209] Attorneys are nevertheless expected to execute an engagement letter with the inventor, and attorneys must also commit to providing any information needed for reports to the USPTO.[210] In general, the volunteer attorney will draft and file one nonprovisional U.S. patent application, will prosecute the patent application until either (1) a response is filed to a final Office action, or (2) the application issues as a patent, and will commit to monitor and docket all deadlines.[211] The attorney is not responsible for filing any requests for continued examination, appeals, challenges to a USPTO decision in a court of law, prosecution after issue or response to final Office Action, foreign filings or additional U.S. application filings.[212] However, the attorney's services may be expanded by mutual agreement between the inventor and the attorney, which should be in writing.[213]

The Illinois program matches inventors or small businesses with attorneys based on the field of the invention and the preferred technical fields of expertise of the attorney.[214]

---

[204] *Information for Inventors*, IIT CHI.-KENT C. LAW, http://www.kentlaw.iit.edu/seeking-legal-help/illinois-patent-pro-bono/inventor-information (last visited Aug. 19, 2015).
[205] *Id.*
[206] *Id.*
[207] *Id.*
[208] *Id.*
[209] *Information for Volunteer Attorneys*, IIT CHI.-KENT C. LAW, http://www.kentlaw.iit.edu/seeking-legal-help/illinois-patent-pro-bono/volunteer-attorney-information (last visited Aug. 19, 2015).
[210] *Id.*
[211] *Id.*
[212] *Id.*
[213] *Id.*
[214] *Id.*

D.   *Expansions and Breakaways*

While new state and region-specific programs have been emerging, existing programs have also been expanding and spinning off new efforts to provide greater support to underserved innovators throughout the United States. In the second half of 2014, Minnesota's LegalCORPS program joined with William Mitchell College of Law to provide patent pro bono services to residents in four surrounding states: Wisconsin, North Dakota, South Dakota, and Iowa.[215] Through this effort, LegalCORPS still provides free patent services to Minnesota residents, but now individuals and business owners in the other four surrounding states may seek help from William Mitchell's Inventor Assistance Program.[216]

The Inventor Assistance Program is administered by the law school's intellectual property clinic, which conducts applicant intake and screening.[217] Like LegalCORPS, William Mitchell uses an income level of 300% of the federal poverty guidelines for both inventors and small business owners.[218] Additionally, like LegalCORPS, the William Mitchell Inventor Assistance Program requires inventors to have already filed a provisional application, and be a resident of one of the states for which the program provides service.[219] Law students, under

---

[215]   *Inventor Assistance Program*, WM. MITCHELL C. LAW, http://web.wmitchell.edu/intellectual-property/inventors/ (last visited Aug. 19, 2015).
[216]   *Ways We Can Help Inventors*, WM. MITCHELL C. LAW, http://web.wmitchell.edu/intellectual-property/inventors/ways-we-can-help-inventors/ (last visited Aug. 19, 2015).
[217]   *See Clinic-Intellectual Property Law Clinic*, WM. MITCHELL C. LAW, http://web.wmitchell.edu/students/course-description/?course=5111 (last visited Aug. 19, 2015).
[218]   *Ways We Can Help Inventors, supra* note 216 ("William Mitchell will apply pre-determined income guidelines . . . .").
[219]   *See id.* However, inventors who have not filed a provisional application may request assistance form the William Mitchell Intellectual Property Clinic. *Id.*

the supervision of William Mitchell's patent law faculty, help file and prosecute patent applications referred through the expanded program.[220]

Moreover, in the second half of 2014, the Colorado program, ProBoPat, expanded its service area to include Wyoming, Utah, and New Mexico.[221] Similarly, the Ohio program, operated through Case Western Reserve University School of Law, expanded to accept applicants from nearby Kentucky.[222] The NC LEAP program began to accept requests from Tennessee individuals and small businesses.[223] The Washington DC program began serving residents of West Virginia and Delaware.[224] And the Greater Philadelphia program expanded to accept all inventors in Pennsylvania.[225]

Two significant expansions in late 2014 opened up the growing patent pro bono movement to a large number of people in the northeastern United States. The New York Volunteer Lawyers for the Arts program expanded its coverage to include residents living or working in New Jersey and Connecticut.[226] Similarly, the Massachusetts program began to serve individuals residing in Maine,

[220] Caitlin Hill, *LegalCorps Provides Pricey Patent Help for Free*, MINN. BUS. MAG. (Mar. 25, 2015), http://minnesotabusiness.com/legalcorps-provides-pricey-patent-help-free ("[The program] enables free legal representation for low-income inventors seeking to patent their inventions with the USPTO, connecting them to law school students and volunteer attorneys.").
[221] *See* Alicia Wallace, *Mi Casa-based Pro Bono Patent Program Expands to Neighboring States*, DENVER POST, (May 12, 2015 3:51 PM), http://www.denverpost.com/business/ci_28101567/mi-casa-based-pro-bono-patent-program-expands.
[222] The USPTO brings the person seeking assistance to the Case Western University School of Law *IP Venture Clinic* homepage when one clicks on the Kentucky link. *See Patent Pro Bono Program*, USPTO, http://www.uspto.gov/patents-getting-started/using-legal-services/pro-bono/patent-pro-bono-program (last visited Aug. 19, 2015) [*hereinafter USPTO Patent Pro Bono Program*].
[223] *Frequently Asked Questions*, N.C. B. ASS'N, http://www.ncbar.org/public-resources/nc-leap/faqs/ (last visited Aug. 19, 2015). The NC LEAP program won the 2015 NCBF/LexisNexis Partnerships for Success Award for its inventor assistance efforts. *See Inventor Assistance Program Receiving Award*, N.C. B. ASS'N, http://www.ncbar.org/news/inventor-assistance-program-receiving-award/ (last visited Aug. 19, 2015).
[224] *PTO Pro Bono Program*, FED. CIR. B. ASS'N, http://www.fedcirbar.org/olc/pub/LVFC/cpages/misc/pto.jsp (last visited Aug. 20, 2015).
[225] *See Philadelphia Patent Pro Bono Program, supra* note 130.
[226] *TRI-STATE Patet Pro Bono Program to Launch in New York, New Jersey, and Connecticut*, ABA CENTER FOR PRO BONO EXCHANGE (Feb. 10, 2015), https://centerforprobono.wordpress.com/2015/02/10/tri-state-patent-pro-bono-program-to-launch-in-new-york-new-jersey-and-connecticut/.

New Hampshire, Vermont, and Rhode Island by offering access to the Boston-based inventor assistance program.[227] In a June 22, 2015 press conference, Senator Patrick Leahy announced his support for the northeastern Patent Pro Bono Program's efforts to assist Vermont inventors and small businesses, commenting: "The Patent Pro Bono program will make sure that anybody with an innovative invention, regardless of income, has the ability to take advantage of the crucial protection that patents afford."[228]

As a federal coordinator in this national effort, the USPTO is sensitive to the needs of local inventor assistance programs to address the particular needs of their respective communities. To that end, the USPTO is also prepared to provide support to new programs as comprehensive as what the above-described programs have enjoyed. The USPTO is working with various groups in Washington state, Delaware and Tennessee to establish programs specific to those states, apart from their current regional programs.

IV.   A CLOSER LOOK AT THE PROGRAM'S SUCCESS

Beyond a qualitative overview of the Patent Pro Bono Program's trajectory, it is also helpful to evaluate the effectiveness of a particular program in some quantitative detail. Given the rapid expansion of programs across the country in a relatively short period of time, data on the work of most programs is very limited. Future analysis of data from all the regional programs will be appropriate for a more robust assessment. The earliest program, however—in Minnesota—has now

---

[227] *See Pro Bono Patent Program of New England*, ARTS & BUS. COUNCIL GREATER BOS., http://www.artsandbusinesscouncil.org/programs/patent-program.html (last visited Aug. 19, 2015).
[228] *Leahy Kicks Off Vermont Launch Of Patent Pro Bono Program*, U.S. SENATOR PATRICK LEAHY VERMONT (June 22, 2015), http://www.leahy.senate.gov/press/leahy-kicks-off-vermont-launch-of-patent-pro-bono-program.

been in operation for close to four years and offers an initial longitudinal view of the Patent Pro Bono Program's benefits.

A. *Minnesota: The Basic Numbers*

In its first year of operation (July 1, 2011 through June 30, 2012), the Minnesota program received thirty-seven inventor requests for assistance.[229] From these requests, seventeen inventors met the screening criteria and were matched with volunteer attorneys.[230] Of the seventeen inventors paired with free patent counsel, twelve eventually received patents.[231] One applicant abandoned the application, another declined to proceed after the search report was generated, and three more remain unpublished.[232] Because the Minnesota program requires applicants to have filed a provisional application in order to meet the Inventor Assistance Program's screening criteria,[233] the program in its first year of operation also referred thirteen inventors to the William Mitchell Intellectual Property Clinic for assistance with filing provisional applications.[234]

In the second year of operation (July 1, 2012 through June 30, 2013), the program received forty requests for assistance.[235] Of these, fourteen resulted in matches with volunteer attorneys.[236] Of the fourteen matches, seven applications have issued as patents.[237] Six more are pending, including two that have just been docketed and are ready for examination and three more for which the attorneys have currently filed responses to USPTO office actions.[238] One application has received a final rejection. In the second year, the program also referred thirteen inventors to the William Mitchell Intellectual Property Clinic.[239]

---

[229] *See infra* Table 2. The authors are grateful to LegalCORPS staff and volunteers for generously providing Minnesota program data. No information contained in this Article is confidential. Only published information on applications and patents is reported.

[230] *Id.*

[231] *Id.*

[232] *Id.*

[233] *See supra* Part III.A.1.

[234] *Id.*

[235] *See infra* Table 3.

[236] *Id.*

[237] *Id.*

[238] *Id.*

[239] *Id.*

In the third year (July 1, 2013 through June 30, 2014), the Minnesota program received 38 requests for assistance.[240] Of these, seventeen were matched with volunteer attorneys.[241] From these matches, two applications have issued as patents, and twelve applications are currently pending.[242] The twelve pending applications include three newly docketed cases ready for examination, three more applications for which examiners have issued Office Actions and await an applicant reply, one application for which the applicant has filed a response, and one application for which the USPTO has issued an advisory action to the applicant.[243] One application was abandoned by the inventor,[244] and two more applications were not filed because the inventors declined to proceed.[245] In the third year, the program also referred two inventors to the William Mitchell Intellectual Property Clinic.[246]

In all three years for which Minnesota program data is available, the patent applications encompass nearly all the major technology categories, including computer and communications, drugs and medical, electrical and electronic, and mechanical.[247] Likewise, the

---

[240] *See infra* Table 4.
[241] *Id.*
[242] *Id.*
[243] *Id.*
[244] *Id.*
[245] *Id.*
[246] *Id.*
[247] *See* CLASSES WITHIN THE U.S. CLASSIFICATION SYSTEM: ARRANGED BY RELATED SUBJECT MATTER, USPTO (2012), *available at* http://www.uspto.gov/sites/default/files/patents/resources/classification/classescombined. pdf. These categorizations are based on the U.S. Patent Classification System into which all applications and patents are ordered, and on the National Bureau of Economic Research six-category system, which is keyed to the USPC. *See generally The NBER U.S. Patent Citations Data File: Lessons, Insights, and Methodological Tools*, NBER, http://www.nber.org/patents/ (last updated May 16, 2012).

cases referred to the William Mitchell Intellectual Property Clinic also
encompass most of the major technology areas, including mechanical,
chemical, electrical, and business method inventions. These various
data are summarized in Tables 2–4.

These bare numbers from the Minnesota program reveal that, even
at the small-scale level of a single state's patent pro bono initiative,
inventors are availing themselves of help in a variety of technological
areas. They also reveal that the law school clinic model is, indeed, a
meaningful complement to pro bono services in empowering low-
income innovators while educating future lawyers both in real-world IP
and business counseling and in the legal profession's ethic of public
service.

B.   Impact of the Pro Bono Filings

To understand the impact of patent pro bono services beyond this
basic summary information, it is useful to consider the disparity in
patent prosecution outcomes between applicants who proceed *pro se*
and those who are represented by a USPTO-registered practitioner. We
draw this comparison in two steps. First, to place our analysis in
context with underlying (and unobservable) differences among
macroeconomic and other regional factors, we compare various
outcome statistics for USPTO applications originating from Minnesota
and USPTO applications overall. Second, we then compare the
outcomes for applications supported through LegalCORPS in the
Minnesota patent pro bono program both to overall Minnesota
applications filed *with* an attorney and to overall Minnesota
applications filed *without* an attorney, i.e., *pro se*. The particular
outcomes we compare in all cases are as follow:

- the rate at which the USPTO examiner's first action on the
  merits is to allow the application to issue as a patent;
- the rate at which the USPTO examiner allows the application
  to issue as a patent within one round of examination, i.e.,
  without a request for continued examination (RCE) or an
  appeal;
- the rate at which the USPTO examiner allows the application
  to issue as a patent with up to one rejection; and
- the rate at which the application goes abandoned.

Even with the small sample size of the Minnesota patent pro bono
population, the results are illuminating. As Figure 1 shows, the general

run of patent applications from Minnesota fare differently, to a statistically significant extent, from USPTO applications overall.

The rate of first-action allowance is indistinguishable between Minnesota-originating applications and USPTO applications overall. Minnesota-originating applications receive first-action allowances in 6.78% of cases, and USPTO applications overall receive first-action allowances in 7.01% of cases. The difference is not statistically significant ($p = 0.9808$). However, Minnesota applications are allowed more often without RCE or appeal, are more often allowed with up to one rejection, are abandoned less frequently, and remain pending longer than applications overall.

In turn, comparing applications within Minnesota more specifically, the rate of first-action allowances for LegalCORPS patent pro bono applications are virtually indistinguishable from overall Minnesota applications *filed with an attorney*. LegalCORPS applications receive first-action allowances in 6.67% of cases, and overall Minnesota applications with an attorney receive first-action allowances in 6.65% of cases, with a statistically insignificant difference ($p = 0.9963$). By contrast, overall Minnesota *pro se* applications receive first-action allowances in only 2.13% of cases, and this difference is somewhat significant ($p = 0.0868$).

The rate of allowance without RCE or appeal is considerably higher for Minnesota applications *with* attorneys (39.9%) than for Minnesota *pro se* applications (12.3%), and the rate for LegalCORPS applications (46.7%) quite closely resembles the former. The difference between LegalCORPS applications and Minnesota applications *with* attorneys is insignificant ($p = 0.4492$), but the difference between LegalCORPS and Minnesota *pro se* applications is significant ($p = 0.000$).

Likewise, the rate of allowance with up to one rejection is considerably higher for Minnesota applications *with* attorneys (36.0%)

than for Minnesota *pro se* applications (10.0%), and the rate for
LegalCORPS applications (40.0%) quite closely resembles the former.
Again, the difference between LegalCORPS and Minnesota *with*
attorneys is insignificant (p = 0.6500), but the difference between
LegalCORPS and Minnesota *pro se* applications is significant (p =
0.000).

These findings indicate that support from LegalCORPS's patent
practitioners in the Minnesota patent pro bono program does
significantly improve an inventor's likelihood of receiving a favorable
outcome in the patent application process, as evidenced by three basic
measures of patent allowance. Our initial comparison demonstrates a
significant difference between USPTO applications overall and the
subset of applications from Minnesota, meaning that Minnesota
applications with and without attorneys are, indeed, the appropriate
reference point for LegalCORPS's outcomes—rather than the general
population of USPTO applications. Our second comparison then shows
that inventors supported by LegalCORPS's patent pro bono attorneys
fare as well as the average Minnesota inventor who is represented by
counsel—and significantly better than the average Minnesota inventor
who proceeds *pro se*.

It is also important to consider two additional prosecution outcome
measures—abandonment   and   pendency—that   are   particularly
important to under-resourced innovators. The rate of abandonment
among applications supported by LegalCORPS (10.0%) is roughly the
same as that among Minnesota *pro se* applications (13.9%), with a
statistically insignificant difference (p = 0.5343). By contrast, the rate
of abandonment is lower for LegalCORPS applications than for overall
Minnesota applications filed with an attorney (25.5%), and to a
somewhat statistically significant extent (p = 0.0520).

This abandonment finding suggests a possible selection effect
arising from the small size and scarce resources of an inventor or firm
that was eligible for pro bono assistance in the first place. Such a firm
might only begin the patent application process after carefully vetting
applicants, and would presumably be less likely to abandon its
investments in patent prosecution. However, this is difficult to establish
with the small sample size of LegalCORPS's work to date. In general,
the abandonment rate among Minnesota applicants claiming "large
entity" status (16.2%) in the USPTO is notably higher than for those
claiming "small entity" status (2.86%), and the difference is significant
(p = 0.0000). Yet, the LegalCORPS abandonment rate (10.0%) is

indistinguishable both from that of large entities (p = 0.8601) and from that of small entities (p = 0.3599), meaning that the precise effect of size and resources cannot be resolved without a larger data set of patent pro bono outcomes.

C. Two Case Studies

In addition to statistical inferences from these comparisons of the Minnesota patent pro bono program applications to larger, more general populations, two cases studies from the program also bear closer scrutiny.

In November 2011, Travis Kelley, a *pro se* inventor in Backus, Minnesota, sought legal help through the pro bono program to patent his door-installation invention, called the CHEATAH.[248] LegalCORPS connected Mr. Kelley with a volunteer patent lawyer, Kate DeVries Smith, who filed and prosecuted his application.[249] By March 2014, he had received U.S. Patent No. 8,677,636.[250] During the same year, he would go on to be named a runner up in the Minnesota Cup, a statewide entrepreneurship competition.[251]

Mr. Kelley's company JenTra Tools has now manufactured over 6,000 units of his invention, all within the United States, generating over $150,000 in gross revenue.[252] As the invention employs a leveler

---

[248] *'Minnesota   Cup'   Honors   IAP   Participant*,   LEGALCORPS, http://www.legalcorps.org/minnesota-cup-honors-iap-participant (last visited Aug. 19, 2015).

[249] Caitlin Hill, *supra* note 220.

[250] *See* U.S. Patent No. 8,677,636 (issued Mar. 25, 2014).

[251] *See 'Minnesota Cup' Honors IAP Participant, supra* note 248.

[252] *See Patent Pro Bono Program Grows: My Interview with Jennifer McDowell, Coordinator of the U.S. Patent Pro Bono Program*, L. OFFICE KATHLEEN LYNCH PLLC (Dec. 16, 2014), http://kliplaw.com/blog/2014/12/16/patent-pro-bono-program-grows-my-interview-with-jennifer-mcdowell-coordinator-of-the-us-patent-pro-bono-program (*hereinafter Interview with Jennifer McDowell*).

and spacer kit to enable faster and more precise door installation,[253] it is
of particular relevance to the door manufacturing industry. In order to
reach a greater segment of that industry, JenTra Tools has now hired
three employees in Minnesota to expand its operational capacity.[254] On
the small scale of an individual firm, Mr. Kelley's successful patent
prosecution reflects many of the aims of a well-functioning innovation
system: production of a new and useful good, complementary benefits
to existing industry, and local job creation.

A second Minnesota inventor, a seventy-one-year-old retiree
named Jim Lemke, had initially tried to file a patent application on his
own, but was unable to do so.[255] In June 2011, LegalCORPS matched
Mr. Lemke with volunteer patent attorneys Amy Salmela and Christian
Girtz.[256] They filed a provisional application and, subsequently, a
nonprovisional utility application for his invention, a device to remove
ice clumps from behind car wheels.[257] Colorfully named the Snow
Booger Remover, the device is now protected under U.S. Patent No.
8,533,896.[258]

Mr. Lemke began marketing his device locally in the Twin Cities
area and through his website,[259] and LegalCORPS then also assisted
Mr. Lemke with obtaining a trademark for his device.[260] As part of his
ongoing efforts to commercialize his invention, Mr. Lemke has
attended trade shows, advertised on the radio, and visited with local
meteorologists.[261] With his business operation now approaching 1,000
units sold, he is preparing to license his invention to retail stores across
the United States, secure in the intellectual property rights that give him
a more equal bargaining position with large well-funded distribution
chains.[262] In these licensing discussions, too, Mr. Lemke has returned

---

[253] *CHEETAH Door Level Features*, JENTRA TOOLS, http://www.jentratools.com/cheatah-door-level-features/ (last visited Aug. 19, 2015).
[254] *Interview with Jennifer McDowell, supra* note 252.
[255] Neal St. Anthony, *LegalCorps Cited by White House for Helping Low-income Inventors*, STAR TRIB. (Mar. 1, 2014), http://www.startribune.com/legalcorps-cited-by-white-house-for-helping-low-income-inventors/247896711/.
[256] *See* Phone Interview with Jim Lemke (document on file with author).
[257] *See* Neal St. Anthony, *supra* note 255.
[258] *See id.*; U.S. Patent No. 8,533,896 (issued Sept. 17, 2013).
[259] *See* SNOW BOOGER REMOVER, http://www.snowboogersbegone.com/ (last visited Aug. 6, 2015).
[260] *See* Phone Interview with Jim Lemke, *supra* note 256.
[261] *Id.*
[262] *Id.*

to LegalCORPS for counsel.[263] As with Mr. Kelley, Mr. Lemke's case began from modest means and personal initiative before he sought help and was able to receive it from the Minnesota patent pro bono program.

It is unlikely that these inventors' intellectual property rights would have been protected at all, or adequately, without the help of competent patent counsel. Given this support, they now contribute their innovations to their local economies with not only the ambition, but the means, to contribute to the national economy.

V.   CONCLUSION

The patent pro bono movement is an illuminating example of socially and economically conscious investments that yield returns many times over. Beyond the direct benefits to inventors and to their local economies and communities, the innovation system as a whole functions more smoothly through such investments. The complexities of filing and prosecuting patent applications often leave otherwise capable inventors and startups stymied.

The USPTO, for its part, continues to develop its programs of assistance to unrepresented inventors, such as the Pro Se Assistance Program,[264] a redesigned website geared towards first-time users of the patent system,[265] and Patent and Trademark Resource Centers located all across the country.[266] Yet, the benefits of representation by patent counsel remain clear. Unnecessary errors, overlooked formalities, and ultimately abandoned applications consume the USPTO's resources,

---

[263] *Id.*
[264] *See Pro Se Assistance Program*, USPTO, http://www.uspto.gov/patents-getting-started/using-legal-services/pro-se-assistance-program (last visited Aug. 19, 2015).
[265] *See* USPTO, http://www.uspto.gov/ (last visited Aug. 19, 2015).
[266] *PTRC Locations By State*, USPTO, http://www.uspto.gov/learning-and-resources/support-centers/patent-and-trademark-resource-centers-ptrc/ptrc-locations (last visited Aug. 19, 2015).

including examiner time spent assisting *pro se* applicants—often before an invention even receives substantive evaluation on the merits, let alone approaches an issued patent. By pairing inventors with volunteer attorneys, these up-front inefficiencies in the patent system are greatly reduced.

The positive economic impacts of patent pro bono initiatives are a principal reason why the USPTO is committed to making the program available to low-income residents across the United States. Together with small inventor-friendly policies such as reduced fee structures, these efforts help level the playing field for innovators to compete on the strength of their innovations.

The USPTO's significant commitment of pro bono lawyers and its initial commitment of financial resources provided the kick start the program needed to expand nationwide. Now, going forward, the USPTO must transition primary responsibility for the vision and sustainability of the patent pro bono initiative to those outside of the federal government. Given the successes already seen during the short duration of the program, market forces appear likely to bear the minimal operational burden required not only to expand but to flourish. In this, the Pro Bono Advisory Council (PBAC) is well prepared to lead the way forward.

Key challenges remain in broadening the participation of patent professionals as well as inventors and small businesses in the program. For attorneys, especially those without portable professional liability insurance (such as in-house counsel), a regional programs' provision of malpractice insurance becomes a necessity for participation. To this end, in late 2014, the PBAC established a subcommittee to explore malpractice issues, and by mid-2015, found multiple insurers willing to work with the regional programs to provide adequate malpractice coverage. This alone increases the capacity of patent pro bono programs through greater volunteer attorney participation, which, in turn, makes it possible to provide service to more inventors and startups.

Another key challenge is the ability of every regional program to become self-sustaining. Currently, most programs operate through corporate sponsorship and other donations. Some, such as the California program, recover some costs through administrative fees. Others, such as the Midwest program, are exploring a mode of expansion by which revenue from successful applicants may help fund future operations. In all cases, sustainable sources of funding must eventually be built into each program's business model. With direction and guidance from the dozens of IP professionals on the PBAC, the program is poised to thrive.

The USPTO's Pro Bono Program team remains committed to offering enthusiastic guidance and coordination to the PBAC, to the regional programs already established, and to the new inquiries that come to the office daily. The USPTO's responsible stewardship of the program requires that the program's future viability be pursued in a realistic and thoughtful way by each regional program, so that all American can reap the benefits this program has to offer.

TABLES AND FIGURES

Table 1. Law School Clinic Certification Program Participants

Patents	Trademarks	Both
Brooklyn Law School	American University, Washington College of Law	Arizona State University College of Law
Case Western Reserve University School of Law	California Western School of Law	Fordham University School of Law
New York Law School	Howard University School of Law	Indiana University Maurer School of Law

University of Colorado Law School	Lewis & Clark College School of Law	Lincoln Law School of San Jose
University of Detroit Mercy School of Law	Loyola University Chicago School of Law	North Carolina Central University School of Law
Wayne State University Law School	Northwestern University School of Law	South Texas College Of Law
	Roger Williams University School of Law	Southern Methodist University Dedman School of Law
	Rutgers Law School—Newark	Texas A&M University School of Law
	Saint Louis University School of Law	The John Marshall Law School
	The George Washington University School of Law	Thomas Jefferson School of Law
	University of Akron School of Law	University of California, Los Angeles School of Law
	University of Idaho College of Law	University of Connecticut School of Law
	University of New Hampshire School of Law	University of Maryland School of Law
	University of North Carolina at Chapel Hill School of Law	University of Notre Dame Law School
	University of San Francisco School of Law	University of Puerto Rico School of Law

	University of Tennessee College of Law	University of Washington School of Law
	Vanderbilt Law School	William Mitchell College of Law
	West Virginia University School of Law	
	Western New England University School of Law	

Table 2. Minnesota Patent Pro Bono Program Summary: July 2011– June 2012

Month of Att'y-Client Match	Application Serial No.	USPTO Art Unit	U.S. Patent Class	NBER Category	Status
Sep-2011	12/363,787	3656	074	Mech	Patented Case
Nov-2011	13/315,450	2685	340	Cmp&Cmm	Patented Case
Nov-2011	13/371,004	2856	033	Others	Patented Case
Dec-2011	Unpublished	—	—	—	—

Dec-2011	13/462,444	3788	206	Others	Patented Case
Jan-2012	12/803,309	3611	040	Others	Abandoned -- Failure to Respond to an Office Action
Jan-2012	Unpublished	—	—	—	—
Feb-2012	12/785,303	3716	463	Others	Patented Case
Mar-2012	Unpublished	—	—	—	Client did not proceed after search
Mar-2012	Unpublished	—	—	—	—
Mar-2012	13/065,596	3632	248	Others	Patented Case
May-2012	12/587,881	3652	294	Mech	Patented Case
May-2012	12/962,974	3764	482	Mech	Patented Case
May-2012	13/334,698	2848	174	Elec	Patented Case
Jun-2012	13/555,555	3644	043	Others	Patented Case
Jun-2012	12/804,100	3781	220	Others	Patented Case
Jun-2012	13/612,372	3739	607	Drgs&Med	Patented Case

Table 3. Minnesota Patent Pro Bono Program Summary: July 2012–June 2013

Month of Att'y-Client Match	Application Serial No.	USPTO Art Unit	U.S. Patent Class	NBER Category	Status
Jul-2012	29/442,338	2912	D02	Design	Patented Case
Aug-2012	13/330,183	3654	254	Mech	Patented Case
Aug-2012	13/586,128	3721	053	Others	Response to Non-Final Office Action Entered and Forwarded to Examiner
Aug-2012	13/302,210	3679	403	Others	Response to Non-Final Office Action Entered and Forwarded to Examiner
Oct-2012	13/764,535	3788	206	Others	Docketed New Case - Ready for Examination
Nov-2012	Unpublished	—	—	—	Final rejection

Jan-2013	12/930,778	3727	015	Others	Patented Case
Feb-2013	13/860,385	3643	054	Others	Response to Non-Final Office Action Entered and Forwarded to Examiner
Feb-2013	Unpublished	—	—	—	Active
Mar-2013	13/010,254	3739	607	Drgs&Med	Patented Case
Apr-2013	13/485,792	1792	426	Others	Patented Case
May-2013	12/930,263	2886	356	Elec	Patented Case
Jun-2013	14/262,331	3765	036	Others	Docketed New Case - Ready for Examination
Jun-2013	14/188,726	2837	084	Others	Patented Case

Table 4. Minnesota Patent Pro Bono Program Summary: July 2013–
June 2014

Month of Att'y-Client Match	Application Serial No.	USPTO Art Unit	U.S. Patent Class	NBER Category	Status
Jul-2013	14/104,952	3634	043	Others	Docketed New Case - Ready for Examination
Aug-2013	13/017,019	2614	345	Cmp&Cmm	Patented Case
Aug-2013	14/081,713	3746	417	Mech	Docketed New Case - Ready for Examination
Oct-2013	14/285,757	2875	362	Elec	Docketed New Case - Ready for Examination
Nov-2013	14/106,407	3672	405	Others	Patented Case
Nov-2013	Unpublished	—	—	—	Client did not proceed

Nov-2013	14/211,017	3634	160	Others	Non Final Action Mailed
Nov-2013	Unpublished	—	—	—	Client did not proceed
Nov-2013	13/209,503	3753	137	Others	Abandoned -- Failure to Respond to an Office Action
Feb-2014	14/318,670	3625	705	Cmp&Cmm	Non Final Action Mailed
Feb-2014	Unpublished	—	—	—	Active
Mar-2014	14/226,516	3711	273	Others	Non Final Action Mailed
May-2014	Unpublished				Active
May-2014	13/507,951	3731	606	Drgs&Med	Advisory Action Mailed
May-2014	Unpublished	—	—	—	Active
May-2014	Unpublished	—	—	—	Active
Jun-2014	14/034,759	3677	063	Others	Response after Final Action Forwarded to Examiner

Figure 1. Prosecution Statistics for Minnesota vs. Overall Applications

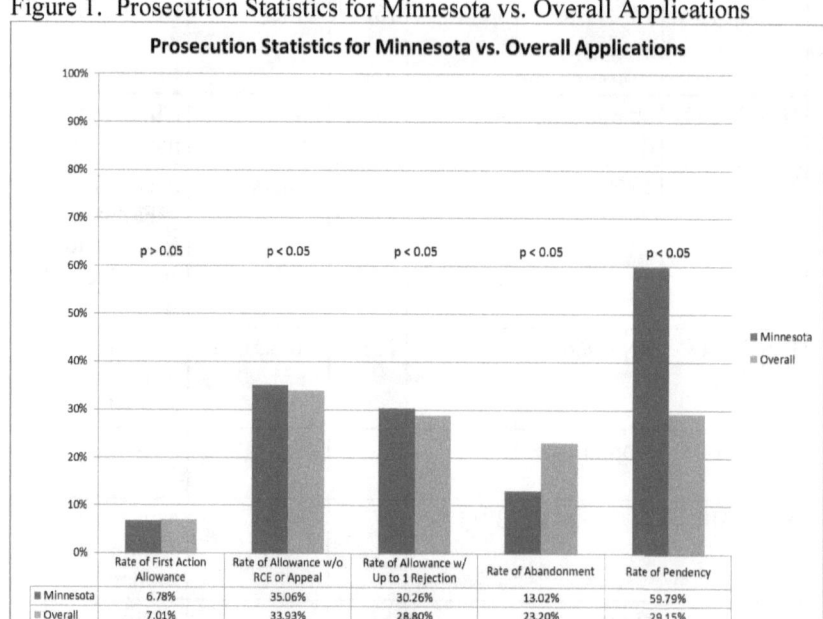

Figure 2. Prosecution Statistics for LegalCORPS vs. Minnesota w/ and w/o Att'y

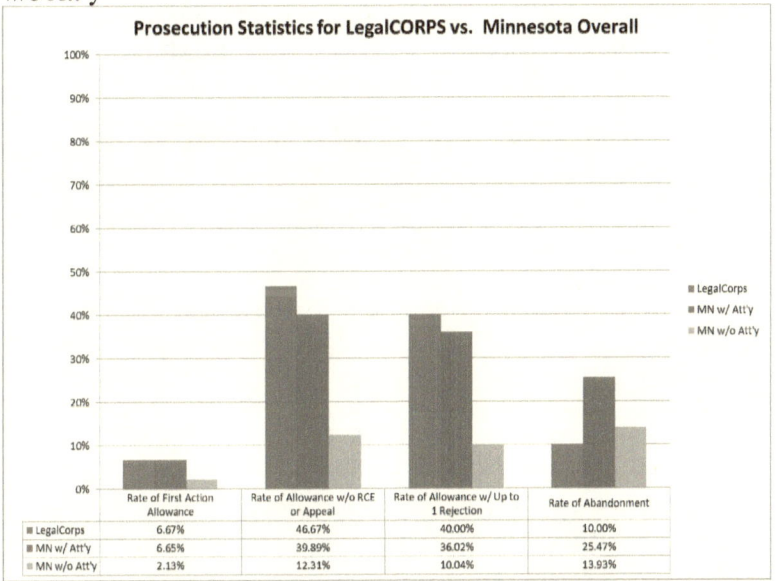

Measure	LegalCORPS vs. MN w/ Att'y	LegalCORPS vs. MN w/o Att'y
Rate of First Action Allowance	p > 0.05	p > 0.05
Rate of Allowance w/o RCE or Appeal	p > 0.05	p < 0.05
Rate of Allowance w/ Up to 1 Rejection	p > 0.05	p < 0.05
Rate of Abandonment	p > 0.05	p > 0.05

EXCEPTIONS TO PROSECUTION HISTORY ESTOPPEL ARE HARDLY A DIME A DOZEN: AN ANALYSIS OF THE FEDERAL CIRCUIT'S APPLICATION OF THE NARROW EXCEPTIONS TO PROSECUTION HISTORY ESTOPPEL TWELVE YEARS AFTER *FESTO*

RACHEL C. HUGHEY[1] & LINHDA NGUYEN[2]

[1] Rachel C. Hughey is a shareholder with the law firm of Merchant & Gould, P.C., in Minneapolis, MN. She is the co-chair of the firm's appellate practice. The authors would like to thank Elisabeth Muirhead and Joseph Dubis for their assistance on this article.
[2] Linhda Nguyen is an associate with the law firm of Merchant & Gould, P.C., in Minneapolis, MN.

In *Festo Corp. v. Shoketsu Kinzoku Kogyo Kabushiki Co.* (*Festo VIII*),[3] the Supreme Court rejected the Federal Circuit's bright-line rule that prosecution history estoppel bars infringement under the doctrine of equivalents when a patent applicant makes a narrowing amendment for reasons related to patentability. The Court specified three narrow potential exceptions by which a patentee could overcome the presumption of prosecution history estoppel.[4] More than ten years after the *Festo* decision, however, courts and patent practitioners alike are left with little guidance as to when and why the narrow exceptions apply to a particular case.

Part I of this article introduces the doctrine of equivalents, prosecution history estoppel, and the *Festo* decisions that created the exceptions thereto. Part II discusses a decade of Federal Circuit cases following the Supreme Court's *Festo* decision that consider the tangential exception to prosecution history estoppel. Part III provides a discussion of Federal Circuit cases addressing the unforeseeability exception. Part IV discusses the last exception, whether the patentee has "some other reason" why the applicant could not have been expected to draft the patent claims to cover the accused equivalent. Part V includes a table of all relevant Federal Circuit decisions relating to the exceptions to prosecution history estoppel, including authoring judge and panel members. The article concludes, in Part VI, with a discussion of scenarios where the exceptions to prosecution history estoppel are likely to apply.

---

[3] 535 U.S. 722 (2002). This Article shall adopt the notation used by both Sharp and Walter for numbering each of the individual *Festo* cases. *See* Marc D. Sharp, Note, Festo X: *The Complete Bar by Another Name?*, 19 BERKELEY TECH. L.J. 111 (2004); Derek Walter, Note, *Prosecution History Estoppel in the Post-Festo Era: The Increased Importance of Determining What Constitutes a Relevant Narrowing Claim Amendment*, 20 BERKELEY TECH. L.J. 123 (2005).
[4] *Festo VIII*, 535 U.S. at 740–41.

I.   BACKGROUND ON THE DOCTRINE OF EQUIVALENTS,
       PROSECUTION HISTORY ESTOPPEL, AND EXCEPTIONS
       THERETO.

A. *The Doctrine of Equivalents: An Exception to Literal
    Infringement.*

It is hornbook law that a patent is only literally infringed if every limitation in a claim, as properly construed, reads exactly on an accused product.[5] This bright-line rule could allow accused infringers to avoid infringement by making "unimportant and insubstantial changes" to patented inventions.[6] To avoid the harsh effects of the limits of literal infringement, courts created a judicial mechanism to expand protection to patentees: the doctrine of equivalents ("DOE").[7] The Supreme Court affirmed, in *Graver Tank & Manufacturing Co. v. Linde Air Products Co.,*[8] that under the DOE, a patentee may assert infringement over a product that "performs substantially the same function in substantially the same way to obtain the same result," even if it does not literally infringe.[9]

The expanded protection patentees receive under the DOE arguably conflicts with the notice function of patent claims.[10] The Patent Act requires a patent applicant to particularly point out and distinctly claim the subject matter of his invention in order to provide fair notice to the public about the "metes and bounds of the claimed invention."[11] With proper notice of the claimed invention, competitors are able to avoid infringement by designing around the patent.[12] The patent system encourages competitors to create new inventions by making substantial changes to a patented invention.[13] Competitors would not be able to design around patents, however, if the DOE were

---

[5] Strattec Sec. Corp. v. Gen. Auto. Specialty Co., 126 F.3d 1411, 1418 (Fed. Cir. 1997).

[6] Graver Tank & Mfg. Co. v. Linde Air Prods. Co., 339 U.S. 605, 607 (1950).

[7] *Id.* at 608.

[8] 339 U.S. 605 (1950).

[9] *Id.* at 608 (internal quotation marks omitted).

[10] Warner-Jenkinson Co. v. Hilton Davis Chem. Co., 520 U.S. 17, 29 (1997).

[11] Wallace London & Clemco Prods. v. Carson Pirie Scott & Co., 946 F.2d 1534, 1538 (Fed. Cir. 1991); *see also* 35 U.S.C. § 112 (2012).

[12] *Wallace,* 946 F.2d at 1538.

[13] *Id.*

applied so broadly that the public no longer had clear notice of the scope of the invention.[14]

Cognizant of the tension between the desire to properly protect patent owners and encourage patent innovation, and the desire to protect the rights of the public to know what is and is not an infringement, courts have allowed the application of the DOE, while recognizing that its reach must be carefully limited. These competing interests—and the inherent uncertainty surrounding the DOE—have caused courts trouble as they try to define the proper scope of the doctrine.

B. *Prosecution History Estoppel: An Exception to an Exception.*

Prosecution history estoppel ("PHE") is a legal instrument that courts use to strike a balance between the notice function of patent claims and the expanded protection that results when the DOE is applied.[15] PHE serves to limit, and is available as a defense to, the DOE.[16] In *Warner-Jenkinson Co. v. Hilton Davis Chemical Co.,*[17] the Supreme Court held that a patentee may be estopped from relying on the DOE to assert infringement of a claim if the patentee amended the claim to avoid prior art.[18] In this way, PHE tempers the patentee's ability to assert infringement under the DOE after disclaiming subject matter by narrowing the scope of a claim in order to secure the grant of a patent.[19]

The *Warner-Jenkinson* Court placed the burden on the patentee to demonstrate that the reason for an amendment was

---

[14] *Warner-Jenkinson*, 520 U.S. at 29 ("It is important to ensure that the application of the doctrine, even as to an individual element, is not allowed such broad play as to effectively eliminate that element in its entirety."); *Wallace*, 946 F.2d at 1538 ("Application of the doctrine of equivalents is the exception, however, not the rule, for if the public comes to believe (or fear) that the language of patent claims can never be relied on, and that the doctrine of equivalents is simply the second prong of every infringement charge, regularly available to extend protection beyond the scope of the claims, then claims will cease to serve their intended purpose.").

[15] *Warner-Jenkinson*, 520 U.S. at 33.

[16] *Id.* at 30, 40.

[17] 520 U.S. 17 (1997).

[18] *Id.* at 30.

[19] Exhibit Supply Co. v. Ace Patents Corp., 315 U.S. 126, 136 (1942) ("[I]t has long been settled that recourse may not be had to [the doctrine of equivalents] to recapture claims which the patentee has surrendered by amendment.").

unrelated to patentability in order to maintain an infringement claim under the DOE.[20] If the reason for a narrowing amendment is not apparent from the prosecution history, the Court applies a rebuttable presumption that the amendment was made for reasons related to patentability.[21] If the patentee is unable to rebut the presumption with an appropriate reason for the amendment, then PHE bars the patentee from asserting infringement under the DOE.[22] PHE allows the public to rely on a patent's prosecution history, and the estoppel resulting from a narrowing amendment, to avoid infringement of an amended claim.[23]

C. *The Rise of the Three Exceptions to Prosecution History Estoppel: The* Festo *Decisions.*

1. Festo VII: *The Federal Circuit declares that PHE is unrebuttable.*

The Federal Circuit, sitting en banc in 2000, considered the limits of PHE in *Festo Corp. v. Shoketsu Kinzoku Kogyo Kabushiki Co.*[24] Festo had sued Shoketsu Kinzoku Kogyo Kabushiki Co. ("SMC") for infringement of two of its patents, the "Stoll patent" and "Carroll patent," which relate to magnetically coupled rodless cylinders.[25] The district court held that SMC infringed the Carroll patent under the DOE

---

[20] *Warner-Jenkinson*, 520 U.S. at 33.

[21] *Id.*

[22] *Id.* In *Conoco, Inc. v. Energy & Environmental International, L.C.*, the patentee was able to rebut the presumption of PHE. 460 F.3d 1349 (Fed. Cir. 2006). Conoco's patent application claimed the use of fatty acid waxes such as stearamides. *Id.* at 1354. The patent examiner rejected the claims in light of prior art use of metal stearates, which it deemed to be functionally equivalent. *Id.* Conoco canceled the original claims and submitted twenty-two new claims, with all but one of the new claims containing a "fatty acid wax" limitation. *Id.* The examiner later amended the remaining claim to include the "fatty acid wax" limitation. *Id.* at 1354–55. The defendant argued that Conoco was barred by PHE from asserting infringement over any equivalents of "fatty acid wax," because it was a narrowing amendment made during prosecution. *Id.* at 1363. The Federal Circuit instead held that the amendment was not made for patentability reasons, but to correct an obvious omission. *Id.* at 1364. The prosecution history showed that the applicant and examiner continually argued about whether "fatty acid wax" was novel over metal stearates and treated the limitation as if it were present throughout prosecution. *Id.*

[23] *Festo VIII*, 535 U.S. 722, 727 (2002).

[24] Festo Corp. v. Shoketsu Kinzoku Kogyo Kabushiki Co. (*Festo VII*), 234 F.3d 558 (Fed. Cir. 2000).

[25] *Id.* at 578.

and granted partial summary judgment to Festo.[26] At trial, the jury found that SMC also infringed the Stoll patent under the DOE.[27] On appeal before a Federal Circuit panel, the court affirmed the district court's decision.[28] The Supreme Court, however, vacated and remanded the case for reconsideration in light of its recent decision in *Warner-Jenkinson*.[29]

On remand, in *Festo VII*, an eight-to-four majority of the Federal Circuit en banc panel held that "a narrowing amendment made for any reason related to the statutory requirements for a patent will give rise to prosecution history estoppel with respect to the amended claim element."[30] The court noted that, while the Supreme Court's focus in *Warner-Jenkinson* was on amendments made to avoid prior art and not amendments made for other reasons related to patentability, amendments made for "substantial reason[s] related to patentability" extend beyond the statutory requirements of novelty and nonobviousness.[31] The Federal Circuit determined that its holding was not inconsistent with *Warner-Jenkinson*.[32]

The en banc majority further held that, when an amendment to a claim element creates PHE, a patentee is completely barred from asserting the DOE with respect to that claim element.[33] The court found there was a need for certainty regarding the territory of surrender when patent claims are amended, and with a complete bar the public could be certain the scope of the amended claim element did not extend beyond the literal terms of the claim.[34] A complete bar to the application of the DOE, according to the majority, would underscore the importance of the notice function of claims.[35]

---

[26] Festo Corp. v. Shoketsu Kinzoku Kogyo Kabushiki Co. (*Festo I*), 1993 U.S. Dist. LEXIS 21434 (D. Mass. 1993).
[27] *Id.*
[28] Festo Corp. v. Shoketsu Kinzoku Kabushiki Co. (*Festo II*), 72 F.3d 857 (Fed. Cir. 1995).
[29] Festo Corp. v. Shoketsu Kinzoku Kabushiki Co. (*Festo IV*), 520 U.S. 1111 (1997).
[30] *Festo VII*, 234 F.3d at 566.
[31] *Id.* at 567–68. The court cited the patentable subject matter requirement of 35 U.S.C. § 101, as well as the written description, enablement, definiteness, and best mode requirements of 35 U.S.C. § 112, as statutory requirements for patentability that do not involve overcoming prior art. *Id.*
[32] *Id.*
[33] *Id.* at 569.
[34] *Id.* at 577.
[35] *Id.* at 575.

Addressing Festo's Stoll patent, the Federal Circuit held that PHE barred Festo from asserting any range of equivalents for its "magnetizable sleeve" and "sealing ring" elements.[36] Festo's original independent claim 1 contained neither of the two elements at issue, which were found in the original dependent claims instead.[37] In response to a 35 U.S.C. § 112 rejection addressed to whether the claim was directed to a motor or clutch, the applicant amended the independent claim to recite the "magnetizable sleeve" element as well as "first sealing rings" and "second sealing rings" and canceled the dependent claims, one of which generally recited "sealing rings."[38] In the same office action response, the applicant cited two German patents and argued that the claims were distinguishable over the patents.[39] The Federal Circuit reversed the jury's finding of infringement under the DOE because it held that both the "magnetizable sleeve" and "sealing ring" elements were narrowing amendments made for patentability reasons because they were made in response to a 35 U.S.C. § 112 rejection.[40] To further support its conclusion that the "sealing ring" limitation was amended for a reason related to patentability, the court pointed to the applicant's statement that the limitation distinguished the invention from the two German prior art references, which did not disclose sealing rings.[41]

Festo's Carroll patent claimed a "pair of resilient sealing rings," which the district court held was infringed under the DOE.[42] Festo argued that PHE should not apply because the original patent applicant (from whom Festo acquired the patent) voluntarily amended the claim to add the limitation during a reexamination of the patent.[43] Festo argued the amendment was not made for patentability reasons because it did not distinguish the invention from the German patent cited as prior art during reexamination, which also disclosed a pair of

---

[36] *Id.* at 588, 591.

[37] *Id.* at 582–83.

[38] *Id.* at 583.

[39] *Id.*

[40] *Id.* at 588–89. The Federal Circuit noted that the "magnetizable sleeve" limitation did not address the patent examiner's § 112 rejection, but there was nothing in the prosecution history that indicated that the amendment was made for clarification purposes rather than patentability reasons. The court also held that because the "sealing ring" limitation was added to satisfy the § 112 rejection, the amendment was made for patentability reasons. *Id.*

[41] *Id.* at 589.

[42] *Id.* at 589–90.

[43] *Id.* at 590.

sealing rings.[44] The Federal Circuit rejected this argument and reversed the district court's grant of summary judgment, holding that a voluntary amendment does not escape PHE.[45] The court further held that Festo could not overcome the presumption that the amendment was made for patentability reasons because, while the "pair of resilient sealing rings" limitation alone may not have distinguished the prior art, the combination of elements was patentable over prior art.[46]

Judges Michel, Rader, Linn, and Newman dissented from the majority's holding that a patentee is completely barred from relying on the DOE for claims amended for any reason related to patentability.[47] Judge Michel asserted that the Supreme Court's *Warner-Jenkinson* opinion struck the appropriate balance between the notice function of claims and the unfairness patentees face if they are limited to protection from literal infringement, a balance which the majority now disrupted by creating the complete bar to the DOE.[48] Judge Michel performed an extensive analysis of past Supreme Court cases as well as Federal Circuit cases and argued the cases supported a flexible application of PHE.[49] All of the dissenting judges agreed that the complete bar to the DOE would effectively allow copyists to avoid infringement by making insubstantial changes to claim elements that had been amended during prosecution.[50]

2.   Festo VIII: *The Supreme Court rejects the complete bar and provides three exceptions to prosecution history estoppel.*

---

[44] *Id.*
[45] *Id.* at 591.
[46] *Id.*
[47] Judge Michel wrote an opinion concurring-in-part and dissenting-in-part and was joined by Judge Rader. *See Id.* at 598 (Michel, J., concurring-in-part, dissenting-in-part). Judge Rader wrote a separate opinion concurring-in-part and dissenting-in-part. *Id.* at 619 (Rader, J., concurring-in-part, dissenting-in-part). Judge Linn, also joined by Judge Rader, wrote a third opinion concurring-in-part and dissenting-in-part. *Id.* at 620 (Linn, J., concurring-in-part, dissenting-in-part). Judge Newman wrote a fourth separate opinion, concurring-in-part and dissenting-in-part. *Id.* at 630 (Newman, J., concurring-in-part, dissenting-in-part).
[48] *Id.* at 598 (Michel, J., concurring-in-part, dissenting-in-part).
[49] *See id.* at 601–15.
[50] *See id.* at 616, 627.

The Supreme Court accepted certiorari and affirmed the Federal Circuit's holding that a claim amendment made for any reason related to patentability triggers a presumption of PHE.[51] The Court explained that, while an amendment to satisfy the 35 U.S.C. § 112 written description, enablement, and best mode requirements may be clarifying rather than narrowing, if the amendment narrows the claim, estoppel may apply.[52] A narrowing amendment to overcome a patentability rejection, according to the Court, reflects a patentee's concession that his invention is not as broad as his original claim.[53] Were it otherwise, the patentee could have chosen to appeal the patent examiner's rejection.[54]

The Supreme Court, however, overturned the Federal Circuit's finding that once a narrowing amendment for reasons related to patentability is made, it is a complete bar to the DOE.[55] The Court recognized that words cannot always capture the essence of an invention, and the purpose of the DOE is to allow a patent's scope to cover equivalents that do not fit the literal terms of the patent.[56] While a narrowing amendment is a concession that the invention is not as broad as the original claim, the Court reasoned, it does not follow that the amended claim is able to capture the invention so precisely that all equivalents should be foreclosed.[57]

Rather than a complete bar to the DOE, when a patent applicant makes a narrowing amendment, the Supreme Court held that there is a *presumption* that an amendment surrenders the equivalent in question and the patentee then has the burden of overcoming the presumption.[58] The Court specified three instances where a patentee could overcome the presumption that PHE applies and demonstrate an amendment does not surrender an equivalent: 1) the rationale underlying the amendment has a mere tangential relation to the accused equivalent; 2) the accused equivalent was unforeseeable at the time of the amendment; or 3) there was some other reason that the patentee

---

[51] *Festo VIII*, 535 U.S. 722, 736 (2002).

[52] *Id.* at 736–37.

[53] *Id.* at 737.

[54] *Id.* at 734 ("While the patentee had the right to appeal, his decision to forego an appeal and submit an amended claim is taken as a concession that the invention as patented does not reach as far as the original claim.").

[55] *Id.* at 737.

[56] *Festo VIII*, 535 U.S. at 731–32.

[57] *Id.* at 738.

[58] *Id.* at 740.

could not have been expected to describe the accused equivalent.[59] The Supreme Court then remanded the case for the Federal Circuit to consider whether Festo was able to rebut the presumption that its narrowing amendments surrendered the equivalents at issue.[60]

> 3. Festo X: *The Federal Circuit provided further guidance on the three exceptions to prosecution history estoppel.*

On remand from the Supreme Court, the Federal Circuit found that PHE still applied to Festo's Stoll and Carroll patents.[61] In its opinion, the court provided guidance on how to approach the three exceptions to PHE laid out by the Supreme Court in *Festo VIII*.[62] First, the court acknowledged that PHE applies only to amendments that narrow the scope of a claim. If an amendment is determined to be narrowing, then, under *Warner-Jenkinson*, there is a rebuttable presumption that the amendment was made "for a substantial reason related to patentability."[63] The patentee then carries the burden to rebut the presumption using only evidence from the prosecution history.[64] The patentee can successfully rebut the presumption if it can show that the amendment was not made for reasons related to patentability.

If the patentee is unable to rebut the *Warner-Jenkinson* presumption, or if the reason given for the amendment in the prosecution history is related to patentability, then the *Festo* presumption applies.[65] In other words, there is a second presumption that the narrowing amendment surrendered all equivalents that fall in the territory between the unamended and amended claim limitation.

The patentee then has the burden of proving that it did not surrender the accused equivalent using one of the three exceptions the Supreme Court set forth: 1) the tangential exception, 2) the unforeseeability exception, or 3) the "some other reason" exception.

The court was clear that when an equivalent is found in the cited prior art, none of the three exceptions are available and PHE

---

[59] *Id.* at 740–41.
[60] *Id.* at 741–42.
[61] Festo Corp. v. Shoketsu Kinzoku Kogyo Kabushiki Co. (*Festo X*), 344 F.3d 1359 (Fed. Cir. 2003).
[62] *Id.* at 1366–67.
[63] *Id.* at 1366.
[64] *Id.* at 1367.
[65] *Id.*

applies.[66] The court explained that if the accused equivalent is found in the prior art in the same field of invention, it should have been foreseeable to one of skill in the art at the time of the amendment.[67] In addition, if the amendment was made to overcome prior art containing the equivalent, the reason for the amendment is directly related to the equivalent.[68] Lastly, the court held that a patentee could not have any other reason for not being able to describe the accused equivalent if it was in the prior art.[69]

The court evaluated the Stoll and Carroll patents under these guidelines. It determined PHE presumptively applied because the amendments narrowed the claims and were made for patentability reasons. The court further found that Festo was unable to rebut the presumption that the amendments disclaimed the territory between the original limitations and the amended limitations.

The court found that because the applicant amended the Stoll patent during prosecution to add the "magnetizable" limitation, one of the two limitations at issue, the applicant presumptively disclaimed nonmagnetizable sleeves. Festo argued that the tangential exception applied. Specifically, Festo asserted that Stoll added the limitation when he rewrote multiple claims as a single independent claim in response to a 35 U.S.C. § 112 rejection, which meant that the "magnetizable" limitation was only tangential to the 35 U.S.C. § 112 rejection.[70] The Federal Circuit disagreed, determining that Festo failed to show that "the rationale for the 'magnetizable' amendment was only tangential to the *accused equivalent*."[71] The court concluded Festo could not satisfy the tangential exception for the "magnetizable" limitation, as the court could not discern the reason for the amendment from the prosecution history.[72] Without a rationale for the amendment,

---

[66] *See id.* at 1369–70.

[67] *Id.* at 1369.

[68] *Id.* ("Although we cannot anticipate the instances of mere tangentialness that may arise, we can say that an amendment made to avoid prior art that contains the equivalent is not tangential; it is central to allowance of the claim.").

[69] *Id.* at 1370 ("[A] patentee may not rely on the third rebuttal criterion if the alleged equivalent is in the prior art, for then 'there can be no other reason the patentee could not have described the substitute in question.'" (quoting Pioneer Magnetics, Inc. v. Micro Linear Corp., 330 F.3d 1352, 1357 (Fed. Cir. 2003)).

[70] *Id.* at 1371–72.

[71] *Id.* at 1372 (emphasis added).

[72] *Id.* at 1371–72. *See supra* Part I.C.1. The applicant added the "magnetizable" sleeve limitation after the patent examiner issued a § 112 rejection, but the amendment did not address the examiner's rejection.

Festo could not show that the rationale was only tangential to the accused aluminum sleeve equivalent.[73]

Regarding the second "sealing ring" limitations at issue in both the Stoll and Carroll patents, the Federal Circuit also held that Festo was unable to overcome the presumption that the narrowing amendments surrendered the equivalents at issue using the tangential exception.[74] The patent applicant amended the Stoll patent, which originally recited "sealing means," to recite "first sealing rings" and "second sealing rings." The court thus presumed that Stoll surrendered all "sealing means" other than structures with two sealing rings.[75] Festo argued the amendment to the Stoll patent was to "clarify" the invention in response to a 35 U.S.C. § 112 rejection.[76] As for the Carroll patent, although the original claims did not refer to any sealing rings, Festo amended the patent during reexamination to add the "pair of resilient sealing rings" limitation.[77] Festo argued that, because the German prior art patent at issue during reexamination already disclosed sealing rings, the amendment was not necessary to distinguish the prior art.[78]

The Federal Circuit reiterated its holding in *Festo VII*, which was unaffected by the Supreme Court's decision in *Festo VIII*, that both of the "sealing ring" limitations in the Stoll and Carroll patents were added to distinguish prior art.[79] Specifically, the court held that Festo overcame two prior art references by adding the "sealing rings" limitation to the Stoll patent.[80] Likewise, Festo overcame the sealing ring limitation disclosed in the German prior art patent by claiming a *pair* of sealing rings during reexamination of the Carroll patent.[81] Thus, the court concluded that PHE presumptively applied and the reasons for the amendments were not tangentially related to the accused product, a single two-way sealing ring.[82]

The Federal Circuit next found that Festo's arguments were insufficient to show that there was "some other reason" that the applicant could not have been expected to draft the patent claims to

---

[73] *Id.* at 1371–72.
[74] *Id.* at 1373.
[75] *Id.* at 1373–74.
[76] *Id.* at 1373.
[77] *Id.* at 1372.
[78] *Id.* at 1373.
[79] *Id.* (citing *Festo VII*, 234 F.3d 558, 589, 591 (Fed. Cir. 2000)).
[80] *Id.* at 1372.
[81] *Id.*
[82] *Id.*

cover the accused equivalent.[83] Festo argued that it "could not reasonably have been expected to have drafted a claim to cover what was thought to be an inferior and unacceptable design."[84] The court held that Festo's reasoning indicated that Festo could have chosen to draft a claim to cover an aluminum sleeve, but chose not to because the element was "inferior."[85] The court also found a lack of linguistic or "other" limitation that rendered the patent applicant unable to describe the accused equivalent, as the applicant could have claimed a nonmagnetizable sleeve just as he had claimed a magnetizable sleeve or could have generally claimed a "metal" sleeve.[86] The Federal Circuit rejected Festo's similar argument that it could not have been expected to draft a claim to cover the accused sealing ring equivalent, which was inferior.[87] If the patent applicant knew about the equivalent and chose not to claim it, the court reasoned, Festo could not argue that the applicant was unable to describe the equivalent.[88] The court also found that Festo's original claim of the Stoll patent, which recited "sealing means," was broad enough to literally encompass the accused equivalent.[89] This was at odds with Festo's argument that the applicant could not have been expected to broaden its original claim to capture the equivalent.[90] The court lastly held that there was no linguistic barrier preventing Festo from describing the single two-way sealing ring equivalent, because the difference between the claimed "sealing rings" and the equivalent was simply a matter of quantity.[91]

The court remanded the case for the district court to consider whether Festo could rebut the presumption that it surrendered the accused equivalent under the unforeseeability exception because issues of fact existed as to the objective unforeseeability of the accused equivalents at the time of the amendment.[92]

---

[83] *Festo X*, 344 F.3d at 1373.
[84] *Id.*
[85] *Id.*
[86] *Id.* at 1372.
[87] *Id.* at 1373.
[88] *Id.* 1372.
[89] *Id.* at 1373.
[90] *Id.*
[91] *Id.* at 1373.
[92] *Id.* at 1374.

> 4. Festo XI: *The Federal Circuit provided further guidance on the foreseeability exception to prosecution history estoppel.*

On remand after *Festo X*, the district court determined that Festo was unable to show that the accused aluminum sleeve and single two-way sealing ring equivalents were unforeseeable at the time of the amendment.[93] Festo appealed once again.

On appeal, in *Festo XI*,[94] the Federal Circuit held that "[a]n equivalent is foreseeable if one skilled in the art would have known that the alternative existed in the field of art as defined by the original claim scope, even if the suitability of the alternative for the particular purposes defined by the amended claim scope were unknown."[95] The court expressly rejected Festo's argument that the test for the unforeseeability exception should be the same test as determining infringement by equivalents, i.e. whether a person of ordinary skill in the art, at the time of the amendment, is able to foresee that the equivalent performs the same function, in the same way, with the same result or that the differences are merely insubstantial.[96]

The court found that Festo's original broader, independent claim did not require a sleeve to be made of "magnetizable" material, which meant that the sleeve could have been made of any material; the "magnetizable sleeve" was a limitation in another dependent claim.[97] The court noted that a German prior art patent cited in the prosecution history expressly claimed a sleeve made of "non-magnetic material."[98] Because a non-magnetizable alternative was foreseeable and Festo chose not to claim it, the court concluded that Festo surrendered the aluminum sleeve equivalent.[99] Festo was therefore estopped from maintaining an assertion of infringement under the DOE because none of the exceptions to PHE applied.

---

[93] Festo Corp. v. Shoketsu Kinzoku Kogyo Kabushiki Co. (*Festo XI*), 493 F.3d 1368, 1375–76 (Fed. Cir. 2007).
[94] 493 F.3d 1368 (Fed. Cir. 2007).
[95] *Id.* at 1382.
[96] *Id.*
[97] *Id.*
[98] *Id.*
[99] *Id.* at 1383. Because the court found that Festo was barred by PHE for the "magnetizable sleeve" limitation, it did not reach the "sealing rings" limitation. *See id.*

II.   THE FEDERAL CIRCUIT'S POST-*FESTO* APPLICATION
OF THE TANGENTIAL EXCEPTION TO PROSECUTION HISTORY
ESTOPPEL.

The Supreme Court held that a patentee may overcome PHE if the patentee is able to show that the *reason* for the narrowing amendment is merely "tangential" *to the accused equivalent*.[100] How this rule applies to various factual scenarios, however, is not always clear. This section of the article attempts to discern the scope of the application of the tangential exception to PHE by examining Federal Circuit cases decided since the Supreme Court's *Festo VIII* decision, and to provide some guidance to evaluate when and why the tangential exception applies.

A. *The Reason for the Allegedly Tangential Amendment Must be Discernible Solely from the Intrinsic Record.*

The Federal Circuit, in *Festo X*, held that the tangential exception is an objective inquiry and the reason for the amendment must be discernible from the intrinsic record, i.e. the prosecution history.[101] Unlike the foreseeability exception, extrinsic evidence may not be used in evaluating whether an amendment is merely tangential to the accused equivalent.[102] Allowing the patentee to rely on extrinsic evidence, according to the court, would undermine the public notice function of a patent and its prosecution history.[103] Thus, only intrinsic evidence (such as the prosecution history) may be considered in evaluating whether the tangential exception applies.[104]

---

[100] *Festo VIII*, 535 U.S. 722, 740–41 (2002).

[101] *Festo X*, 344 F.3d 1359, 1369–70 (Fed. Cir. 2003).

[102] *Id.* The court held that extrinsic evidence such as expert testimony should only be used when necessary to interpret the prosecution history. *Id.*

[103] *Id.*

[104] *Id.* at 1367 ("In this regard, we reinstate our earlier holding that a patentee's rebuttal of the *Warner-Jenkinson* presumption is restricted to the evidence in the prosecution history record."); *see also* Talbert Fuel Sys. Patents Co. v. Unocal Corp., 347 F.3d 1355, 1360 (Fed. Cir. 2003) (citing *Festo X*, 344 F.3d at 1369–70) ("This court's remand decision in *Festo* generally prohibits evidence outside the prosecution record in deciding this ground of rebuttal."); Pioneer Magnetics Inc. v. Micro Linear Corp., 330 F.3d 1352, 1356 (Fed. Cir. 2003) ("First, we do not consider the Beecher declaration in determining the reason for the amendment to the claim. Only the public record of the patent prosecution, the prosecution history, can be a basis for such a reason. Otherwise the public notice function of the patent record would be undermined.").

As discussed in Part I.C.3, in *Festo X*, the Federal Circuit held that the tangential exception did not apply because the court could not discern the reason for the amendment from the prosecution history.[105] Without a rationale for the amendment, Festo could not show that the rationale was tangential to the accused equivalent.[106] And since the Federal Circuit's decision in *Festo X*, the Federal Circuit has required that the patentee proffer a reason for the amendment that is tangential to the accused equivalent and has routinely considered only intrinsic evidence in evaluating whether the tangential exception applies.[107]

> B. *Even if an Applicant Did Not Need to Amend A Claim in a Specific Way to Overcome the Prior Art, the Tangential Exception May Not Apply to that Added Limitation.*

---

[105] *Festo X*, 344 F.3d at 1371–72. The applicant added the "magnetizable" sleeve limitation after the patent examiner issued a § 112 rejection, but the amendment did not address the examiner's rejection. *See supra* Part I.C.1.

[106] *Festo X*, 344 F.3d at 1371–72.

[107] *See, e.g.*, A G Design & Assocs. LLC v. Trainman Lantern Co., 271 Fed. App'x. 995, 998 (Fed. Cir. 2008) (The Federal Circuit held that AG conflated the tangential exception with the function-way-result test for infringement under the doctrine of equivalents by arguing that "[t]he addition of ports in the reflector bears only a tangential relationship to the equivalent in question," which lacks a plurality of ports, because the accused product performs the claimed function in the same way. Because "AG has not put forth a rationale for the amendment that is tangential to the equivalent in question," PHE precluded a finding of infringement under the doctrine of equivalents.); Voda v. Cordis Corp., 536 F.3d 1311 (Fed. Cir. 2008) (holding that PHE barred a finding of equivalence because the patentee did not make any argument to overcome the presumption of PHE); O2 Micro Int'l Ltd. v. Beyond Innovation Technology Co., 521 F.3d 1351, 1364 (Fed. Cir. 2008); Business Objects, S.A. v. MicroStrategy, Inc., 393 F.3d 1366, 1374 (Fed. Cir. 2005) (The Federal Circuit held that the patentee overcame prior art by amending the method claim to add an "associating" step, because the prior art did not associate WHERE clauses with a familiar name. The accused equivalent, a method that associates something equivalent to a WHERE clause to a familiar name, was therefore directly rather than tangentially related to the reason for the amendment.); Terlep v. Brinkman Corp., 418 F.3d 1379, 1385–86 (Fed. Cir. 2005) ("Terlep asserts that the prosecution history shows that the addition of the term 'clear' was merely to describe the plastic used for the claimed 'plastic holder,' and thus the addition of that term is not directly relevant to the accused equivalent. However, as discussed *supra*, Terlep amended claim 1 and argued patentability based on the diffusion characteristics of prior art LED devices and the absence of diffusion in the clear plastic tubular holder of the claimed invention. Thus, it cannot be said that the reason for adding 'clear' was tangential to the accused equivalents, which are holders that are ribbed and diffuse light."); Biagro Western Sales, Inc. v. Grow More, Inc., 423 F.3d 1296, 1306 (Fed. Cir. 2005).

Federal Circuit decisions indicate that when claim limitations were previously missing and added for patentability reasons, the presence of those limitations were likely at issue during prosecution. Therefore, the patentee could not later claim that the *reason* for the amendment is only tangential to an equivalent of the disputed limitation.[108]

> 1. Chimie v. PPG: *The tangential exception does not apply even though the claimed equivalent was not in the prior art.*

In *Chimie v. PPG Industries*, the Federal Circuit held that the tangential exception did not apply to Chimie's "dust-free and non-dusting" limitation.[109] Chimie had a patent covering silica of a particular spheroidal shape and size, which is used as fillers in elastomeric products such as automobile tires.[110] The district court found, and Chimie conceded on appeal, that Chimie added the "dust-free and non-dusting" limitation to its claim to distinguish the invention from prior art, which consisted of "powdered or granulated silicas."[111] Thus prosecution history presumptively applied.

The court rejected Chimie's argument that the *reason* for the amendment adding "dust-free and non-dusting" was merely tangential to the accused equivalent, "spray-dried silica microspheres."[112] Chimie argued that the amendment was tangential because the accused equivalent was not in the prior art.[113] According to Chimie's reasoning, the amendment was not made to overcome prior art that contained the equivalent, and thus the tangential exception should apply.[114] The Federal Circuit disagreed.[115] It explained that while an amendment made to distinguish prior art that contains the equivalent is not tangential to the equivalent, the inverse is not necessarily true.[116] The

---

[108] *Festo X*, 344 F.3d at 1369 ("In other words, this criterion asks whether the reason for the narrowing amendment was peripheral, or not directly relevant, to the alleged equivalent.").
[109] 402 F.3d 1371 (Fed. Cir. 2005).
[110] *Id.* at 1374.
[111] *Id.* at 1380, 1382.
[112] *Id.* at 1383.
[113] *Id.*
[114] *Id.*
[115] *Chimie*, 402 F.3d at 1383.
[116] *Id.* ("It does not follow, however, that the equivalents not within the prior art must be tangential to the amendment.").

Federal Circuit concluded that Chimie surrendered all equivalents of silica that did not fit within the literal scope of the added limitation of "dust-free and non-dusting," as Chimie's patent covers an improvement over granulated silica in the prior art and the dustiness of the claimed silica was at issue during prosecution.[117] Chimie was thus estopped from recapturing the accused "spray-dried silica microspheres," which had dust levels higher than "dust-free and non-dusting."[118]

>   2.   Felix v. American Honda: *Silence does not overcome the presumption of PHE and it is irrelevant if the narrowing amendment did not secure allowance of the claim.*

In *Felix v. American Honda Motor Co.*, the Federal Circuit explained silence does not overcome the presumption of PHE, and it is irrelevant if the narrowing amendment did not secure allowance of the claim.[119] In that case, patentee Felix made a first amendment cancelling original independent claim 1 and re-writing dependent claim 7 (which included channel and gasket limitations not present in claim 1) in independent form.[120] Even after Felix re-wrote claim 7, the PTO did not allow the claim.[121] Felix then re-wrote claim 8, which contained additional limitations, in independent form, and the claim was allowed.[122]

Felix then accused a product of infringing where the gasket of the accused compartment was not securely affixed to the compartment, even though the claims literally required "a weathertight gasket mounted on said flange and engaging said lid in its closed position."[123] Felix argued that the amendment adding the gasket limitation was tangential to patentability and thus the tangential exception to PHE applied.[124] The district court found that the amendment was not tangential, such that PHE applied, and Felix appealed.[125]

---

[117] *Id.*
[118] *Id.*
[119] 562 F.3d 1167 (Fed. Cir. 2009).
[120] *Id.* at 1182.
[121] *Id.*
[122] *Id.*
[123] *Id.* at 1173, 1181.
[124] *Id.* at 1181.
[125] *Felix*, 562 F.3d at 1181.

The Federal Circuit agreed with the district court that the addition of the channel and gasket limitations and cancellation of claim 1 created a presumption of PHE with respect to the added elements in claim 7.[126] Felix argued that prosecution history estoppel did not apply to equivalents containing a gasket because "the first amendment 'was made because the applicant thought the prior art lacked a channel,' not because of the presence or position of a gasket."[127] The court rejected this argument, reasoning that "[i]f Felix had intended only to add a channel and not add a gasket, he could easily have simply amended original claim 1 to add limitation (e) and not limitation (f)."[128] The court rejected the suggestion that silence could overcome the presumption of PHE: "Felix has identified no explanation in the prosecution history for the addition of the gasket limitation, and Felix therefore cannot meet his burden to show that the rationale for adding the gasket limitation was tangential to the presence and position of a gasket."[129]

The court also rejected Felix's argument that PHE should not apply because the amendment was not successful in obtaining the claim and that a further amendment was needed:

> The fact that the first amendment did not succeed and that a further amendment was required to place the claim in allowable form, however, is of no consequence as to the estoppel. It's the patentee's response to the rejection—not the examiner's

---

[126] *Id.* at 1181–82 (citing Honeywell Int'l, Inc. v. Hamilton Sundstrand Corp., 370 F.3d 1131, 1139 (Fed. Cir. 2004) (en banc)); *see infra* Part II.C.

[127] *Felix*, 562 F.3d at 1184 (emphasis in original).

[128] *Id.* (emphasis in original).

[129] *Id.*; *see also* Honeywell Int'l, Inc. v. Hamilton Sundstrand Corp., 523 F.3d 1304, 1316 (Fed. Cir. 2008) ("Silence does not overcome the presumption."); O2 Micro Int'l Ltd. v. Beyond Tech. Co., 521 F.3d 1351, 1365 (Fed. Cir. 2008) ("The 'objectively apparent' reason for the patentee's amendment was to require the feedback circuit to be operational 'only if said feedback signal is above a predetermined threshold,' as the claim language clearly states. No other reason is provided or suggested by the prosecution history."); Biagro W. Sales, Inc. v. Grow More, Inc., 423 F.3d 1296, 1306 (Fed. Cir. 2005) ("Biagro also argues that because only the lower limit of the claimed range was necessary to distinguish over prior art, the reason for the amendment is merely tangential to an accused equivalent at the upper end of the range. . . . [I]n this case, since the prosecution history shows no reason for adding an upper limit to the concentration range, Biagro cannot claim that the rationale for the amendment is merely tangential.").

ultimate allowance of a claim—that gives rise to
prosecution history estoppel.[130]

3.   Integrated v. Rudolph: *Tangential exception did not
apply because while the applicant may not have
needed to add the limitation to overcome the prior
art, it did add the limitation and that was a potential
reason for overcoming the prior art.*

In *Integrated Technology Corp. v. Rudolph Technologies,
Inc.*,[131] the Federal Circuit reversed the district court and held that PHE
barred Integrated from recovering under the DOE.[132] At issue was the
accused infringement of a patent directed at the inspection equipment
for probe cards used to test chips on semiconductor wafers.[133] The
patented system allowed individuals to view whether the probes had
become misaligned based on the three-dimensional relationship to each
other, as measured by taking the coordinates in a first and second
state.[134]

As originally filed, the patent application claimed "a window
with a flat surface contacted by said probe tip."[135] This claim was rejected
as anticipated under 35 U.S.C. § 102(b) and as indefinite under 35 U.S.C. §
112, second paragraph.[136] Integrated amended the claim to recite "in a first
state where said probe tip is driven in contact with said window with a first
force, and in a second state where said probe tip is driven in contact with
said window with a second force."[137] The accused Rudolph instrument
took an image in the first state above the viewing window.[138] In this
manner, the Rudolph instrument was a no-touch product and thus did not
literally infringe. Integrated argued there was infringement under the DOE,
and Rudolph argued that PHE applied to bar equivalents infringement.[139]

This district court found that PHE did not apply.[140] The court
reasoned that because both the original and issued claims required contact

---

[130] *Felix*, 562 F.3d at 1182–83.
[131] 734 F.3d 1352 (Fed. Cir. 2013). The authors were involved with this case.
[132] *Id.* at 1355.
[133] *Id.*
[134] *Id.*
[135] *Id.* at 1356.
[136] *Id.*
[137] *Id.* at 1355 (emphasis omitted).
[138] *Id.*
[139] *Id.*
[140] *Id.* at 1356.

between the plate and the probe, there had been no narrowing amendment.[141] On appeal, the Federal Circuit disagreed and held that there had been a narrowing amendment because the original claims did not require contact in both states, and the amended claims did.[142] Thus, PHE presumptively applied.[143]

The Federal Circuit further concluded that the tangential exception to prosecution history estoppel did not apply. The Federal Circuit held that the reasoning for the amendment was not "objectively apparent from the prosecution history."[144] While Integrated may not have needed to surrender lack of physical contact to overcome prior art that disclosed contact between the plate and probe, Integrated chose to add language requiring that the probe tip be driven into contact with the plate in a first and second state, and that did distinguish the prior art. The Court likened the case to its decision in *Felix v. American Honda Motor Co*, because like that case, the patentee chose to add two limitations when only one non-tangential limitation was required to distinguish the prior art.[145] The Federal Circuit also noted that during prosecution, Integrated represented to the public that it relied on physical contact to overcome the prior art.[146] Thus, the Court concluded that Integrated did not meet its burden to rebut the presumption of PHE by showing that the narrowing amendment was only tangentially related to the equivalent.[147]

4. Intervet v. Merial: *Amendment was tangential to one equivalent, but not to another.*

In *Intervet Inc. v. Merial Ltd.*,[148] the Federal Circuit applied the tangential exception. The patent at issue in that case covered PCV-2, a pathogenic type of porcine circovirus.[149] The patentee, Merial, identified five strains that are representative of PCV-2, deposited the five strains with the USPTO, and disclosed the full DNA sequence for

---

[141] *Id.*

[142] *Id.* at 1357–58.

[143] *Id.*

[144] *Id.* at 1358.

[145] *Id.* (citing Felix v. Am. Honda Motor Co., 562 F.3d 1167, 1184 (Fed. Cir. 2009)).

[146] *Id.* at 1359.

[147] *Id. See also* Lucent Techs., Inc. v. Gateway, Inc., 525 F.3d 1200, 1218 (Fed. Cir. 2008) ("It is not relevant to the determination of the scope of the surrender that the applicant did not need to amend the claims [as they were amended] in order to overcome the prior art.").

[148] 617 F.3d 1282 (Fed. Cir. 2010).

[149] *Id.* at 1285.

four of the strains.[150] The four representative PCV-2 strains that are sequenced have ninety-six percent nucleotide homology with each other but only seventy-six percent nucleotide homology with a representative strain of PCV-1, named PK/15, which is nonpathogenic. Merial also identified thirteen open reading frames ("ORFs") in one of the four representative PCV-2 sequences.[151]

During patent prosecution, Merial originally claimed "ORFs 1-13" without specifying that they were limited to PCV-2.[152] The patent examiner rejected the claim because 1) it captured ORFs from all organisms rather than just porcine circovirus, and 2) the claim was anticipated by PCV-1, as four of the thirteen ORFs are found in both PCV-1 and PCV-2.[153] Merial overcame the rejection by amending the claim to read ORFs 1 to 13 "of porcine circovirus type II."[154]

Intervet's accused vaccine product had a nucleotide sequence that had 99.7% homology to one of Merial's five deposited sequences.[155] The district court held that Intervet did not literally infringe because the nucleotide sequence was not the exact same as any of the deposited sequences and that Merial could not assert infringement by equivalents because of PHE.[156] Because the district court's claim construction was flawed, the Federal Circuit reversed and remanded the case for consideration of literal infringement.[157] The Federal Circuit also considered the district court's holding that Merial was barred from asserting infringement under the DOE due to PHE.[158]

The Federal Circuit held that the amendment was narrowing and that Merial surrendered the territory between PCV-1 and PCV-2.[159] As the court explained, "PCV-2" was previously missing from the claim set, but Merial added the limitation and narrowed its claim.[160] Merial was therefore estopped from asserting any equivalents of PCV-2.

---

[150] *Id.*

[151] *Id.* Open reading frames are portions of the nucleotide sequence between the start and stop codons that code for proteins.

[152] *Id.* at 1291.

[153] *See id.*

[154] *Id.*

[155] *Id.* at 1286.

[156] *Id.* 1290.

[157] *Id.*

[158] *Id.*

[159] *Id.* at 1291.

[160] *Id.*

However, the Federal Circuit held that PHE did not preclude Merial from arguing that "a pathogenic porcine viral sequence with over ninety-nine percent nucleotide homology with one of the five representative strains is equivalent to that strain."[161] The Federal Circuit held that the reason for the amendment, to limit the *claimed ORFs to PCV-2*, was only tangential to accused equivalents that could be *characterized* as PCV-2.[162] The court remanded the case for consideration of infringement under the DOE in addition to literal infringement.[163] The patentee was therefore allowed to argue that the ninety-nine percent homologous sequence is an equivalent to the claimed sequence, as long as the patentee could show that the accused equivalent could be characterized as PCV-2.

5.   *Discussion.*

The Federal Circuit's *Festo X* and *Chimie* decisions indicate that when a patent applicant adds a limitation to a claim that was previously missing from a claim set to overcome the prior art, it is likely that the court will find that the added limitation is directly rather than tangentially related to the accused equivalent, even if it was not necessary to add the limitation. Because the patent applicants added the claim limitations in order to distinguish their inventions from the prior art, the applicants conceded the true boundaries of their invention. The applicants could not later claim that the reasons for adding those limitations are only tangentially related to equivalents that fall outside the boundaries they established.

The court's decision in *Intervet* is likewise consistent with *Festo X* and *Chimie*, as the patentee was still estopped from asserting infringement under the DOE for any accused equivalent of PCV-2, which was the limitation the patent applicant added to overcome a patentability rejection.

C.   *If an Applicant Amends an Independent Claim for Patentability Reasons to Recite a Limitation Previously Found in a Dependent Claim, the Tangential Exception Is*

---

[161] *Id.* at 1292.
[162] *Id.* Although Merial could not assert the DOE to capture equivalents of PCV-2, Merial could assert the DOE to capture equivalents of the claimed ORFs that fall within the literal construed definition of PCV-2.
[163] *Id.*

Available for Aspects of the Limitations That Were Not at Issue During Prosecution.

The Federal Circuit has found that the tangential exception may apply in cases where a patent applicant narrowed an independent claim by including a limitation that was previously in a dependent claim.

> 1. Insituform v. Cat: *When it was clear from the prosecution history that the amended language was not relevant to the amendments over the prior art, the tangential exception applied.*

Insituform Technologies, Inc. v. Cat Contracting Inc., like *Festo X*, was a case where the Federal Circuit reconsidered its decision after the Supreme Court overturned the short-lived complete bar to the DOE for any amended claim element.[164] It is also the first case after *Festo VIII* where the Federal Circuit found that the tangential exception to PHE applied.

Insituform's patent application covered a process for impregnating a liner with resin and installing the liner into an underground pipe in order to repair it while in the ground.[165] The claimed process involved application of a vacuum inside the liner. The claim, as originally drafted, was rejected over prior art that disclosed "use of a continuous vacuum and the creation of that vacuum from only a single vacuum source at the far end of the tube opposite the resin source."[166] Insituform amended its independent claim 1 to include the limitations in dependent claims 2–4 and also to require the vacuum source to be located closer to the resin source.[167] In doing so, Insituform thereby imported the limitation, "a cup," from dependent claim 4 into the independent claim. Specifically, Insituform amended original claim 1 in relevant part as follows, with the underlined material added and removed material stricken, with the amended language at-issue in bold:

---

[164] *See* Insituform. Techs., Inc. v. Cat Contracting, 385 F.3d 1360 (Fed. Cir. 2004).
[165] *Id.* at 1362.
[166] *Id.* at 1369.
[167] *Id.*

A method of impregnating a flexible tube comprising with a curable resin an inner layer of resin absorbent material and disposed in an elongate flexible tube having an outer layer in the form offormed by an impermeable film, wherein the method comprising the resin absorbent layer is impregnated with a curable resin by applying steps of . . . (3) drawing through the inflow a vacuum to the inside ofin the interior of the tube downstream of said one end by disposing over the window **a cup** connected by a flexible tube whilst the resin is brought into impregnation contact with the resin absorbent material, the impermeable film serving as a means to prevent hose to a vacuum source which cup prevents ingress of air into the interior of the tube whilst the impregnation process is taking placewhile the tube is being evacuated, the other lawyer of the tube being substantially impermeable to air. . . .[168]

The defendant argued that PHE barred Insituform from asserting infringement by the DOE over its product, which used multiple cups rather than a single cup.[169] The Federal Circuit disagreed, holding that the *number* of cups in Insituform's claim was never at issue during patent prosecution.[170] The court pointed to the prosecution history, where Insituform expressly argued to the patent examiner that its invention was patentable over prior art because the *location* of the suctioning cup was closer to the resin source.[171] The Federal Circuit concluded that the *reason* for the amendment, to alter the location of the vacuum, was merely tangential to the accused multiple-cup *equivalent.*[172]

    2.   Funai v. Daewoo: *When a dependent claim is re-written as independent, the tangential exception*

---

[168] *Id.* at 1364, 1368–69 (represented as amended claim 1 would appear in the prosecution history).
[169] *Id.* at 1370.
[170] *Id.* at 1369.
[171] *Id.*
[172] *Id.* at 1370.

> *applies to the original elements of the dependent
> claim if they were not at-issue during prosecution.*

Funai Electric Co., Ltd. v. Daewoo Electronics Corp.[173] involved a similar narrowing amendment. Funai was in the business of making video cassette players and recorders ("VCRs") and had a patent over a process of limiting noise and vibration created by a VCRs driving motor.[174] During prosecution, the patent examiner rejected independent claim 1 and dependent claims 2–3 as obvious in view of two prior art patents that disclosed electrically insulating the motor.[175] Because the examiner stated that dependent claim 4 was allowable, the patent applicant canceled claims 1–3 and rewrote claim 4 in independent form. Thus, the original language in claim 4, including "wherein said bearing holder is made of an insulating material," was imported into new independent claim 1.[176]

The defendant argued that Funai was barred by PHE from asserting infringement by equivalents over its VCR product, which had a bearing holder material that was only ninety-two percent insulating.[177] The Federal Circuit disagreed, holding that Funai was not estopped from asserting the DOE because the *nature* of the insulating material was never at issue during prosecution.[178] The reason for the amendment was to require electrical insulation, which was merely tangential to the alleged equivalent of the defendant's ninety-two percent insulating material.[179]

> 3.   Honeywell v. Hamilton: *When a dependent claim is re-written as independent, the tangential exception does not apply if the original elements of the dependent claim were at-issue during prosecution and necessary to overcome the prior art.*

---

[173] Funai Elec. Co., Ltd. v. Daewoo Elecs. Corp., 616 F.3d 1357 (Fed. Cir. 2010).

[174] *Id.* at 1362, 1368.

[175] *Id.* at 1369.

[176] *Id.*

[177] *Id.* at 1367. The district court held that the accused product did not literally infringe because it was only ninety-two percent insulating. *Id.*

[178] *Id.* at 1369.

[179] *Id.*

In *Honeywell International, Inc. v. Hamilton Sundstrand Corp.*,[180] on the other hand, the court declined to apply the tangential exception. Honeywell's patent was directed to a surge control system for controlling airflow in aircraft engines.[181] At issue during litigation was Honeywell's "inlet guide vane" limitation, which was absent from the original independent claim but present in dependent claims.[182] The court referred to the "inlet guide vane" limitation as including both the inlet guide vane's structure and function.[183] During prosecution, after the patent examiner rejected the independent claim as obvious in light of prior art, the patent applicant added the "inlet guide vane" limitation by rewriting the dependent claim in independent form and canceling the original independent claim.[184]

The Federal Circuit affirmed the district court's holding that Honeywell was estopped from asserting infringement by equivalents over the defendant's surge control system, which also included an inlet guide vane, but did not literally infringe because it performed its function differently.[185] The court held that, because the patent applicant added the "inlet guide vane" limitation to overcome an obviousness rejection, the reason for the adding limitation was directly rather than merely tangentially related to the accused equivalent.[186]

Judge Newman dissented from the panel majority's decision, pointing out that the "inlet guide vane" limitation itself was never amended during prosecution.[187] She argued that the majority's decision meant that the tangential exception never applies when a limitation asserted against an infringer was imported from an original dependent claim into an amended independent claim.[188]

4.   *Discussion.*

When a limitation is already present in the claim set and merely imported from a dependent claim to an independent claim, it may be easier to discern how the amendment overcame prior art

---

[180] 523 F.3d 1304 (Fed. Cir. 2008).
[181] *Id.* at 1307.
[182] *Id.* at 1308.
[183] *Id.* at 1316.
[184] *Id.* at 1308.
[185] *Id.* at 1315.
[186] *Id.* at 1316.
[187] *Id.* at 1317 (Newman, J., dissenting).
[188] *Id.* at 1322.

rejections and which aspects of the limitation were affected by the amendment. In *Insituform* and *Funai* the aspects of the limitation such as quantity and type, respectively, were not affected by the amendment. The Federal Circuit, therefore, held that the patentees were not estopped from asserting the DOE.[189]

At first blush, *Honeywell* appears to be inconsistent with *Insituform* and *Funai*. All three cases involved narrowing amendments where a limitation was imported from a dependent claim to an independent claim in order to overcome prior art.[190] The Federal Circuit, however, applied the tangential exception in *Insituform* and *Funai*, but not in *Honeywell*.[191] The reason for the different treatment between these cases—at least the one the Federal Circuit appeared to rely upon—could simply be that the limitations in *Insituform* and *Funai* were not relevant during prosecution and the limitation in *Honeywell* was.

One point of distinction that the Federal Circuit did not specifically draw is that *Honeywell* involved an amendment that affected the same aspect of the imported limitation as the equivalent, i.e. the inlet guide vane's function, whereas the amendments in *Insituform* and *Funai* affected different aspects of the invention, i.e. quantity and type, respectively. The *Honeywell* court expressly noted that the "inlet guide vane" limitation refers to both the structure and function.[192] By adding the "inlet guide vane" limitation, the reason for the amendment was to make both the structure and function of the inlet guide vane distinguishing features in order to overcome a patentability rejection. Honeywell, therefore, could not show that the reason for the amendment was only tangentially related to the accused equivalent, an inlet guide vane that functioned in a different manner.

D.   *The Tangential Exception Applies to Claim Elements That Were Never Narrowed During Patent Prosecution.*

The Federal Circuit has found that the tangential exception applies to overcome the PHE presumption when the claims at issue

---

[189] *Id.* at 1318.

[190] *See id.* at 1306; Insituform. Techs., Inc. v. Cat Contracting, 385 F.3d 1360 (Fed. Cir. 2004); Funai Elec. Co., Ltd. v. Daewoo Elecs. Corp., 616 F.3d 1357, 1369 (Fed. Cir. 2010).

[191] *Compare supra* Part 2.C.3, *with supra* Parts II.C.1, II.C.2.

[192] *Honeywell*, 523 F.3d at 1316.

were narrowed during prosecution, but the claim elements asserted against the equivalents were not.

> 1. Regents v. DakoCytomation: *When the amendment relates to a claim element that was not at issue and not specifically narrowed throughout the claim in relevant part, the tangential exception applies.*

In *Regents of the University of California v. DakoCytomation California, Inc.,*[193] the claimed invention covered a method of staining chromosomal DNA where nucleic acids are used to block repetitive sequences while probes target unique sequences.[194] The claim at issue, in its original form, was rejected in view of a prior art reference that disclosed the use of unique sequence probes rather than blocking, and a second prior art reference that disclosed use of the blocking method but not to target unique sequences.[195] The patent applicant overcame the prior art rejections by narrowing the claims to the blocking method and pursuing other embodiments of the invention in other applications.[196] In doing so, the applicant amended the claim language "blocking the labeled repetitive nucleic acid fragments" to read "employing said . . . blocking nucleic acid . . . so that labeled repetitive sequences are substantially blocked."[197]

The accused product used peptide nucleic acids, which are synthetic nucleic acids, rather than human DNA.[198] The district court granted the defendants summary judgment of noninfringement, holding that the defendants did not literally infringe because the accused products did not use human DNA and that the patentee was barred from asserting the DOE because the patentee amended the "blocking nucleic acid" limitation during prosecution and narrowed its scope.[199] On appeal, the patentee argued that there was no narrowing amendment because "nucleic acid" limitation was never narrowed during

---

[193] 517 F.3d 1364 (Fed. Cir. 2008).
[194] *Id.* at 1368
[195] *Id.* at 1378.
[196] *Id.*
[197] *Id.* at 1377–78.
[198] *Id.* at 1376.
[199] *Id.*

prosecution.[200] The patentee also argued, in the alternative, that any narrowing amendment was tangential to the accused equivalent.[201]

While the Federal Circuit agreed with the district court that the presumption of PHE applied because "the patentees limited the claim to the blocking method at least in part to overcome the examiner's rejections, the patentees presumptively surrendered all equivalents of the 'blocking nucleic acid' limitation."[202] But the court further concluded that the presumption was overcome because the tangential exception applied.[203] The Federal Circuit found that the *type* of nucleic acid was never at issue during patent prosecution, as evidenced by the office action, summary of the interview between the patent applicant and examiner, and patentees' remarks.[204] The court further noted that the "nucleic acid" limitation was never narrowed.[205] Thus, the Federal Circuit concluded that the patentee overcame the presumption of PHE because the reason for the amendment (adding the method of "blocking" to distinguish the method over the prior art) was tangential to the claimed equivalent (the particular type of nucleic acid), and remanded the case to the district court to consider infringement under the DOE.[206]

> 2.   Primos v. Hunter: *When the amendment relates to a claim element that was not at issue and not specifically narrowed throughout the claim in relevant part, the tangential exception applies.*

Similarly, the Federal Circuit found the tangential exception applied in *Primos, Inc. v. Hunter's Specialties, Inc.*, which involved a claim element that was arguably never narrowed during prosecution.[207] Primos's patented invention was a game call device hunters used to simulate animal sounds.[208] The amendment during prosecution required

---

[200] *Id.*
[201] *Id.*
[202] *Id.* at 1377–78.
[203] *Id.* at 1378.
[204] *Id.*
[205] *Id.*
[206] *Id.*
[207] *Primos, Inc. v. Hunter's Specialties, Inc.*, 451 F.3d 841 (Fed. Cir. 2006).
[208] *Id.* at 843-44.

the claim element at issue, a "plate," to 1) have a "length" and 2) be "differentially spaced" above a membrane.[209]

The defendant argued that Primos was barred from asserting the DOE to capture the accused device, which had a "dome" rather than a "plate" as construed by the district court.[210] The district court held that adding the "length" limitation did not alter the claim scope.[211] The court held that the addition of the "differentially spaced" limitation, on the other hand, did narrow the scope of the claim and further assumed that the amendment was made for reasons related to patentability.[212] However, the district court held that the patentee surrendered only plates that are not "differentially spaced" above the membrane.[213]

On appeal, the Federal Circuit agreed with the district court that the addition of the term "length" was not a narrowing amendment because "every physical object has a length."[214] The court also agreed that the "differentially spaced" limitation was a narrowing amendment presumptively made for reasons related to patentability.[215] The Federal Circuit then held that the territory Primos surrendered included all equivalents that were not differentially spaced above the membrane, because the patentee distinguished prior art that contained a structure positioned on top of a membrane without any spacing.[216] Because the accused device had a dome that was differentially spaced above the membrane, the reason for the amendment requiring a plate that was differentially spaced was merely tangential to the accused equivalent.[217] In other words, while the narrowing amendment affected the *position* of the plate relative to other claim elements, the "plate" element itself was never narrowed. Equivalents were therefore available for the "plate" element (such as the accused "dome"), irrespective of the equivalent's size, shape, color, etc.

---

[209] *Id.* at 849.

[210] *Id.* at 848.

[211] *Id.* at 845.

[212] *Id.* at 845.

[213] *Id.*

[214] *Id.* at 849.

[215] *Id.*

[216] *Id.* at 849.

[217] *Id.* While the Federal Circuit cited the correct legal standard, "*the rationale* underlying the amendment may bear no more than a tangential relation to the equivalent in question," its conclusion stated, "*the amendment* was merely tangential to the contested element." *Id.* (emphasis added). The authors believe that the Federal Circuit is applying the correct law, but note that the Federal Circuit may misstate the law from time to time in its decisions.

3. *Discussion.*

Both *Regents* and *Primos* were cases where the specific claim elements asserted against the equivalent were never narrowed during prosecution, although the same language may have been added elsewhere during prosecution. Any amendments to the claims as a whole were therefore tangential to accused equivalents of the unamended claim elements.

In fact, it is arguable that PHE should not have attached in the first place in these cases, as there was not a narrowing amendment to the relevant portion of the claim, in which case the Federal Circuit did not need to perform the tangential exception analysis. In *Festo X*, the Federal Circuit clarified that PHE applies to an amendment that narrows the literal scope of a claim.[218] Presumably the rule should apply to amendments that narrow the literal scope of a claim *element*, instead of any part of the claim. Such a rule would more directly address the ultimate question of whether PHE should apply and would allow the court to avoid an unnecessary tangential exception analysis. Because the same claim element was added elsewhere, though, the court may have felt it necessary to apply the prosecution history presumption and then consider the exceptions.

In *Regents*, the court expressly recognized that the "nucleic acid" limitation was never narrowed, but continued to hold that the amendment was not tangential to the accused equivalent.[219] The court's statement that "[t]he prosecution history therefore reveals that in narrowing the claim to overcome the prior art rejections, the focus of the patentees' arguments centered on the method of blocking—not on the particular type of nucleic acid that could be used for blocking," suggests that it will perform the tangential exception analysis if the claim is narrowed, even if the claim element at issue was not. [220]

E. *The Tangential Exception Does Not Apply to Asserted Equivalents of Claim Elements Relied Upon to Overcome 35 U.S.C. § 112 Rejections.*

---

[218] *Festo X*, 344 F.3d 1359, 1366 (Fed. Cir. 2003).
[219] Regents of the Univ. of Cal. v. DakoCytomation Cal., Inc., 517 F.3d 1364, 1376 (Fed. Cir. 2008).
[220] *Id.* at 1378.

In two cases where the Federal Circuit considered claim limitations that were added to overcome 35 U.S.C. § 112 rejections, it declined to apply the tangential exception to allow the patentees to assert infringement under the DOE to capture equivalents of those limitations.[221] Section 112, paragraphs 1 and 2, require patent applicants to draft the specification to describe the "manner and process of making and using it, in such full, clear, concise, and exact terms," as well as, "conclude with one or more claims particularly pointing out and distinctly claiming the subject matter."[222]

> 1. Cross Medical v. Medtronic: *The tangential exception does not apply to an amendment that is made to overcome a § 112 rejection that is necessary and narrows the patent's scope.*

Cross Medical Products v. Medtronic Sofamor Danek, Inc.[223] was a *per curiam* decision that did not garner a majority vote from the three-judge Federal Circuit panel. Cross Medical's patent was directed to a device for stabilizing bone segments of the spine.[224] The claim limitation at issue recited, "seat means including a vertical axis and first threads which extend . . . to a depth below the diameter of the rod."[225] This limitation was not in the claim as originally drafted, but was added in response to the patent examiner's rejection of the claim as lacking an antecedent basis and support in the specification under 35 U.S.C. § 112, paragraphs 1 and 2.[226]

Medtronic's accused polyaxial screw device had a groove or "undercut" below the rod rather than threads.[227] The district court held that the accused product did not literally infringe the asserted claim because it lacked threads.[228] But the district court held that despite Cross Medical's narrowing amendment involving the asserted thread depth limitation to overcome a 35 U.S.C. § 112 rejection, the amendment was merely tangential to the accused equivalent.[229] The

---

[221] *See infra* Parts 2.E.1–2.E.2.
[222] 35 U.S.C. § 112 (2012).
[223] 480 F.3d 1335 (Fed. Cir. 2007).
[224] *Id.* at 1339.
[225] *Id.*
[226] *Id.* at 1340.
[227] *Id.* at 1339.
[228] *Id.*
[229] *Id.* at 1340.

district court granted summary judgment of infringement under the DOE, and Medtronic appealed.[230]

On appeal, the Federal Circuit considered whether Cross Medical was able to overcome the presumption of PHE due to its narrowing amendment to overcome the patent examiner's 35 U.S.C. § 112 rejection involving the thread depth limitation. The court held that, "if a § 112 amendment is necessary and narrows the patent's scope— even if only for the purpose of better description—estoppel may apply."[231] The court found that the prosecution history revealed that the reason for the amendment was to overcome the 35 U.S.C. § 112 rejection by describing how the invention operated.[232] As the court explained,

> In other words, the prosecution history explains that the thread depth limitation was added to capture the manner in which the stabilizer aspect of the invention operated and thereby overcome the 35 U.S.C. § 112 rejections. Thus, the accused equivalent, which does not include threads extending "to a depth below the top of the stabilizer" and correspondingly does not capture this aspect of the invention, relates to the amendment as shown even by the applicant's own statements. For this reason, the district court erred in reliance on the tangential rebuttal principle to avoid the doctrine of equivalents.[233]

Because the accused equivalent operated in a different manner, it was not tangential to the amendment.[234] The court emphasized that the tangential exception is "very narrow" and held that Cross Medical was unable to overcome the presumption of PHE under the narrow exception.[235]

Judge Rader wrote a concurring opinion to express his dissatisfaction with the tangential exception.[236] He argued that the

---

[230] *Id.* at 1337.
[231] *Id.* at 1341 (citing Honeywell Int'l, Inc. v. Hamilton Sundstrand Corp., 370 F.3d 1131, 1142 (Fed. Cir. 2004)).
[232] *Id.* at 1343.
[233] *Id.*
[234] *Id.*
[235] *Id.* at 1341–42.
[236] *Id.* at 1346 (Rader, J., concurring).

tangential exception conflicts with the policy behind public notice of the claimed invention.[237] According to Judge Rader, the reasons that would support an application of the tangential exception would not be found in the prosecution history because a patentee would assert reasons that are unrelated to narrowing amendments that surrender the equivalent at issue.[238] He asserted that the tangential exception produces the perverse result where a patentee is rewarded by providing vague explanations so that it can later argue that the amendment is merely tangential to the accused equivalent.[239] The public, relying on the prosecution history for narrowing amendments and believing the patentee to have surrendered certain equivalents, would fall prey to infringement charges when the patentee comes forth with some reasoning why the reason for the amendment is merely tangential to the accused equivalent.[240]

2. International Rectifier v. IXYS: *The tangential exception does not apply to an amendment that is made to overcome a § 112 rejection, even if the amendment was not necessary.*

In *International Rectifier Corp. v. IXYS Corp.*,[241] the Federal Circuit again declined to apply the tangential exception to a claim limitation that was added in order to overcome a 35 U.S.C. § 112 rejection.[242] International Rectifier's ("IR's") patent was drawn to semiconductor transistors, and the claim at issue recited a structure with "adjoining" components.[243] IR added the "adjoining" limitation to its claim in response to the patent examiner's rejection of the original claim under 35 U.S.C. § 112 because the claimed structures were not supported by the specification.[244]

IR argued that the reason for the "adjoining" limitation was tangential to the accused equivalent of non-adjoining components because IR added the limitation when amending the claim to recite

---

[237] *Id.* at 1347.
[238] *Id.*
[239] *Id.*
[240] *Id.*
[241] 515 F.3d 1353 (Fed. Cir. 2008).
[242] *Id.* at 1359.
[243] *Id.* at 1355.
[244] *Id.* at 1359.

structures that were supported by the specification.[245] The Federal Circuit rejected the argument, holding that, as "IR recited precisely the structure it disclosed, and thereby overcame the examiner's 35 U.S.C. § 112 rejection," the reason for the amendment was not tangential to the accused equivalent of non-adjoining components.[246] The Federal Circuit held that it was irrelevant whether IR was required to add the limitation in order to overcome the examiner's rejection of the claim.[247]

3. *Discussion.*

In both *Cross Medical* and *International Rectifier*, the Federal Circuit declined to apply the tangential exception to equivalents of claim elements amended in response to 35 U.S.C. § 112, paragraphs 1 and 2. In both cases, equivalents were unavailable because the patent examiners required the patent applicants to recite the *exact* invention in order to overcome the 35 U.S.C. § 112 rejection. Because the limitations that would encompass the accused equivalents were added to overcome these patentability rejections, the reasons for the amendments were directly rather than tangentially related to the claimed equivalents.

III.   THE FEDERAL CIRCUIT'S POST-*FESTO* APPLICATION OF THE UNFORESEEABILITY EXCEPTION TO PROSECUTION HISTORY ESTOPPEL.

In *Festo VIII*, the Supreme Court also created the "unforeseeability" exception to the DOE, reasoning that a patent applicant cannot surrender what is unforeseeable when it makes a narrowing amendment.[248] In *Festo X*, the Federal Circuit held that the test for the unforeseeability exception is whether one of ordinary skill in the art would have foreseen the alleged equivalent at the time of the amendment.[249] The court explained that the inquiry is objective, and a district court may consider evidence outside of the prosecution history such as expert testimony.[250]

---

[245] *Id.*

[246] *Id.*

[247] *Id.*

[248] *Festo VIII*, 535 U.S. 722, 738 (2002).

[249] *Festo X*, 344 F.3d 1359, 1369 (Fed. Cir. 2003).

[250] *Id.*

The Federal Circuit did not find that the unforeseeability exception applied in the *Festo* litigation, nor in any case following *Festo*.[251] In cases since *Festo* where the Federal Circuit has considered and rejected the unforeseeability exception, the court has unequivocally held, consistent with its guidance in *Festo X*, that an accused equivalent is foreseeable if it was known in the field of the invention at the time of the narrowing amendment.[252]

A. Honeywell v. Hamilton: *Expert testimony may be used to evaluate the unforeseeability exception.*

In *Honeywell International v. Hamilton Sundstrand Corp.*,[253] the court accepted expert testimony when determining whether the alleged equivalent was foreseeable to a person of skill in the art at the time of the amendment.[254] While the patentee argued that using the inlet guide vane position to distinguish between high flow and low flow to control surge in auxiliary power units of aircrafts was unforeseeable at the time of the amendment, the patentee's expert conceded that controlling surge requires accounting for the position of the inlet guide vane.[255] The Federal Circuit affirmed the district court's finding that it was foreseeable to use the position of the inlet guide vane to determine high flow and low flow at the time of the amendment.[256]

B. Research Plastics v. Federal Packaging: *The unforeseeability exception does not apply if the amendment demonstrates that the equivalent was foreseeable.*

The patent applicant in *Research Plastics, Inc. v. Federal Packaging Corp.*[257] amended its claim, which did not originally specify a location for the ribs, to cover only ribs located at the "rear end" of the tube in order to distinguish prior art that had ribs located on the nozzle end of a caulking tube.[258] The Federal Circuit held that the amendment

---

[251] *See supra* Part I.C.3.
[252] *See supra* Part I.C.3.
[253] 523 F.3d 1304 (Fed. Cir. 2008).
[254] *Id.* at 1314.
[255] *Id.* at 1313–14.
[256] *Id.* at 1314.
[257] 421 F.3d 1290 (Fed. Cir. 2005).
[258] *Id.* at 1293.

demonstrated that the applicant was able to foresee that the placement of the ribs was a point of differentiation and therefore could not rely on the DOE to cover the accused equivalent, which had ribs located inside of the rear end.[259]

> C.   Schwartz v. Paddock: *The unforeseeability exception does not apply if the alleged equivalent was foreseeable in the field of the invention.*

In *Schwartz Pharma, Inc. v. Paddock Laboratories, Inc.,*[260] the patentee argued that PHE did not apply because the amendment was unforeseeable.[261] "Originally, the independent claims recited a 'metal containing stabilizer' and 'an alkali or alkaline earth-metal salt,' respectively . . . ."[262] Following an obviousness rejection, "each was amended to instead recite 'an alkali or alkaline earth metal carbonate.'"[263]

On appeal, the patentee did "not seriously dispute [that the accused equivalent, magnesium oxide (MgO),] was known as a stabilizer by those of skill in the art at the time of the amendment."[264] Instead, the patentee asserted "that MgO had to have been known as a stabilizer against the specific degradation pathway of cyclization or for the specific drug category of ACE inhibitors in order to have been foreseeable as an equivalent."[265] The Federal Circuit disagreed.[266]

The Federal Circuit held that the field of the invention, for foreseeability purposes, is defined by the language of the claim.[267] The court determined that the field of invention in that case was pharmaceutical compositions, based on the preamble of the pre-

---

[259] *Id.* at 1299.
[260] 504 F.3d 1371 (Fed. Cir. 2007).
[261] *Id.* at 1374–75.
[262] *Id.*
[263] *Id.*
[264] *Id.* at 1377.
[265] *Id.*
[266] *Id.*
[267] *Id.* The court applied a similar reasoning in *Duramed Pharmaceuticals, Inc. v. Paddock Labs, Inc.*, where it held the alleged equivalent was known in the field of pharmaceutical compositions at the time of the amendment and was thus foreseeable. 644 F.3d 1376, 1380–81 (Fed. Cir. 2011). The court rejected the patentee's argument that the alleged equivalent had to have been known specifically "for use *with conjugated estrogens*," because such characterization of the field of the invention is too restrictive. *Id.* at 1380 (emphasis in original).

amendment claim, and that MgO was a known stabilizer in that field.[268] Thus, the court rejected the patentee's argument that the equivalent was unforeseeable.[269]

> D. Amgen v. Hoechst Marion *and* Glaxo v. Impax: *An alleged equivalent is foreseeable if the patentee knew of the equivalent at the time of the narrowing amendment or if the equivalent was disclosed in the prior art.*

An alleged equivalent is also foreseeable if the patentee knew of the equivalent at the time of the narrowing amendment. In *Amgen Inc. v. Hoechst Marion Roussel, Inc.*,[270] the court affirmed the district court's finding that the patentee admitted to knowing about the alleged equivalent when it made the amendment and therefore could not claim that the alleged equivalent was unforeseeable.[271]

In *Glaxo Wellcome, Inc. v. Impax Laboratories, Inc.*,[272] the Federal Circuit held that the unforeseeability exception was unavailable when prior art cited during prosecution disclosed the alleged equivalent.[273] Despite evidence in the record showing that hydroxypropylmethyl cellulose (HPMC) was the only sustained release compound that had been tested with the bupropion hydrochloride drug, the alleged equivalent, hydroxylpropyl cellulose (HPC), was a known sustained release compound in the field of pharmaceutical formulation.[274] Furthermore, the record showed that the patentee disclosed a reference to the USPTO that described the alleged equivalent.[275] The court concluded that the alleged equivalent was

---

[268] *Schwarz Pharma*, 504 F.3d at 1377.
[269] *Id.* In a similar case, *Cross Medical Products v. Medtronic Sofamar Danek, Inc.*, the Federal Circuit held that the alleged equivalent was foreseeable at the time of the amendment because it was "an old and well known fundamental of basic machining." 480 F.3d 1335, 1343 (Fed. Cir. 2007).
[270] 457 F.3d 1293 (Fed. Cir. 2006).
[271] *Id.* at 1313.
[272] 356 F.3d 1348 (Fed. Cir. 2004).
[273] *Id.* at 1355; *see also* Pioneer Magnetics, Inc. v. Micro Linear Corp., 330 F.3d 1352, 1357 (Fed. Cir. 2003) (holding that the alleged equivalent was foreseeable because it was contained in the prior art that the patentee sought to avoid through the narrowing amendment); Okor v. Atari Games Corp., 76 Fed. App'x 327, 332 (Fed. Cir. 2003) (The patentee expressly discussed the alleged equivalent as prior art in his comments during prosecution.).
[274] *Glaxo Wellcome*, 356 F.3d at 1355.
[275] *Id.*

therefore foreseeable to a person or ordinary skill in the art at the time of the amendment.[276]

On the other hand, in a companion case, *SmithKline Beecham Corp. v. Excel Pharmaceuticals, Inc.*,[277] the Federal Circuit remanded the case for a determination of whether polyvinyl alcohol (PVA) was a known sustained release agent or whether it was an unforeseeable equivalent of HPMC.[278] As the record was undeveloped, the Federal Circuit was unable to determine whether PVA qualified as later-developed technology, rendering it "a [sic] undeniable ground for unforeseeability."[279]

E.   Mycogen v. Monsanto *and* Talbert v. Unocal: *If the claim originally included a range and then was narrowed, the original range was foreseeable.*

When a patent applicant has drafted a claim that covers a range of values and later narrowed it for reasons related to patentability, the Federal Circuit has held that the patentee cannot argue that an accused equivalent, which was captured by the broader claim but later falls outside the narrowed range of values, is unforeseeable. In *Mycogen Plant Science, Inc. v. Monsanto Co.*,[280] the court held that the patentee could not claim that the accused equivalent, a gene that is only seventy-eight percent homologous to the claimed gene sequence, was unforeseeable, because the applicant canceled a claim that originally covered sequences that were eighty-five percent homologous.[281] The patentee had to narrow its claims to the specific gene sequence that was ultimately allowed by the examiner.[282] Therefore, the court concluded that the patent applicant was able to foresee the possibility of a gene with less homology to the claimed sequence.[283]

Likewise, in *Talbert Fuel Systems Patents Co. v. Unocal Corp.*,[284] the Federal Circuit held that the patentee could not "credibly argue[]" that it could not foresee fuels with a boiling point range higher

---

[276] *Id.* at 1355–56.

[277] 356 F.3d 1357 (Fed. Cir. 2004).

[278] *Id.* at 1364–65.

[279] *Id.*

[280] 91 Fed. App'x. 666 (Fed. Cir. 2004).

[281] *Id.* at 668.

[282] *Id.* at 667.

[283] *Id.* at 668.

[284] 347 F.3d 1355 (Fed. Cir. 2003).

than that ultimately claimed, because the patentee had amended its claim to distinguish prior art that contained higher boiling point fuels.[285]

F.   Ranbaxy v. Apotex: *It is irrelevant if the patentee did not foresee the surrender.*

The patentee in *Ranbaxy Pharmaceuticals, Inc. v. Apotex, Inc.*[286] attempted to argue that it was not foreseeable that amending its claim to cover only formic acid would result in surrender of acetic acid, which was an "obvious structural equivalent (homolog)."[287] The court clarified that "foreseeability relates to the equivalent, not to whether an amendment may result in prosecution history estoppel."[288] The court held that by arguing that acetic acid, the alleged equivalent, is a known homolog to the claimed compound, formic acid, the patentee demonstrated that it would have been foreseeable to include the equivalent when drafting the claim.[289]

G.   *Discussion.*

Because the Federal Circuit has never applied the foreseeability exception, it is difficult to pinpoint the factual circumstances that would merit the use of this exception. It is clear that in determining whether an alleged equivalent was foreseeable, it is appropriate to rely on extrinsic evidence such as expert testimony. It is also true that if the amendment was known by the patentee, or disclosed in the prior art, or a range in the original claims, the foreseeability exception does not apply. But when the exception would apply remains unclear. By definition, a claim must literally include the alleged equivalent and then be narrowed to exclude the equivalent for the question of PHE and the exceptions to be in consideration. In any situation where the alleged equivalent is explicitly removed—such as a range, or specific discussion of the equivalent—it is, by definition foreseeable. Likewise, an alleged equivalent in the prior art is also foreseeable.

---

[285] *Id.* at 1359–60.

[286] 350 F.3d 1235 (Fed. Cir. 2003).

[287] *Id.* at 1241.

[288] *Id.*

[289] *Id.*

IV.   "SOME OTHER REASON" EXCEPTION TO PROSECUTION
        HISTORY ESTOPPEL.

     The Supreme Court in *Festo VIII* held that a patentee could
overcome the presumption that it surrendered the accused equivalent by
showing that there is "some other reason" that it could not have been
expected to claim the equivalent.[290] In *Festo X*, the Federal Circuit held
that, as with the tangential exception, the evidence available to support
the "some other reason" exception should be limited to the prosecution
history, "when at all possible."[291] Specifically, the court explained that
"if the alleged equivalent is in the [cited] prior art, there can be no other
reason the patentee could not have described the substitute in
question."[292] The court expressly declined to reach the question of what
evidence outside of the prosecution history, if any, should be
considered to determine whether the patentee has rebutted the
presumption of PHE.[293]
     There has not been a single case where the Federal Circuit has
held that the "some other reason" exception applies to rebut the *Festo*
presumption. In cases since *Festo* where the Federal Circuit has
considered and rejected the "some other reason" exception, the court
continued to apply its holding that a patentee could not argue that there
was "some other reason" that it could not have been expected to
describe an alleged equivalent if the equivalent is found in the prior art.

     A. Pioneer Magnetics v. Micro Linear *and* Okor v. Atari:
         *The "some other reason" exception does not apply if the
         alleged equivalent was in the cited prior art.*

     In *Pioneer Magnetics Inc. v. Micro Linear Corp.*,[294] the
Federal Circuit held that "there can be no other reason the patentee
could not have described the substituted in question" because the
alleged equivalent was in the prior art cited against the patentee during
prosecution.[295] Likewise, because the patentee in *Okor v. Atari Games*

---

[290] *Festo VIII*, 535 U.S. 722, 740–41 (2002).
[291] *Festo X*, 344 F.3d 1359, 1370 (Fed. Cir. 2003).
[292] *Id.* (internal citations omitted) (citing Pioneer Magnetics, Inc. v. Micro Linear Corp.,
330 F.3d 1352 (Fed. Cir. 2003).
[293] *Id.*
[294] 330 F.3d 1352 (Fed. Cir. 2003).
[295] *Id.* at 1357.

Corp.[296] distinguished its invention from the prior art, which contained the alleged equivalent, it could not point to some other reason that it could not have drafted its claim to cover the equivalent.[297]

> B. Amgen v. Hoechst: *The "some other reason" exception does not apply if the patentee was aware of the alleged equivalent.*

The Federal Circuit has also held that the patentee could not rely on the "some other reason" exception if the patentee knew about the alleged equivalent at the time of the amendment. The court held that the patentee in *Amgen Inc. v. Hoechst Marion Roussel, Inc.*[298] could not argue that there was some other reason it could not have been expected to draft its claim to cover the alleged equivalent, a 165-amino acid erythropoietin (EPO) sequence, because the patentee submitted information to the USPTO about the 165-amino acid sequence but chose only to claim a 166-amino acid EPO sequence.[299] The district court had found that the patentee succeeded in demonstrating that there was "some other reason" it could not have claimed the accused equivalent, because a person of ordinary skill in the art would have interpreted the amended claim to cover the 165-amino acid sequence.[300]

The Federal Circuit reversed, holding that "whether the patentee, the examiner, or a person of skill in the art may have thought the claims encompassed EPO with 165 amino acids does not excuse the patentee's failure to claim the equivalent."[301] Because the patentee knew about the alleged equivalent, and because there was no linguistic barrier to describing the equivalent, the patentee could not rely on the "some other reason" exception to PHE.

> C. Festo X: *The "some other reason" exception does not apply if the claim as originally drafted included the alleged equivalent.*

---

[296] 76 Fed. App'x. 327 (Fed. Cir. 2003).
[297] *Id.* at 332–33.
[298] 457 F.3d 1293 (Fed. Cir. 2006).
[299] *Id.* at 1315.
[300] *Id.* at 1315–16.
[301] *Id.* at 1316.

From the *Festo X* decision, it appears that the "some other reason" exception does not apply when the original claim literally encompassed the accused equivalent, because the patentee cannot argue that he is incapable of drafting a claim to cover the equivalent.[302] In addition, the court's reasoning that the patentee could have claimed a nonmagnetizable sleeve as easily as it claimed a magnetizable sleeve suggests that a patentee is bound by the level of specificity that it chooses to describe its invention.[303]

In *Research Plastics*, the Federal Circuit similarly held that the patentee could have described the alleged equivalent, because it amended its original claim, which was broad enough to cover the equivalent, to describe only ribs located at the rear end of the caulking tube, when it could have instead described the ribs as being located anywhere along the tube, as long as they were not adjacent to the nozzle.[304]

D. *Discussion.*

Like the unforeseeability exception, it is unclear when the "some other reason" exception to prosecution estoppel could apply because the Federal Circuit has never found the exception to apply. Like the unforeseeability exception, the "some other reason" exception does not apply if the alleged equivalent was in the prior art, if the patentee was aware of the equivalent, or if the original claim language explicitly included the alleged equivalent. It is also unclear when and to what extent the court will allow extrinsic evidence to be considered in evaluating the "some other reason" exception.

V.   TABLE OF RELEVANT DECISIONS CONSIDERING THE TANGENTIAL EXCEPTION, INCLUDING AUTHORING JUDGE AND PANEL.

There are few cases that substantively consider the narrow exceptions to PHE, and even fewer that find the exceptions apply. Indeed, the only exception the court has ever found applied was the

---

[302] *Festo X*, 344 F.3d 1359, 1373 (Fed. Cir. 2003). The Federal Circuit held that the "sealing rings" limitation in the original claim in the Stoll patent was broad enough to cover the accused equivalent, a two-way sealing ring. *Id.* at 1373–74.
[303] *Id.* at 1372.
[304] Research Plastics, Inc. v. Fed. Packaging Corp., 421 F.3d 1290, 1298 (Fed. Cir. 2005).

tangential exception. The court only seriously considered the tangential exception in twenty-eight cases, and the tangential exception was only found to apply in five of them.

While there are not enough cases to make a confident prediction by a judge, a review of the cases where the court has seriously considered the tangential exception suggests that some judges may be more receptive to the exceptions than others. For example, former Chief Judge Rader considered eight cases where the tangential exception was seriously in dispute. In each case—whether he was the authoring judge or not—the court found the exception did not apply. Likewise, Judge Newman has been on nine panels where the tangential exception was considered. In two of those cases, the court found the tangential exception applied, and in two more she dissented and suggested that it should apply. This could have nothing to do with the judges' views on the exceptions and everything to do with the facts of the specific cases (although Judge Newman's two dissents occurred in cases where Judge Rader was in the majority), but it could indicate some judges view the exceptions more favorably than others.

With the caveat that the case sample size is very small, and that the judges' decisions could have little to do with their viewpoints on the exception and more to do with the specific facts of the case, these are the judges who appear less receptive to the tangential exception (and potentially less receptive to the other exceptions as well):

- Retired Judge Rader (on eight panels finding no tangential exception, authored three; never found tangential exception applied)
- Retired Judge Gajarsa (on seven panels finding no tangential exception, authored three; never found tangential exception applied)
- Senior Judge Clevenger (on six panels finding no tangential exception; never found tangential exception applied)
- Judge Dyk (on four panels finding no tangential exception; never found tangential exception applied)

With the same caveat, these are the judges who appear more receptive to the tangential exception (and potentially more receptive to the other exceptions as well):

- Judge Newman (considered tangential exception in seven cases; on two panels finding tangential exception applied, authored one; dissented on two cases that tangential exception should apply)
- Judge Lourie (considered tangential exception in seven cases; on three panels finding tangential exception applied, authored two of them)
- Senior Judge Mayer (considered tangential exception in four cases; on two panels finding tangential exception applied; dissented on one case that tangential exception should apply)

The full table showing the panel compositions of the relevant cases, including authoring judge, follows:

Judge	*Found tangential exception applied*		
	Authored opinion finding tangential exception	On panel finding tangential exception	Dissent (i.e. would find not tangential)
Prost	23	11	16
Newman	24	11	
Lourie	11, 16	24	
Dyk			23***
Moore			
Senior			
Bryson		23	
Clevenger			
Linn		24	
Plager			
Mayer		5, 16	
Schall	5		
Retired			
Rader			
Michel		5	
Garjasa			
Friedman			

	Found tangential exception did not apply			Festo VII	
Judge	**Authored opinion finding no tangential exception**	**On panel/majority finding no tangential exception**	**Dissent (i.e. would find tangential)**	**Per curiam decision finding no tangential exception**	**Absolute Bar**	**Not Absolute Bar**
Prost	17, 18, 20	6, 15, F		13		
Newman	3	7, 9	19, F **	1, 2		X
Lourie	14, F	18, 20		1	X	
Dyk		10, 15, 19, F			X	
Moore	25	14				
Senior						
Bryson		8, 9, 21, F		4	X	
Clevenger		7, 12, 18, 25, F		4	X	
Linn	8, 15, 22	20, F		4		X
Plager	10	F			X	
Mayer		21	F **	1	X	
Schall	12	6, 17, F		13	X	
Retired						
Rader	6, 13*, 19	3, 17, 22, 25, F		2		X
Michel		3, 12, 14, F		2		X
Garjasa	7, 9, 21	8, 10, F			X	
Friedman		22				

*wrote separately to concur with per curium opinion of no tangential
**would remand to the district court for factfinding
***would find claim not literally infringed or infringed under doe b/c of claim construction, did not opine separately on tangential

1.   Pioneer Magnetics, Inc. v. Micro Linear Corp., 330 F.3d 1352 (Fed. Cir. 2003).

2. Okor v. Atari Games Corp., 76 Fed. Appx. 327 (Fed. Cir. 2003).
3. Talbert Fuel Sys. Patents Co. v. Unocal Corp., 347 F.3d 1355 (Fed. Cir. 2003).
4. Mycogen Plant Sci., Inc. v. Monsanto Co., 91 Fed. Appx. 666 (Fed. Cir. 2004).
5. Insituform Techs., Inc. v. Cat Contr., Inc., 385 F.3d 1360 (Fed. Cir. 2004).
6. Business Objects, S.A. v. MicroStrategy, Inc., 393 F.3d 1366 (Fed. Cir. 2005).
7. Chimie v. PPG Indus., 402 F.3d 1371 (Fed. Cir. 2005).
8. Terlep v. Brinkmann Corp., 418 F.3d 1379 (Fed. Cir. 2005).
9. Research Plastics, Inc. v. Fed. Packaging Corp., 421 F.3d 1290 (Fed. Cir. 2005).
10. Biagro Western Sales, Inc. v. Grow More, Inc., 423 F.3d 1296 (Fed. Cir. 2005).
11. Primos, Inc. v. Hunter's Specialties, Inc., 451 F.3d 841 (Fed. Cir. 2006).
12. Amgen Inc. v. Hoechst Marion Roussel, Inc., 457 F.3d 1293 (Fed. Cir. 2006).
13. Cross Med. Prods. v. Medtronic Sofamor Danek, Inc., 480 F.3d 1335 (Fed. Cir. 2007).
14. Schwarz Pharma, Inc. v. Paddock Labs., Inc., 504 F.3d 1371 (Fed. Cir. 2007).
15. Int'l Rectifier Corp. v. IXYS Corp., 515 F.3d 1353 (Fed. Cir. 2008).
16. Regents of the Univ. of Cal. v. DakoCytomation Cal., Inc., 517 F.3d 1364 (Fed. Cir. 2008).
17. A G Design & Assocs. LLC v. Trainman Lantern Co., 271 Fed. Appx. 995 (Fed. Cir. 2008).
18. O2 Micro Int'l Ltd. v. Beyond Innovation Tech. Co., 521 F.3d 1351 (Fed. Cir. 2008).
19. Honeywell Int'l, Inc. v. Hamilton Sundstrand Corp., 523 F.3d 1304 (Fed. Cir. 2008).
20. Lucent Techs., Inc. v. Gateway, Inc., 525 F.3d 1200 (Fed. Cir. 2008).
21. Voda v. Cordis Corp., 536 F.3d 1311 (Fed. Cir. 2008).
22. Felix v. Am. Honda Motor Co., 562 F.3d 1167 (Fed. Cir. 2009).
23. Intervet Inc. v. Merial Ltd., 617 F.3d 1282 (Fed. Cir. 2010).

24. Funai Elec. Co., Ltd. v. Daewoo Elecs. Corp., 616 F.3d 1357 (Fed. Cir. 2010).
25. Integrated Tech. Corp. v. Rudolph Techs., Inc., 734 F.3d 1352 (Fed. Cir. 2013).
F. Festo Corp. v. Shoketsu Kinzoku Kogyo Kabushiki Co., 344 F.3d 1359 (Fed. Cir. 2003) (en banc) ("Festo X").

Festo Corp. v. Shoketsu Kinzoku Kogyo Kabushiki Co., 304 F.3d 1289 (Fed. Cir. 2000) (*en banc*) ("Festo VII").

VI. SUGGESTED APPLICATIONS OF THE THREE EXCEPTIONS TO PROSECUTION HISTORY ESTOPPEL.

The Supreme Court set out a series of steps for determining whether PHE applies. The first step is to determine whether the amendment is narrowing. If the answer is "no," there is no surrender of subject matter. If the answer is yes, the next step is to determine whether the reason for that amendment was substantially related to patentability. If the answer is "no," there is no surrender of subject matter. If the answer is "yes," there is a presumption that the patentee has surrendered all territory between the original claim and the amended claim. The patentee may then attempt to rebut the presumption with the *Festo* exceptions.

A. *Tangential Exception.*

The Supreme Court's statement of the law for the tangential exception is that a patentee does not surrender an equivalent when amending a claim for patentability reasons if "the *rationale* underlying the amendment [ ] bear[s] no more than a tangential relation to the *equivalent in question*."[305] The Federal Circuit has interpreted this to mean "the reason for the narrowing amendment was peripheral, or not directly relevant, to the alleged equivalent."[306] The Federal Circuit has made clear that where an amendment was made to overcome prior art that contains the accused equivalent, the reasoning for the amendment is directly related to rather than tangential to the equivalent.[307]

---

[305] *Festo VIII*, 535 U.S. 722, 740 (2002) (emphasis added).
[306] *Festo X*, 344 F.3d at 1369.
[307] *See supra* Part I.C.3.

This does not mean, however, that "the equivalents not within the prior art must be tangential to the amendment."[308] Indeed, the Federal Circuit has declined to apply the tangential exception to PHE in cases that where the patentees made narrowing amendments that were potentially unnecessary to overcome the prior art.[309] In such cases, the Federal Circuit held that, while the patentees may not have been required to make the amendments they did, because the prosecution history was either silent or not "objectively apparent" as to the reasons for the amendments, the patentees were bound by their choices of amendments.

From the Federal Circuit's various post-*Festo* cases, it appears in a patentee's best interest to ensure that any narrowing amendment made to overcome prior art during patent prosecution is accompanied by a clear reason for the amendment. If there are potentially multiple reasons for an amendment, the patentee should clarify which reason is associated with distinguishing the invention from the prior art. A court would then be able to rely on this stated reason to determine whether the reason is directly related to or merely peripheral to the alleged equivalent. Patentees should also be wary of surrendering more territory than necessary to overcome prior art, as it will likely be foreclosed from recapturing the surrendered territory under the DOE.

In addition, the court's particular viewpoints on the appropriateness of the tangential exception may have some variation depending on the panel. From the few available decisions where the Federal Circuit has applied the tangential exception to PHE, some judges seemed more open to applying the exception than others.[310]

B. *Unforeseeability Exception.*

In the twelve years since the Supreme Court articulated the unforeseeability exception to PHE in its *Festo VIII* decision, the Federal Circuit has yet to apply the exception. It is therefore unclear when the unforeseeability exception would apply to rebut the presumption that the patent applicant surrendered the accused equivalent by making a narrowing claim amendment. The Federal Circuit's decisions make clear that the exception *does not* apply where

---

[308] Chimie v. PPG Indus., 402 F.3d 1371, 1383 (Fed. Cir. 2005).
[309] *See* Integrated Tech. Corp. v. Rudolph Techs., Inc., 734 F.3d 1352 (Fed. Cir. 2013); Felix v. Am. Honda Motor Co., 562 F.3d 1167 (Fed. Cir. 2009).
[310] *See supra* Part V.

the equivalent is found in the cited prior art.[311] The Court in *Festo X*, however, did offer some guidance as to when the exception may apply: "Usually, if the alleged equivalent represents later-developed technology . . . or technology that was not known in the relevant art, then it would not have been foreseeable."[312] The court therefore views after-arising technology and existing technology in other fields of invention potential unforeseeable equivalents that a patent applicant does not surrender when making narrowing amendments.[313]

The unforeseeability exception may allow a patentee to rebut the presumption of PHE and assert infringement by equivalents over after-arising technologies that are marked improvements, and perhaps separately patentable, over the patented invention. Such a rule may lead to the perverse and undesirable consequence of allowing a patentee to expand its patent protection to cover after-arising, innovative technology by merely claiming that the equivalent was unforeseeable at the time of the amendment.

On the other hand, even if the court applies the unforeseeability exception and the patentee rebuts the presumption of PHE, that may not necessarily be the end of the inquiry. With the ability to assert infringement under the DOE, the patentee would still have to show that the accused equivalent is in fact an equivalent of the claimed element, i.e. it performs the same function in the same way with the same results or that any changes are insubstantial. As the Supreme Court stated in *Graver Tank*, the inquiry is whether, "the substitution [of the equivalent], under the circumstances of this case, and in view of the technology and the prior art, is a change of such substance as to make the doctrine of equivalents inapplicable."[314] The DOE is not without boundaries, as the patentee still has the burden of proving that the accused infringer only made colorable changes to the claimed invention.

C. *"Some Other Reason" Exception.*

---

[311] *See supra* Part III.

[312] *Festo X*, 344 F.3d 1359, 1369 (Fed. Cir. 2003).

[313] In *Festo VII*, Judge Rader noted the harshness of the complete bar as applied to after-arising technology, because a patentee would be estopped from asserting the DOE to capture after-arising technology, even if he could not have known about the technology and therefore could not have surrendered it when narrowing his claim. 234 F.3d 558, 619–20 (Fed. Cir. 2000) (Rader, J., dissenting).

[314] Graver Tank & Mfg. v. Linde Air Products Co., 339 U.S. 605, 610 (1950).

As with the unforeseeability exception, the Federal Circuit has yet to apply to "some other reason" exception created by the Supreme Court in *Festo VIII*. The Federal Circuit has made clear that the "some other reason" exception is not available where the claim at issue, as originally drafted, literally covers the accused equivalent.[315] The exception is also not available if the accused equivalent is found in the prior art.[316] From the post-*Festo* decisions described in Part III, it appears that the "some other reason" exception will be rarely, if ever, applied. While the court may be amenable to applying the exception if there is a linguistic barrier that prevents the patent applicant from being able to describe the accused equivalent, it is unclear what the court will consider to be a sufficient linguistic barrier. This exception, however, remains available as a "catch-all" exception to PHE.

VII.   CONCLUSION.

The Federal Circuit's post-*Festo* cases in the twelve years since the decision confirm that the three potential exceptions to PHE are indeed narrowly applied. The cases do, however, provide guidance for a number of common factual scenarios in whether the exceptions will apply.

---

[315] *See supra* Part IV.
[316] *See supra* Part IV.

#TRADEMARKLAW: PROTECTING AND MAXIMIZING THE VALUE OF TRADEMARKS IN AN EVOLVING SOCIAL MEDIA MARKETPLACE

BETSY A. BUTWIN[1]

I.   INTRODUCTION

Trademark law in the United States serves both commerce and consumers. Its primary purpose is to protect consumers from confusion as to the source of goods and services. Trademark law serves to protect businesses by ensuring exclusivity in the brands they curate. Once a business has chosen a name and cultivated a brand, that branding becomes identifiable to consumers as the source of the business' goods or services.[2] With the upsurge in social media, there are more vast and accessible marketing outlets available to businesses and their branding than ever in the history of American commerce. It has become essential

---

[1] Betsy is an attorney at Bernick Lifson, P.A. and a 2008 graduate of Brooklyn Law School.

[2] See 15 U.S.C. § 1051 (2012) ("The application shall include . . . the goods in connection with which the mark is used, and a drawing of the mark.").

for businesses to establish brand visibility across social media platforms. While there are countless benefits to social media marketing, there are certain drawbacks and likely pitfalls as well. This article explores the difficulty in controlling brand identity in light of almost unrestricted third-party participation in social media and the particular trademark problems posed by the prevalence of hashtags in social media marketing.

Social media turned the once simple octothorpe, symbolizing the words "pounds" and "number," into a very powerful marketing tool. "A 'hashtag' is a form of metadata comprised of a word or phrase prefixed with the symbol '#.'"[3] By applying a hashtag to the beginning of a word or phrase on social media outlets, like Instagram and Twitter, users turn that word or phrase into a searchable expression.[4] Business owners and marketing professionals alike tout the power of hashtagging a trademark or service mark into a searchable, trend-able expression.

The scope and necessity of social media marketing is observable in the use of business' allocated marketing budgets. Adweek.com reported the following from a poll of 5,000 marketers conducted in early 2015 by Salesforce:[5]

> 70% planned to increase social media ad spending;[6]
> 70% planned to increase spending on non-paid social media marketing;[7]
> 66% responded that "social media was core to their business;"[8] and
> 38% planned to shift a portion of their marketing budgets previously allocated to traditional marketing to digital marketing.[9]

While it is free to use and engage in social media outlets, marketers spend these dollars on sponsored advertisement buys and social media expertise. Social media marketing experts strategically maximize a

---

[3] TMEP § 1202.18 (8th ed. Oct. 2015) (entitled "Hashtag Marks").
[4] *See id.* ("Hashtags are often used in social-networking sites to identify or facilitate a search for a keyword or topic of interest.").
[5] Shea Bennett, *70% of Marketers Will Increase Social Media Spend in 2015,* SOCIALTIMES (Jan. 12, 2015, 6:00 PM), http://www.adweek.com/socialtimes/social-marketing-2015/504357.
[6] *Id.*
[7] *Id.*
[8] *Id.*
[9] *Id.*

brand's social media prevalence with sponsored advertisements, posting content, and, yes, strategic use of hashtags.

Twitter and Instagram are the two primary social media outlets to revolutionize the hashtag. Twitter is a service on which any user may share an idea, an experience, or a thought in 180 characters of text or less, a photo, or a video, each called a "tweet."[10] Hashtags with accompanying words or phrases appropriate the corresponding tweet to a topic embodied by such word or phrase.[11] Each Twitter user has a timeline on his or her profile displaying tweets in reverse chronological order.[12] The timeline and profile of a business become the Twitter face of the brand. Instagram is "a fun and quirky way to share your life with friends through a series of pictures."[13] Similarly, each user has a profile and timeline of photos or videos displayed in reverse chronological order. Users can provide comments, including hashtags, to photo or video posts. Placing a hashtag at the beginning of a word or phrase on both Twitter and Instagram turns the word or phrase into a hyperlink that leads to topically related posts.[14]

Perhaps the greatest advantage social media outlets like Twitter and Instagram pose to marketers is the ability to interact with their audience.[15] When a user tweets or posts on Instagram, other users may then comment, repost, share directly, and basically participate in the conversation surrounding the tweet or post. This audience interaction provides valuable insight to marketers and inflames the reach of a simple marketing effort, sometimes virally. Including a hashtag word or phrase makes such conversations sortable by topic.[16] If the hashtag goes viral, the social media marketplace considers it to be a trending topic, a pinnacle for any social media marketing effort. It is this audience interaction that makes the hashtag such a powerful marketing and branding implement.

---

[10] *See The Story of a Tweet*, TWITTER, https://about.twitter.com/what-is-twitter/story-of-a-tweet (last visited Dec. 27, 2015).

[11] *See id.* ("Hashtags assign a topic to a Tweet.").

[12] *See id.*

[13] *FAQ*, INSTAGRAM, https://www.instagram.com/about/faq/ (last visited Dec. 27, 2015).

[14] *See The story of a Tweet, supra* note 10; *How Do I Use Hashtags?*, INSTAGRAM, https://help.instagram.com/351460621611097 (last visited Dec. 27, 2015).

[15] *See* Stephanie Chandler, *The Hidden Benefits of Social Media Marketing: Why Your Strategy May Be Working Better Than You Think*, FORBES / FORBES WOMEN (March 12, 2013, 3:15 AM), http://www.forbes.com/sites/work-in-progress/2013/03/12/the-hidden-benefits-of-social-media-marketing-why-your-strategy-may-be-working-better-than-you-think/.

[16] *See The Story of a Tweet, supra* note 10; *How Do I Use Hashtags?, supra* note 14.

But, "with great power comes great responsibility."[17] Successful registration of a mark with the United States Patent and Trademark Office provides the owner of that mark the "exclusive right to use the registered mark in commerce on or in connection with the goods or services specified in the registration."[18] The value in trademark ownership lies in the right to exclusive use of the mark. Thus, it is in the trademark owner's best interest to police third-party use of his or her mark in order to protect it from dilution and/or consumer confusion with a similar mark. So, there is a problem. Trademark owners are encouraged to limit third-party use of their marks. However, they are simultaneously well served by encouraging audience participation in their social media marketing, especially to exacerbate the use of their marks as hashtagged trending topics.

II.   TRADEMARK LAW BROADLY.

A.   *Rationale.*

The statute underlying modern trademark law in the United States is the Lanham Act.[19] "The basic goal of the Act . . . was 'the protection of trademarks, securing to the owner the good will of his business and protecting the public against spurious and falsely marked goods.'"[20] A trademark's capability to distinguish the goods or services of this source is referred to as "distinctiveness."[21] A protectable and marketable trademark should be unique among its channel of commerce so that it establishes its own brand as the source of the relevant goods and or services.

---

[17] SPIDER-MAN (Columbia Pictures 2002).

[18] 15 U.S.C. § 1115(a) (2012) ("Any registration issued under the Act of March 3, 1881, or the Act of February 20, 1905, or of a mark registered on the principal register provided by this chapter and owned by a party to an action shall be admissible in evidence and shall be prima facie evidence of the validity of the registered mark and of the registration of the mark, of the registrant's ownership of the mark, and of the registrant's exclusive right to use the registered mark in commerce on or in connection with the goods or services specified in the registration . . . .").

[19] *See* 15 U.S.C. § 1051 (2012).

[20] *In re* E. I. DuPont DeNemours & Co., 476 F.2d 1357, 1360 (C.C.P.A. 1973). *See generally* Jacob Ries Bottling Works, Inc. v. Coca-Cola Co., 138 F.2d 56 (C.C.P.A. 1943); Van Camp Sea Food Co. v. Westgate Sea Prods. Co., 48 F.2d 950, 951 (C.C.P.A. 1931); Skookum Packers Ass'n v. Pac. Nw. Canning Co., 45 F.2d 912 (C.C.P.A. 1930).

[21] *See* Two Pesos, Inc. v. Taco Cabana, Inc., 505 U.S. 763, 768–69 (1992).

B.   *The Standard.*

Trademarks are valuable to marketers because they distinctly represent a particular brand. For that reason, trademark law will generally not allow for simultaneous ownership of confusingly similar marks by representing more than one brand in a particular channel of commerce. This leads to trademark confusion, which is defined as "the incorrect assumption on the part of a hypothetical consumer that the two trademarks belong to the same source."[22] Therefore, the United States Patent and Trademark Office will reject applications for marks for which there is likelihood of confusion with an existing registered mark.

A likelihood of confusion exists when a mark "so resembles a mark registered in the Patent and Trademark Office . . . as to be likely, when used on or in connection with the goods of the applicant, to cause confusion, or to cause mistake, or to deceive."[23] In *In re E. I. DuPont DeNemours & Co.,*[24] the predecessor to the United States Court of Appeals for the Federal Circuit set forth the relevant factors to consider when making this determination:

> (1) The similarity or dissimilarity of the marks in their entireties as to appearance, sound, connotation and commercial impression.

> (2) The similarity or dissimilarity and nature of the goods or services as described in an application or registration or in connection with which a prior mark is in use.

> (3) The similarity or dissimilarity of established, likely-to-continue trade channels.

> (4) The conditions under which and buyers to whom sales are made, i.e. "impulse" vs. careful, sophisticated purchasing.

---

[22] *Confusingly Similar (Likelihood of Confusion),* MARKLAW, http://marklaw.com/index.php/trademark-terms-c/343-trademark-confusion-confusingly-similar-2 (last visited Dec. 27, 2015).

[23] 15 U.S.C. § 1052(d) (2012).

[24] 476 F.2d at 1361.

(5) The fame of the prior mark (sales, advertising, length of use).

(6) The number and nature of similar marks in use on similar goods.

(7) The nature and extent of any actual confusion.

(8) The length of time during and conditions under which there has been concurrent use without evidence of actual confusion.

(9) The variety of goods on which a mark is or is not used (house mark, "family" mark, product mark).

(10) The market interface between applicant and the owner of a prior mark:

    (a) a mere "consent" to register or use.

    (b) agreement provisions designed to preclude confusion, i.e. limitations on continued use of the marks by each party.

    (c) assignment of mark, application, registration and good will of the related business.

    (d) laches and estoppel attributable to owner of prior mark and indicative of lack of confusion.

(11) The extent to which applicant has a right to exclude others from use of its mark on its goods.

(12) The extent of potential confusion, i.e., whether *de minimis* or substantial.

(13) Any other established fact probative of the effect of use.[25]

The key concepts to glean from the *DuPont* case as it relates to the present topic are likelihood of confusion in general and factor number six—the number and nature of similar marks in use on similar goods or services. The law aims to protect the consumer from confusion. Courts have held that "an infringement occurs if it is likely

---

[25] *Id.* at 1361.

to confuse the relevant consumer as to the affiliation, connection or sponsorship,"[26] with or by an existing mark. However, it is important to note that third-party use of a registered mark that does not serve as a source identifier does not amount to infringement.[27] Therefore, using a trademark as a hashtag for purposes of establishing a topical reference will likely not amount to trademark infringement.

DuPont factor number six addresses the occurrence of third-party use of an applied-for mark. When a trademark examining attorney refuses a trademark application under 15 U.S.C. § 1052(d) due to a *likelihood of confusion* with an existing registered mark, the applicant has the chance to respond with an argument that may reference one or several of the DuPont factors. The applicant may address factor number six by pointing to existing concurrent registrations for marks similar to the applied-for mark and existing concurrent third-party use of similar marks in fields similar to the relevant goods or services. This third-party use shows the examining attorney that there is contemporaneous use of similar marks that does not cause detrimental confusion amongst consumers as to the source of the relevant goods or services.

> [T]he theory behind this factor is that the relevant class(es) of consumers have become so conditioned by the presence of a plethora of similar marks in the marketplace that they have been educated or accustomed to distinguish such marks based on differences in the marks that would otherwise be less meaningful.[28]

In this way, concurrent third-party use is actually advantageous. However, concurrent third-party use can be problematic if it indeed does cause consumer confusion or causes attenuation of the mark as a source indicator. For these reasons, it is imperative that trademark owners observe and exert some level of control over third-party use of their marks.

---

[26] THE IP BOOK, 10-134 (Stephen R. Baird et al. eds., 10th ed. 2012), http://www.minncle.org/Materials/OnlineMaterials/77413IPbook.pdf (analyzing Rosetta Stone Ltd. v. Google, Inc., 676 F.3d 144 (4th Cir. 2012).

[27] *See* Multi Time Machine, Inc. v. Amazon.com, Inc., 792 F.3d 1070, 1086–87 (9th Cir. 2015) (holding that Amazon search results for a product are unlikely to cause confusion as a matter of law).

[28] *In re* Tyson Foods Inc., No. 85476655, 2014 WL 788329, at *2 (T.T.A.B. 2014).

Other reasons the United States Patent and Trademark Office may refuse to grant exclusive use of a trademark or services mark are mere descriptiveness, deceptive misdescriptiveness, geographic descriptiveness, geographic misdescriptiveness, primarily merely a surname, and ornamentation.[29] Mere descriptiveness refers to a mark that "merely describes the goods or services on or in connection with which it is used."[30] A brand name or slogan that merely describes goods or services will not qualify as a trademark. To lock up such descriptive terms in association with corresponding goods or services would chill business competition and, ultimately, stymie societal enhancement. Conversely, "[i]f a term immediately conveys such an idea but the idea is false, although plausible, then the term is deceptively misdescriptive."[31] It is important to note that misdescriptive marks may be able to pass muster unless consumers are "likely to believe the misrepresentation."[32] The same concepts apply to geographic descriptiveness and geographic misdescriptiveness with the key distinction that the unregistrable mark contains geographical indications.[33] Finally, ornamentation is subject matter that is merely a decorative feature that does not identify and distinguish the applicant's goods and, thus, does not function as a trademark.[34] A mark embodying solely such decorative subject matter is considered ornamental. A mark must identify the source of the goods or services in a more significant way than merely adorning goods.

---

[29] *Possible Grounds for Refusal of a Mark*, USPTO, http://www.uspto.gov/trademark/additional-guidance-and-resources/possible-grounds-refusal-mark (last visited Jan. 2, 2016).

[30] West Publishing, CORPORATE COUNSEL'S GUIDE TO INTELLECTUAL PROPERTY § 3.7 (2015). *See also In re* Abcor Dev. Corp., 588 F.2d 811, 813 (C.C.P.A. 1978) ("The major reasons for not protecting such marks are: (1) to prevent the owner of a mark from inhibiting competition in the sale of particular goods; and (2) to maintain freedom of the public to use the language involved, thus avoiding the possibility of harassing infringement suits by the registrant against others who use the mark when advertising or describing their own products.").

[31] *In re* Dicom Grid, Inc., Nos. 78741602, 78741064, 2009 WL 129552 (T.T.A.B. 2009).

[32] Binney & Smith Inc. v. Magic Marker Indus., Inc., 222 U.S.P.Q. 1003 (T.T.A.B. 1984) (LIQUID CRAYON held neither common descriptive name, nor merely descriptive, nor deceptively misdescriptive of coloring kits or markers).

[33] 15 U.S.C. §§ 1052(e)(2)–(3) (2012).

[34] Coach Leatherware Co. v. Ann Taylor, Inc., 933 F.2d 162, 171 (2d Cir. 1991).

C.   *Within the Social Media Marketplace.*

The bulk of applicable trademark law was developed prior to the social-media boom. While copyright law has addressed many of the issues brought upon by social media in the Digital Millennium Copyright Act's Safe Harbor provision, trademark law does not have an equivalent standard. The Safe Harbor Act of the Digital Millennium Copyright Act provides copyright owners with the opportunity to have infringing material taken down by filing notice of the infringement with the particular internet service provider. [35] Ultimately, the Act protects the internet service providers from any copyright infringement liability of an end user if the following conditions are met: (1) the internet service provider "does not have actual knowledge that the material or an activity using the material on the system or network is infringing;"[36] (2) the internet services provider "has designated an agent to receive notifications of claimed infringement;"[37] and (3) the internet service provider must remove the allegedly infringing material upon notice from copyright owner.[38]

Some internet service providers will honor the Safe Harbor protocol and apply it to trademark infringement claims as well as copyright infringement claims. However, the Digital Millennium Copyright Act does not apply to trademarks and the internet service providers are under no obligation to treat trademark infringement notices in the same manner.

Many providers have established their own trademark policies and make them available to users via a link at the bottom of their webpages. Twitter's trademark policy says, "Using a company or business name, logo, or other trademark-protected materials in a manner that may mislead or confuse others with regard to its brand or business affiliation may be considered a trademark policy violation."[39] In the event that a trademark owner reports an instance of trademark infringement occurring within its services, Twitter will "review the account and may take the following actions:"[40]

---

[35] 17 U.S.C. § 512 (2012).
[36] 17 U.S.C. § 512 (c)(1)(A)(i).
[37] 17 U.S.C. § 512 (c)(2).
[38] 17 U.S.C. § 512 (c)(1)(C).
[39]   *Trademark Policy*, TWITTER HELP CTR. (Oct. 3, 2012), http://support.twitter.com/articles/18367.
[40] *Id.*

• When there is a clear intent to mislead others through the unauthorized use of a trademark, Twitter will suspend the account and notify the account holder.
• When we determine that an account appears to be confusing users, but is not purposefully passing itself off as the trademarked good or service, we give the account holder an opportunity to clear up any potential confusion. We may also release a username for the trademark holder's active use.
• We are responsive to reports about confusing or misleading Promoted Tweet and Promoted Trend copy, as well as Promoted Account profile information.[41]

Instagram has a form for trademark owners to complete and submit in the event of an occurrence of trademark infringement within its service.[42] Instagram's information on trademarks further clarifies its stance on trademark infringement by encouraging users to reach out directly to an allegedly infringing party without involving Instagram.[43] Instagram's Terms of Use says, "We may, but have no obligation to, remove, edit, block, and/or monitor Content or accounts containing Content that we determine in our sole discretion violates these Terms of Use."[44] The Terms additionally say firmly that users "may not use the Service for any illegal or unauthorized purpose."[45] According to the terms, an Instagram user must:

[R]epresent and warrant that: (i) you own the Content posted by you on or through the Service or otherwise have the right to grant the rights and licenses set forth in these Terms of Use; (ii) the posting and use of your Content on or through the Service does not violate, misappropriate or infringe on the rights of any third party, including, without limitation, privacy

---

[41] Id.
[42] *About Trademark,* INSTAGRAM HELP CTR., http://help.instagram.com/222826637847963 (last visited Jan. 1, 2016).
[43] Id.
[44] *Terms of Use,* INSTAGRAM HELP CTR. (Jan. 19, 2013), https://help.instagram.com/478745558852511.
[45] Id.

rights, publicity rights, copyrights, trademark and/or
other intellectual property rights; (iii) you agree to
pay for all royalties, fees, and any other monies owed
by reason of Content you post on or through the
Service; and (iv) you have the legal right and
capacity to enter into these Terms of Use in your
jurisdiction.[46]

By using the Instagram service, users submit to the above
representation and warranty, which includes that they will not post
intellectual property without proper authorization.[47]

To use a registered trademark as a hashtag on Twitter or
Instagram in an unauthorized manner violates the Terms of Service
policies of each social media platform as well as federal trademark
law.[48] While third-party hashtagging of brand identifiers is potentially
welcomed by the trademark owner, they do have the option to shut
down the third-party use by means of such policies if it amounts to
infringement.[49] Additionally, trademark registrants may always pursue
claims in federal court.[50]

III.   REGISTRANTS.

A.   Hashtags and Registered Marks.

Owners of registered trademarks often use their marks in
conjunction with hashtags in social media contexts for marketing
purposes. Doing so converts the trademark into a categorical topic
which invites the social media marketplace to comment and share. As
discussed above, this type of participation is beneficial to marketers in
that the marketing spreads throughout the particular social media outlet
being used and trademark owners are able to gather informative data
about their audience. But not all third-party hashtags of registered
marks are welcome by owners. Problematic hashtagging occurs when a
brand of similar goods or services uses the mark as a hashtag as either a
source identifier of their own or with the intention (or even the effect)

---

[46] *Id.*
[47] *See id.*
[48] *See id.*
[49] *See id.*
[50] *See id.*

of diverting the trademark owner's consumers to themselves. This likely amounts to infringement and the trademark owner has the opportunity to pursue an infringement claim.

B.   *Registrability of Hashtag Marks.*

In an effort to curb unauthorized third-party use of a word or phrase with a hashtag, marketers may attempt to acquire a trademark registration for a hashtag mark, meaning a term preceded by the hashtag symbol or the word "hashtag." A brand may also attempt trademark registration of a hashtag mark because the symbol or word is actually part of the mark. However, "the addition of the term HASHTAG or the hash symbol (#) to an otherwise unregistrable mark typically cannot render it registrable."[51] In other words, a mark that does not serve to indicate the source of the relevant goods or services is not registrable as a result of applying a hashtag. The reason for this is that the hashtag simply "facilitate(s) categorization and searching within online social media."[52] Therefore, a hashtag mark is only registrable if the mark would be otherwise registrable and the hashtag effectuates the source-indicating function of the overall mark.

IV.   THIRD-PARTY USE.

A.   *Infringement.*

Trademark infringement means the unauthorized third-party use of similar marks for similar goods and/or services as a source identifier. Under the Lanham Act, trademark infringement is defined as:

> (1) Any person who shall, without the consent of the registrant—
> (a) use in commerce any reproduction, counterfeit, copy, or colorable imitation of a registered mark in

---

[51] TMEP § 1202.18 (8th ed. 2015).

[52] *In re* Hotels.com, L.P., 573 F.3d 1300, 1304 (Fed. Cir. 2009) (finding that the addition of a generic top-level-domain to an otherwise unregistrable mark does not typically add any source-identifying significance); Interactive Prods. Corp. v. a2z Mobile Office Sols., Inc., 326 F.3d 687, 691 (6th Cir. 2003) (finding that the post-domain path of a URL does not typically signify source); TMEP §§ 1209.03(m), 1215–.10 (regarding top-level domain names).

connection with the sale, offering for sale, distribution, or advertising of any goods or services on or in connection with which such use is likely to cause confusion, or to cause mistake, or to deceive; or

(b) reproduce, counterfeit, copy or colorably imitate a registered mark and apply such reproduction, counterfeit, copy or colorable imitation to labels, signs, prints, packages, wrappers, receptacles or advertisements intended to be used in commerce upon or in connection with the sale, offering for sale, distribution, or advertising of goods or services on or in connection with which such use is likely to cause confusion, or to cause mistake, or to deceive,

shall be liable in a civil action by the registrant for the remedies hereinafter provided. Under subsection (b) hereof, the registrant shall not be entitled to recover profits or damages unless the acts have been committed with knowledge that such imitation is intended to be used to cause confusion, or to cause mistake, or to deceive.

As used in this paragraph, the term "any person" includes the United States, all agencies and instrumentalities thereof, and all individuals, firms, corporations, or other persons acting for the United States and with the authorization and consent of the United States, and any State, any instrumentality of a State, and any officer or employee of a State or instrumentality of a State acting in his or her official capacity. The United States, all agencies and instrumentalities thereof, and all individuals, firms, corporations, other persons acting for the United States and with the authorization and consent of the United States, and any State, and any such instrumentality, officer, or employee, shall be subject to the provisions of this chapter in the same manner and to the same extent as any nongovernmental entity.[53]

---

[53] 15 U.S.C. § 1114 (2012).

Using a hashtag with a registered trademark on a social media outlet may or may not constitute infringement. As mentioned, when an unauthorized third-party uses a registered mark as a hashtag, and the hashtag has the effect of misidentifying the source of goods or services, such hashtag likely infringes upon the registrant's exclusive trademark rights.[54] If the third-party hashtag is unrelated, related in a way that serves the marketing intentions of the registrant, or does not have a source identifying effect, the hashtag will likely not amount to infringement.[55]

However, the distinction between infringing third-party use and non-infringing third-party use is nuanced and there is little precedent to govern it. Because of the novelty of the issue and parties' ability to resolve such disputes out of court, trademark case law provides very little guidance as to these nuances. One case that does address an interesting nuance is *Eksouzian v. Albanese*.[56] This case revolves around a settlement agreement the parties reached after the defendant sought the use of variations of the plaintiff's registered trademark to identify the source of its own goods, a small device which vaporizes dry or liquefied herbs, such as tobacco, for consumption by smoking.[57] The parties agreed that only the plaintiff could use the word "cloud" standing alone, and not coupled with an additional word or words, as a source identifier.[58] They further agreed that the defendants must cease use of the word "cloud" on their own, and only use it in conjunction with another word.[59] The settlement agreement between the parties states, "[t]he size and relationship of CLOUD with the other word or words used in close association with CLOUD is within Defendants' discretion except that the word coupled with CLOUD must be in close proximity and readable."[60]

Despite this agreement, the plaintiffs used "#cloudpen" on Instagram.[61] The court analyzed whether plaintiff's use of the word "cloud" coupled with the word "pen" in its Instagram hashtag violated

---

[54] *See supra* Part III.A.

[55] *See supra* Part III.A.

[56] Eksouzian v. Albanese, No. CV 13-00728-PSG-MAN, 2015 WL 4720478 (C.D. Cal. Aug. 7, 2015).

[57] CLOUDPEN, https://cloudpenz.com/ (last visited Jan. 25, 2016).

[58] *Eksouzian*, 2015 WL 4720478, at *2.

[59] *Id.*

[60] *Id.*

[61] *Id.* at *7.

the settlement agreement. The court decided this matter in favor of the plaintiff's use of the hashtag "#cloudpen."[62] "Plaintiffs did not materially breach the [settlement agreement] by using the generic descriptor "pen" in close association with "CLOUD" hashtag on Instagram."[63] The Court reasoned that "[p]laintiff's use of the hashtag '#cloudpen' is merely a functional tool to direct the location of [p]laintiff's promotion so that it is viewed by a group of consumers[.]"[64] Therefore, the hashtag did not constitute breach of the settlement agreement or trademark infringement because neither the hashtag nor the descriptive word "pen" amounted to coupling the word "cloud" with another word or phrase.

As more cases like this unfold, trademark law's body of governing precedent will provide further clarity on the various possible issues regarding hashtags and trademark infringement.

B.   *Exclusivity/Policing/Dilution/Generic.*

Exclusivity.

The Lanham Act affords owners of registered trademarks the exclusive rights to use their marks as source identifiers for their goods or services.[65] Because one of trademark law's objectives is to alleviate potential confusion amongst consumers, this exclusive right extends to marks for goods or services that are confusingly similar.[66] The obvious benefit of exclusive use is the ability to establish a brand and differentiate from others in the marketplace.[67] By doing so, the consumer knows exactly what to expect from goods or services bearing the relevant mark.[68] For example, a consumer who buys a can of Campbell's chicken noodle soup knows exactly what to expect because it tastes like every other can of chicken noodle soup on the shelves. The

---

[62] *Id.* at *8.
[63] *Id.*
[64] *Id.*
[65] Lanham Act § 33, 15 U.S.C. § 1115(a) (2012).
[66] B & B Hardware, Inc. v. Hargis Indus., Inc., 135 S. Ct. 1293, 1301 (2015).
[67] Barton Beebe, Search and Persuasion in Trademark Law, 103 MICH. L. REV. 2020, 2042–43 (2005).
[68] 6 J. THOMAS MCCARTHY, MCCARTHY ON TRADEMARKS & UNFAIR COMPETITION § 2:3 (4th ed. 2015).

can bears the Campbell's trademark so consumers knows that his or her expectations will be met every time he or she buys that particular soup.

An additional benefit of exclusive trademark ownership is that the mark becomes an intellectual property asset.[69] The trademark owner then has the opportunity to license the mark for authorized third-party use for a negotiated fee.[70] In this way, the mark has the potential to become a revenue generator. A very lucrative example of this is a professional sports team logo.[71] Professional sports teams are able to license out their logos for use on various types of merchandise items. These licenses give the merchandiser an entire fan base as the market for their goods and garner hefty fees and royalties for the teams.[72] Owners of intellectual property assets, such as trademarks, have real opportunity to generate income because of their exclusive right to license the intellectual property for third-party use.

Policing

Trademark owners have a "duty to police [their] rights against infringers."[73] This means trademark owners must reasonably monitor third-party use of their marks and assert their exclusive rights against infringers.[74] If they fail to effectively police their marks they may lose their exclusivity.[75]

One undesirable consequence of inadequate policing is illustrated by *Black Diamond Sportswear, Inc. v. Black Diamond Equipment*, where the Second Circuit affirmed the district court's holding that the plaintiff's claim was barred by laches on the basis that the plaintiff should have known of the defendant's infringing use of the

---

[69] Cathy Jewell, *Trademarks: Valuable Assets in a Changing World*, WIPO MAG. (July 2009), http://www.wipo.int/wipo_magazine/en/2009/04/article_0002.html.
[70] *Trademark Licensing*, INT'L TRADEMARK ASS'N (Apr. 2015), http://www.inta.org/TrademarkBasics/FactSheets/Pages/TrademarkLicensing.aspx.
[71] Darren Heitner, *Sports Licensing Soars to $698 Million in Royalty Revenue*, FORBES MAG. (Jun. 17, 2014, 5.00 PM), http://www.forbes.com/sites/darrenheitner/2014/06/17/sports-licensing-soars-to-698-million-in-royalty-revenue/.
[72] *Id.*
[73] MCCARTHY, *supra* note 68, § 31:38.
[74] *Id.*
[75] *Id.* at § 17.17 (noting that a markholder's failure to take action against infringers can cause the mark to lose distinctiveness) (citing Wallpaper Mfrs., Ltd. v. Crown Wallcovering Corp., 680 F.2d 755 (C.C.P.A. 1982)).

mark on its ski wear products."[76] The court found that "the plaintiff was aware of the defendants use of the Black Diamond mark on ski equipment . . . and that, had it exercised due diligence in policing its mark, the plaintiff would have readily discovered that the defendant was also selling ski wear in direct competition with the plaintiff's ski wear."[77] In other words, the trademark owner lost its exclusive right to its mark for ski wear due to inadequate policing.

Hashtags and social media pose challenges to trademark owners when it comes to effective policing. The social media marketplace is incredibly vast, making it unlikely that trademark owners would be able to monitor every third-party use of their marks. Further, much of the third-party use of marks, especially as hashtags, is deliberately sought after by marketers. Nonetheless, it is crucial that trademark owners prudently monitor these outlets and uses in order to exercise reasonable control over their exclusive rights in their marks.

Dilution

Another consequence of failing to properly enforce exclusive trademark rights is trademark dilution. The Lanham Act "provides the owner of a famous trademark with injunctive relief against another that engaged in commercial activities that tend to dilute the distinctive quality of the owner's famous mark or tend to tarnish the owner's image, even if there is no likelihood of confusion."[78] The Lanham Act states that a court "may consider all relevant factors including the following:"

> i. The duration, extent, and geographic reach of advertising and publicity of the mark, whether advertised or publicized by the owner or third parties.
> ii. The amount, volume, and geographic extent of sales of goods or services offered under the mark.
> iii. The extent of actual recognition of the mark.

---

[76] Black Diamond Sportswear, Inc. v. Black Diamond Equip., No. 06-3508, 2007 WL 2914452, at 4 (2d Cir. Oct. 5, 2007).
[77] Id.
[78] 15 U.S.C. § 1125(c) (2012).

> iv. Whether the mark was registered under the Act of
> March 3, 1881, or the Act of February 20, 1905, or
> on the principal register.[79]

For famous marks, third-party hashtags need not serve as a diverting or confusing source identifier to amount to infringement. Owners of famous marks can assert their rights over third-party users on dilution grounds if they object to the use. Twitter and Instagram hashtag campaigns may be monitored and easily controlled by the famous mark owner in this way.

Generic.

Even if your mark is not famous, overuse by third parties could cause your mark to become generic. A generic mark is a term that was once a distinct trademark, but through extensive third-party use, has become synonymous with the goods or services it identifies and no longer serves to distinguish the trademark owner from other sources.[80] Consequently, the trademark owner loses its exclusive rights in the mark.[81] "The critical issue in genericness cases is whether members of the relevant public primarily use or understand the term sought to be registered to refer to the category or class of goods or services in question."[82] The court applies a two-prong test to determine if a mark is or has become generic: "First, what is the category or class of goods or services at issue? Second, is the term sought to be registered understood by the relevant public primarily to refer to that category or class of goods or services?"[83]

Genericness can be a double-edge sword for trademark owners. On one hand, trademark owners lose their exclusive rights in their mark. On the other hand, the particular trademark owner has likely become a very commonly known source for its goods or services. Extensive hashtagging of a particular mark may lead to mass awareness of the mark as a source identifier for the relevant goods or services. Occasionally, mass awareness causes a mark to become generic. If the trademark owner wishes to maintain its exclusive rights, keeping the

---

[79] 15 U.S.C. § 1125(c)(2) (2012).

[80] 6 MCCARTHY, *supra* note 68, § 17.8.

[81] *Id.*

[82] *In re* Women's Publ'g Co., 23 U.S.P.Q. 2d 1876, 1877 (T.T.A.B. 1992).

[83] H. Marvin Ginn Corp. v. Int'l Ass'n of Fire Chiefs, Inc., 782 F.2d 987, 991 (Fed. Cir. 1986).

mark's integrity as a source identifier for its own goods or services, the owners should make reasonable efforts to police the mark and educate the public on the topic of the mark's intended meaning.

C.   *Wanted Third-Party Use.*

The above consequences of third-party use of registered trademarks are reason for trepidation on the part of trademark owners in encouraging third-party hashtags of their marks. But paradoxically, those trademark owners stand to benefit greatly from the marketing upside generated by third-party hashtags of their marks. Adweek.com's Shea Bennet highlights this notion in the infographic entitled "The Power of the #hashtag."[84] Bennet describes the hashtag as an invaluable tool for "[i]nstantly linking a social media post to a group of others about the same topic and updating a group of likeminded users on that topic in real time."[85] Bennent's infographic goes on to list some additional advantages of the hashtag such as categorization for easy searching and the potential to use them anywhere within the content of a social media post.[86] All of the above functions of the hashtag are incidental to the audience participation that is so sought after by social media marketers.

The analytics and reporting firm Locowise ran a study on audience engagement rates resulting from hashtags on Twitter and Instagram and gathered the data.[87] On Twitter, 4.75% of tweets studied contained three or more hashtags; and Hashtags had no effect on audience engagement rates.[88] These results can teach trademark owners two lessons: (1) marketing efforts aimed at cultivating third-party hashtagging of their marks on Twitter may be fruitless; and (2) the value of maintaining exclusivity of their marks likely outweighs the benefits of encouraging third-party hashtags on Twitter. However, Locowise's Instagram study yielded a contrasting outcome: "Posts that used three hashtags yielded the highest engagement rate."[89] While the

---

[84] Shea Bennett, *The Power of the #Hashtag [Infographic]*, SOCIAL TIMES (Nov. 12, 2013, 3:00 PM), http://www.adweek.com/socialtimes/hashtag-power/493090.

[85] *Id.*

[86] *Id.*

[87] David Cohen, *Do Hashtags Mean Engagement on Twitter, Instagram?*, SOCIAL TIMES (Nov. 16, 2015, 11:30 AM), http://www.adweek.com/socialtimes/locowise-hashtags-engagement-twitter-instagram/629995.

[88] *Id.*

[89] *Id.*

Instagram data shows more promise for hashtag campaigns, and marketers are well founded in running hashtag campaigns on social media outlets, trademark owners should consider a cost-versus-benefit analysis before launching such a campaign.

D.   *Proposal.*

Some of the value in trademark ownership is the ability to engage in marketing efforts such as hashtag campaigns on social media outlets. So how does a trademark owner protect the exclusivity of the mark while promoting the brand through the very useful social media hashtag?

As mentioned, the trademark owner must diligently monitor third-party use of its mark and prudently maintain control of such use. Trademark owners may set up alerts to notify them of any Internet occurrence of their marks. Also, Twitter and Instagram provide account settings within which their users can clarify any brand affiliation to their marks and/or profile. In certain circumstances, a trademark owner may want to include a rights notification, such as a ®, in the publically visible portion of its user profile.

Additionally, the trademark owner should evaluate each social media campaign with a cost-benefit analysis. Of course, viral hashtagging of a brand's mark is beneficial to the brand from a marketing perspective. The key is to determine the likelihood and scope of the success of each campaign and weigh that against the risk of trademark infringement and its consequences.

Finally, trademark owners ought to address infringing third-party use of their marks with a formal notice and possibly infringement claims.

AT THE CROSSROADS OF INTELLECTUAL PROPERTY AND GOVERNMENT CONTRACTING: CASE STUDIES AND PRACTICAL POINTERS

COURTNEY A. HOFFLANDER[1] &
THEODORE M. THOMPSON II[2]

[1] Courtney A. Hofflander graduated from William Mitchell College of Law *summa cum laude* in 2014. She is admitted to practice law in Minnesota and North Dakota. She is an Associate at Fredrikson & Byron, P.A. where her practice focuses on intellectual property transactions. The author would like to thank Alissa Harrington for her research and dedication to this paper. Harrington is a second year law student at Mitchell Hamline School of Law, expected graduation May 2017, who has worked with government grants both as a contractor and as a government employee.

[2] Theodore M. Thompson II is a 2011 graduate of William Mitchell College of Law. He is admitted to practice in Minnesota and is a licensed patent attorney. He currently works at Medtronic, PLC. None of the views expressed herein are endorsed by or made on behalf of his employer.

I. INTRODUCTION

Contracting with the U.S. federal government can be lucrative for private companies. In fiscal year 2015 alone, the federal government spent over $393 billion on about 2.9 million contracts.[3] The federal government spent an additional $601 billion on grant funding in about 529,000 transactions.[4] With so much money on the line, it is not surprising businesses are eager to get a piece of Uncle Sam's pie. It is also not surprising that the federal government has created complex regulations in order to partially standardize these contracts, namely the Federal Acquisition Regulation (FAR) and its supplements.[5] The largest of these supplements is the Defense Federal Acquisition Regulation Supplement (DFARS).[6] Entities of all sizes need to be aware of the unique risks and considerations of doing business with the government, particularly with respect to intellectual property, in order to make smart choices, mitigate risks, and protect their assets.

This article will explore key areas to consider when contracting with the federal government and will provide practical pointers to use when negotiating and performing under such contracts. First, this article addresses general differences between contracting

---

[3] *Spending Map – FY 2015*, USASPENDING.GOV,
https://www.usaspending.gov/transparency/Pages/SpendingMap.aspx (last visited Nov. 28, 2015).
[4] *Id.* This article focuses on procurement contracts rather than government grants.
[5] *Federal Acquisition Regulation (FAR)*, ACQUISITION.GOV, https://www.acquisition.gov (last visited Nov. 2, 2015).
[6] *Defense Federal Acquisition Regulation Supplement (DFARS) and Procedures, Guidance, and Information (PGI)*, DEF. PROCUREMENT & ACQUISITION POL'Y, http://www.acq.osd.mil/dpap/dars/dfarspgi/current/ (last visited Nov. 2, 2015).

with a private party versus the government.[7] Second, this article
examines how select types of intellectual property are treated under
government contracts, specifically discussing both DFARS and FAR.[8]
Lastly, this article outlines a series of questions that any business
contemplating entering a government contract should review to
determine whether it is, in fact, in the best interest of the business to do
so.[9]

II. DIFFERENCES BETWEEN CONTRACTING WITH A PRIVATE PARTY VERSUS THE GOVERNMENT

A. *Sovereign Immunity Creates Barriers to Suing the Government*

While contracting with the government shares many
similarities with contracting with a private party,[10] the government is
not a "typical litigant." Rather, the government is the benefactor of
special defenses, procedures, and limits on liability.[11] One of the largest
differences between private and government contracts arises from the
status of the United States as a sovereign that, when acting as a
sovereign for the purpose of the general welfare, is immune from
liability unless it consents to waive its immunity.[12] When the
government is contracting as a sovereign, the rights of the other party
will be subordinated.[13]

The Supreme Court stated as early as 1925 the government's
sovereign immunity as a contractor as settled law.[14] In *Horowitz v.
United States*, the Court held that "the United States when sued as a

---

[7] *See infra* Part II.

[8] *See infra* Part III.

[9] *See infra* Part IV.

[10] 1-3 JOHN COSGROVE MCBRIDE & THOMAS J. TOUHEY, GOVERNMENT CONTRACTS:
LAW, ADMIN & PROC § 3.10 (Walter A. I. Wilson ed., 2015).

[11] Gregory C. Sisk, *A Primer on the Doctrine of Federal Sovereign Immunity*, 58 OKLA.
L. REV. 439, 439 (2005).

[12] United States v. Sherwood, 312 U.S. 584, 586 (1941); McBride & Touhey, *supra* note
10.

[13] McBride & Touhey, *supra* note 10 ("[W]hen [the United States] acts as a sovereign, as
distinguished from its action in its individual or proprietary capacity as a contractor, the
rights of the individual doing business with it must be subordinated to the general
welfare."); *see also* Horowitz v. United States, 267 U.S. 458, 461 (1925).

[14] *Horowitz*, 267 U.S. at 461 (citing Wilson v. United States, 11 Ct. Cl. 513, 520 (1875);
Deming v. United States, 1 Ct. Cl. 190, 191 (1865); Jones v. United States, 1 Ct. Cl. 383,
384 (1865)).

contractor cannot be held liable for an obstruction to the performance of the particular contract resulting from its public and general acts as a sovereign."[15] This is in sharp contrast to the basic legal rule that non-performance is a breach.[16] That being said, because overly broad immunity would chill the incentive for businesses to contract with the government, the government has, through legislation, waived sovereign immunity in certain cases arising in contract, tort, and intellectual property infringement.[17] However, waivers of sovereign immunity must be explicit and "not 'enlarged beyond what the language requires.'"[18] For example, as discussed in the case study below, while 28 U.S.C. § 1498 allows a patent owner to bring a claim against the government for patent infringement, the patent owner is expressly limited to remedies for *direct infringement* by the government.[19]

1. *A Case Study:* Liberty Ammunition, Inc. v. United States.

As the Federal Court of Claims stated in *Liberty Ammunition, Inc. v. United States,* "'[a]ctivities of the Government which fall short of direct infringement do not give rise to governmental liability because the Government has not waived its sovereign immunity with respect to such activities. Hence, the Government is not liable for its inducing infringement by others.'"[20]

At issue in *Liberty Ammunition* was a private contractor's claim against the government for developing and manufacturing an infringing bullet.[21] The founder[22] of Liberty Ammunition had created a bullet to address the government's expressed need for a "greener" bullet, containing less lead and other heavy metals, while improving ballistic performance.[23] He had created this bullet independently and

---

[15] *Id.*

[16] RESTATEMENT (SECOND) OF CONTRACTS § 235 (1981).

[17] 1-1 JAMES G. MCEWEN, DAVID S. BLOCH, RICHARD M. GRAY & JOHN T. LUCAS, IP AND TECHNOLOGY IN GOVERNMENT CONTRACTS § 1.02 (Matthew Bender ed., 2015).

[18] U.S. Dep't of Energy v. Ohio, 503 U.S. 607, 615 (1992) (quoting Ruckelshaus v. Sierra Club, 463 U.S. 680, 685–86 (1983)).

[19] Liberty Ammunition, Inc. v. United States, 119 Fed. Cl. 368, 385 (2014), *appeal docketed*, No. 15-5057 (Fed. Cir. Feb. 23, 2015) (quoting Decca Ltd. v. United States, 640 F.2d 1156, 1167 (Ct. Cl. 1980)).

[20] *Id.* (quoting *Decca Ltd.*, 640 F.2d at 1167).

[21] *Id.* at 384.

[22] *Id.*

[23] *Id.* at 377–78. The inventor assigned the patent rights to Liberty Ammunition after filing for the patent. *Id.* at 380.

prior to entering into any government contract.[24] Before receiving prototypes for testing, government officers signed a non-disclosure agreement.[25] The army was not satisfied with the test results,[26] and Liberty Ammunition did not obtain a manufacturing contract.[27] Subsequently the army used a different ammunition manufacturer relying on substantially the same technology covered by Liberty Ammunition's patent.[28] Liberty Ammunition successfully sued under 28 U.S.C. § 1498, alleging infringement of its patent.[29] The Court of Federal Claims explained that the government directly infringes a patent when it "directly uses or manufactures the patented invention without a license, or when, through a procurement contract or otherwise, the government consents to the use or the manufacture of the patented invention for its benefit without first obtaining a license."[30]

In determining whether the patent is infringed by the government, the Court of Federal Claims applies a two-step process which mirrors the process between two private parties: first the court construes the patent claims at issue, then it compares the construed claims against the allegedly infringing product or process.[31] Despite this similarity, a major difference between infringement by a private party and infringement by the government is the damages the patent holder is entitled to under 28 U.S.C. § 1498. The patent holder's relief is limited to a "reasonable royalty,"[32] effectively foreclosing the possibility of treble damages under 35 U.S.C. § 284.[33]

---

[24] *Id.* at 378–82 (describing the beginning of the patent owner's development of the bullet in 2003 and the subsequent events leading to the award of a government contract in 2007).

[25] *Id.* at 378–79.

[26] *Id.* at 381 ("[T]he Army Marksmanship Unit tested ten out of the fifty rounds and found weaknesses in the bullet's muzzle velocity, precision, and target penetration capability.").

[27] *Id.* at 378–79. After preliminary trials, the inventor was told the Army would no longer be considering designs from the industry, but would use a "joint government/ATK [re]design effort" instead. *Id.*

[28] *Id.* at 383.

[29] *Id.* at 406.

[30] *Id.* at 385 (internal citations omitted) (citing Decca Ltd. v. United States, 640 F.2d 1156, 1166–67 (Ct. Cl. 1980); Hughes Aircraft Co. v. United States, 534 F.2d 889, 897 (Ct. Cl. 1976); Parker Beach Restoration, Inc. v. United States, 58 Fed. Cl. 126, 131 (2003)).

[31] *Id.* at 385.

[32] *Id.* at 386 ("Generally, the preferred manner [for computing reasonable and entire compensation] is to require the government to pay a reasonable royalty for its license as

Thus, several differences exist between claims for infringement against the government that contracting parties should keep in mind, which can impact the decision to bring suit. First, the patent owner is limited to recovering a reasonable royalty, not an injunction, and not treble damages.[34] Second, the U.S. government is not liable for claims of inducing patent infringement *unless* it has expressly waived its sovereign immunity for such a claim.[35] With few damage and liability theories available, the prospect of prevailing in litigation may weaken as compared to private party disputes.

B. *Government Can Avoid Performing the Contract in Certain Circumstances*

    1. *Government Agents Do Not Necessarily Have the Authority to Enter Into a Contract on Behalf of a Federal Agency*

As a private party, the appearance of an agent to have authority to enter into a contract can be legally binding. In sharp contrast, the government is not bound unless the agent is acting within the limitations of the agent's authority to do so.[36] It is the burden of the prospective contractor to make sure the government agent has the authority to enter into the contract, and if the matter comes before a court, to offer evidence of the government agent's contracting authority.[37] Thus, the claimant's typical argument that it relied on the words or actions of the other party's agent is not available, "even if a government employee purports to have authority to bind the government, the government will not be bound unless the employee actually has that authority."[38] Said another way, lacking the authority to

---

well as damages for its delay in paying the royalty." (quoting Standard Mfg. Co. v. United States, 42 Fed. Cl. 748, 758 (1999))).

[33] 35 U.S.C. § 284 (2012) ("[T]he court may increase the damages up to three times the amount found or assessed.").

[34] *See generally* Microsoft Corp. v. Motorola, Inc., 696 F.3d 872 (9th Cir. 2012).

[35] Pieczenik v. Cambridge Antibody Tech. Grp., No. 03 Civ. 6336(SAS), 2004 WL 1118500, at *3 (S.D.N.Y. May 14, 2004).

[36] Hawkins & Powers Aviation, Inc. v. United States, 46 Fed. Cl. 238, 246 (2000).

[37] Freed v. United States, 34 Fed. Cl. 715, 720 (1996).

[38] Tracy v. United States, 55 Fed. Cl. 679, 682 (2003).

do so, the agent may not bind the government or even provide binding contract provisions.[39]

For a potential government contractor, this means both the government agency must have the authority to enter into the particular type of contract and the agent, individually, must have the authority to bind the governmental agency for the contract to be enforceable.[40] While it is certainly important, given the severe consequences of not ensuring both types of authority are present in a transaction, problematic incidences occur infrequently.[41] The broad application of other types of government regulations in contracts usually requires a certain level of carefulness on the part of the agency.[42] It would also not be in the best interest of the government to enter into large numbers of transactions with contractors without authority.

> 2. *The Christian Doctrine Subjects a Contractor to the Applicable Regulations, Even If the Requirements are not Expressly Present in the Contract*

Another major way contracting with the government is different than contracting with a private party is that a set of rules (i.e., the regulations) may be "read in" to the contract, regardless of inclusion in the actual instrument.[43] Further, erroneous clauses will be eliminated and clauses intentionally removed but required will even be reinserted by operation of law.[44]

An early case recognizing the enforceability of clauses "read in" to a contract was *G. L. Christian & Associates v. United States*. In *Christian*, a housing contractor for the military objected to a termination for convenience clause being "read in" to the contract when the clause was exercised by the government.[45] The contractor argued that the termination for convenience clause was unenforceable because it was not expressly in the contract, and the implied presence of the clause was based on the regulations rather than directly from the

---

[39] *Freed*, 34 Fed. Cl. at 720.
[40] MCEWEN ET AL., *supra* note 17.
[41] *Id.*
[42] *Id.*
[43] *Id.*
[44] *Id.*
[45] *See* G. L. Christian & Assocs. v. United States, 106 Ct. Cl. 58 (1963).

statute.[46] The court held that "[r]egulations reasonably adapted to the administration of a Congressional act, and not inconsistent with any statute, have 'the force and effect of law.'"[47] In explaining the policy behind the doctrine, the court explained that rendering a regulation powerless to incorporate a clause consistent with the policy of a Congressional act into new contracts "hobble[s] the very policies which the appointed rule-makers consider significant enough to call for a mandatory regulation."[48] Today, it is widely accepted that various clauses are "read in" to government contracts under the regulations.

The doctrine is fairly strong. For example, if a clause has been deleted and the relevant agency has agreed to such omission (and even if such omission has been deemed acceptable by an audit), the court can still "read in" that same clause.[49] The rationale is that government contractors are assumed to have "constructive knowledge" of the government contracting regulations.[50] Notably, as discussed in the case study below, it can be to the contractor's advantage to have a clause "read in" to the contract. For these reasons, it is important to understand the application regulations and what contract clauses are absolutely required before performing (or failing to perform) with the assumption that a particular clause has been added or omitted.[51]

For example, in *Enron Federal Solution, Inc. v. United States*, 80 Fed. Cl. 382 (2008), the court denied a default-terminated contractor's claim for expenses incurred prior to termination. Under the contract, the contractor agreed to pay significant upfront costs for a utility improvement project and to provide ongoing operation services.[52] The contractor was entitled to payments that would refund the upfront project costs over ten years.[53] However, the government terminated the contract before its third anniversary based on the contractor's material breach.[54] As of the termination date, the

---

[46] *Id.* at 67–68.

[47] *Id.* at 65.

[48] *Id.* at 66–67.

[49] *See* General Eng'g & Mach. Works v. O'Keefe, 991 F.2d 775, 780 (Fed. Cir. 1993).

[50] *Id.*

[51] The federal government has conveniently provided information at acquisition.gov on both the general regulations for government contracts and the agency-specific requirements at Supplemental Regulations, https://www.acquisition.gov/?q=Supplemental_Regulations (last visited Oct. 28, 2015).

[52] Enron Fed. Sols., Inc. v. U.S., 80 Fed. Cl. 382, 385 (2008).

[53] *Id.* at 386.

[54] *Id.* at 389.

contractor had spent approximately $7 million more than it had been paid by the government.[55]

The contractor sued the government and argued that the government was required to pay for the improvement costs regardless of why the contract was terminated.[56] The contractor argued that, under the *Christian* doctrine, the operation of the FAR construction provision and the Default Clause (48 CFR 52.249-10) must be incorporated into the contract.[57] Basically, the inclusion of these clauses would entitle the contractor to payment equal to the value of the improvements. The court denied the contractor's claim and held that the *Christian* doctrine does not provide recovery where the government has terminated based on the contractor's default, and "to construe it as such, where the default is the result of a material breach of contract, would be to overturn perhaps centuries of common law contract law applying the doctrine."[58] Thus, the contractor bore the risk of the improvement costs and, because of its default, the contractor could not claim relief by way of the *Christian* doctrine. As a result, the government had the right to use and enjoy those improvements without further payment to the contractor.

While the *Christian* doctrine can seem intimidating and riddled with traps in the government's favor, a contractor should remember that the doctrine can work to its advantage at times. For example, many mandatory FAR regulations are reasonable and entitle a contractor to certain rights even in cases where the contract does not expressly provided for such rights.[59] These implied terms can later be asserted against the government in the event the contractual relationship sours. One point of caution, however, is that the doctrine cannot be relied upon where the contractor is in material breach as illustrated in the *Enron* case.

C. *Production and Ownership Implications Under the Doctrine of Segregability*

Federal contracts are generally ruled by the Federal Acquisition Regulations and the special acquisition regulations of a

---

[55] *Id.*
[56] *Id.* at 392.
[57] *Id.*
[58] *Id.* at 408.
[59] Schoenbrod v. United States, 410 F.2d 400, 403–04.

government agency, and are found in Title 48 of the Code of Federal Regulations.[60] The Doctrine of Segregability most clearly appears in the Defense Federal Acquisition Regulation Supplement (DFARS) and allows for the standards of licensing to differ based on the funding source for each segregable unit.[61]

The leading case on this doctrine is *Bell Helicopter Textron*, where a defense research project had, at a different point in the contract, received government funding and funding from a private contractor.[62] In determining ownership of the work product, the Armed Services Board of Contract Appeals (the "Board") held that the person who shouldered the risk of making a monetary investment to make a speculative idea into a workable item that would likely achieve its intended purpose would be the party that "developed" the idea.[63] The Board went on to define the term "developed" as follows:

> In order to be "developed," an item or component must be in being, that is, at least a prototype must have been fabricated . . . and practicability, workability, and functionality (largely synonymous concepts) must be shown through sufficient analysis and/or test to demonstrate to reasonable persons skilled in the applicable art that there is a high probability the item or component will work as intended. All "development" of the item or component need not be 100 percent complete, and the item or component need not be brought to the point where it could be sold or offered for sale. An invention which has been "actually reduced to practice" under patent law has been "developed," but the converse is not necessarily true in every case.[64]

From this case evolved the general rule that, if a segregable unit is developed with private funding, it is owned by the private developer and the government only obtains limited rights in it.[65] Moreover, it

---

[60] 48 C.F.R. § 1.101 (2015).

[61] MCEWEN ET AL., *supra* note 17, § 2.05.

[62] ASBCA No. 21192, 85-3 ¶18415, 1985 WL 17050 (1985).

[63] *Id.*

[64] *Id.* at 109.

[65] *Id.* at 93.

should be noted that authorities apply the segregability test based on the reality (physical and economical) of the actual development—not the contract terms—to determine which party "developed" a product within the meaning of the statutes and regulations.[66] Therefore, a contractor will not own the work product where the contract recites that the development is privately funded if, in fact, government funds are used. As discussed in the case study below, the application of this test is often less than clear-cut and has interesting licensing implications.

1.   *Segregability in Action*

In *United States v. Honeywell International Inc.*,[67] the plaintiff alleged that Honeywell International Inc. ("Honeywell") fraudulently collected license fees for aircraft navigation software from the government.[68] Honeywell supplied the software as a subcontractor. Throughout negotiations with the prime contractor, Honeywell asserted that its software was a privately developed, "commercial" item (i.e., of the type customarily used by the general public or non-government entities for other than government purposes).[69] The plaintiff, however, argued that Honeywell developed the licensed software in part with government funds and the software was not "commercial."[70] Accordingly, the plaintiff argued the government had acquired rights in the licensed software.[71] Further, the plaintiff alleged that Honeywell committed fraud by collecting more than $250 million in license fees from the government.[72]

While the court did not establish an interpretation of the regulations covering "segregability" and "commercial items," it did not deem Honeywell's interpretation of its software as fraudulent.[73]

---

[66] MCEWEN ET AL., *supra* note 17, § 2.05.

[67] United States *ex rel.* Thompson v. Honeywell Int'l, Inc., No. CV 12-2214-JAK JCG, 2014 WL 7495090, (C.D. Cal. dismissed May 2, 2014). The plaintiff was a private party suing on behalf of the federal government under the False Claims Act.

[68] Stephanie Russell-Kraft, *Honeywell Escapes $250M Software License Fee FCA Suit*, LAW360, Jan. 27, 2014, http://www.law360.com/articles/504432/honeywell-escapes-250m-software-license-fee-fca-suit.

[69] *Id.*; 48 C.F.R. § 2.101 (2015).

[70] Russell-Kraft, *supra* note 68.

[71] *Id.*

[72] *Id.*

[73] Order re Defendant's Motion to Dismiss the Fourth Amended Complaint at 7, U.S. ex rel. Thompson v. Honeywell Int'l, Inc., No. CV 12-2214-JAK JCG, (C.D. Cal. dismissed May 2, 2014), ECF No. 84.

Generally, under the doctrine of segregability, courts look to the "lowest practicable segregable portion of the software" in determining where the funds came from to develop the software and data.[74] Honeywell maintained that the license fees it collected from the government applied only to software units that, when segregated, were developed entirely at private expense and was entitled to keep its licensing fees.[75] While the case was dismissed without resolving the segregability issue directly, the court emphasized that Honeywell's argument was helped by the fact that the government was aware that its software license did not cover the software as a whole, but that only the individual software "functions and capabilities" of that software were "commercial" and presumably segregable from other potentially government-funded software portions.[76]

Honeywell illustrates how government contractors that provide computer software should communicate to the government (and have factual support) that the licensed software was developed at private expense or, in the event it was developed with mixed funding, that the company is charging license fees solely for software that is "commercial" and segregable from government-funded software.

2.   *Segregability and Negotiation Strategy*

A small non-profit entered into a contract to produce a training program for community college instructors to learn how to teach people how to install small wind turbines.[77] The original contract called for the use of subcontractors to put on several training sessions with a developed curriculum and training materials. After signing the contract and moving forward with the project, the subcontractors were uncomfortable with the intellectual property terms of the contract that would have immediately put the materials in the public domain.[78] Given that the subcontractors were professional instructors who made

---

[74] MCEWEN ET AL., *supra* note 17, § 2.05.

[75] Order re Defendant's Motion to Dismiss, *supra* note 73, at 4.

[76] *Id.* at 6.

[77] Interview with Alissa Harrington, former Small and Community Wind Coordinator, Windustry, in Minneapolis, Minn. (July 14, 2015). Information about the case study comes from a discussion with the grants coordinator who was employed to manage the grant. The grant/contract arose from the American Recovery and Reinvestment Act of 2009 and administered through the Minnesota Office of Energy Security. The grant/contract was entered in 2010 and continued through 2011.

[78] *Id.*

their living partially off of materials included in the training materials, they were unwilling to move forward without some kind of accommodation.[79]

Facing the possibility of complete non-performance of the contract, the non-profit reached out to the contracting agency to figure out if there was a way to protect the economic interests of the professional instructors while still providing meaningful development of a small wind-training program.[80] The non-profit was able to convince the contracting agency to execute an amendment to the contract to provide an accommodation.[81] Specifically, the subcontractors would not charge the government for any of the time spent developing the training material and keep the copyright to the material, but would provide the use of the materials by the trainees for a specified period of time.[82] Furthermore, the copyrights for the basic curriculum and training session materials outside of the training materials would go into the public domain.[83]

From this real-world example, a contractor should remember that all is not necessarily lost if it becomes apparent during performance under the contract that the terms are less than ideal. A contractor might reach out to the government and negotiate an amendment to the contract that is amenable to all parties.

III. Unique Factors That Apply to Intellectual Property in
Government Contracts

A. *Intellectual Property as Economic Stimulus Under the Bayh-Dole Act and Similar Legislation*

The federal government recognizes intellectual property as a driver of economic stimulus and commercial innovation as a matter of policy.[84] The Bayh-Dole Act was enacted in 1980 to promote the development of government-funded projects into commercial

---

[79] *Id.*
[80] *Id.*
[81] *Id.*
[82] *Id.*
[83] *Id.*
[84] McEwen et al., *supra* note 17. *See generally* Rebecca S. Eisenberg, Public Research and Private Development: Patents and Technology Transfer in Government-Sponsored Research, 82 Va. L. Rev. 1663, 1664 (1996) (providing a more in-depth and historical prospective relating to the economic advantages of funding IP development).

products.[85] Prior to the act, the government held the position that inventions resulting from federally funded research could only be non-exclusively licensed (including the well-known incident of the Gatorade patents).[86] The act was a reaction to the perception in the 1970s that the U.S. economy had lost its edge; it reversed the previous thirty-five years of public policy by allowing non-profit institutions and small businesses the ability to commercialize inventions resulting from federally funded research.[87]

The Department of Defense has recognized a similar reason for protecting intellectual property.[88] "Intellectual property rights (in the form of patents, trademarks, copyrights and trade secrets) are fundamental to capitalist markets, as they protect firms' creative assets from competitive theft. Intellectual property is the lifeblood of world-class commercial companies engaged in leading-edge technologies."[89]

Despite the philosophical approach underlying the Bayh-Dole Act, which is more pronounced in some agencies than others, the government retains a license to practice an invention, as well as protection for contractor's practicing the invention on the government's behalf under 35 U.S.C. § 202(c)(4).[90]

The Supreme Court discussed patent rights for non-profit organizations receiving government funding at length in *Board of Trustees of the Leland Stanford Junior University v. Roche Molecular Systems, Inc.*[91] At issue in this case were a series of three patents covering inventions by a researcher working at both Stanford

---

[85] 35 U.S.C. § 301 (1980).

[86] Ashley J. Stevens, *The Enactment of Bayh Dole*, 29 J. OF TECH. TRANSFER 93, 94 (2004).

[87] *Id.*

[88] MEMORANDUM FROM DAVE OLIVER, UNDER SEC'Y OF DEF. TO SERV. ACQUISITION EXECS., GEN. COUNSEL OF THE DEP'T OF DEF., DEPUTY UNDER SEC'Y OF DEF., DIR. OF DEF. PROCUREMENT (Jan. 4, 2001),

http://www.acq.osd.mil/dpap/Docs/intellprop010501.pdf.

[89] *Id.*

[90] *See* Madey v. Duke Univ., 413 F. Supp. 2d 601, 611 (M.D.N.C. 2006) (quoting 35 U.S.C. § 202(c)(4) (2006)) ("With respect to any invention in which the contractor elects rights, the Federal agency shall have a nonexclusive, nontransferable, irrevocable, paid-up license to practice or have practiced for or on behalf of the United States any subject invention throughout the world...."). The statute also allows for transfer of foreign patent rights to the invention under specific conditions enumerated in 35 U.S.C. § 202(c)(4) (2015).

[91] Bd. of Trs. of Leland Stanford Junior Univ. v. Roche Molecular Sys., Inc., 563 U.S. 776, 131 S. Ct. 2188, 2189 (2011).

University and a private laboratory.[92] The inventor had originally been hired to work at Stanford University in a federally funded program developing tests to prove the efficacy of drugs combatting the human immunodeficiency virus (HIV) in vivo.[93] The researcher assigned his inventions relating to his work to Stanford through a written agreement.[94] To help the researcher develop laboratory skills, Stanford allowed the researcher to work at a private laboratory for nine months.[95] This researcher assigned his inventions relating to his work, including testing methods, to the private laboratory through a separate written agreement.[96] The researcher returned to Stanford and continued researching blood assay HIV tests.[97] Stanford obtained three patents on the technology.[98] Subsequently, the private laboratory was acquired by another party, Roche, which refined and commercialized tests developed by this researcher.[99]

Stanford sued Roche for patent infringement, alleging that it had superior rights to the inventions developed by the researcher by virtue of having received funding for the research through the Bayh-Dole Act, and that the researcher's assignment in favor of Roche was irrelevant.[100] Roche asserted that it was co-owner of the patents based on its invention assignment from the researcher. Despite initial success in the lower court,[101] the Federal Circuit,[102] and eventually the Supreme Court,[103] held that ownership of a patentable invention does not automatically vest in an institution receiving federal funding under the Bayh-Dole Act. Rather, such institution has to obtain proper assignments and is subject to ownership rules like any other party.

Despite the sweeping policy underlying the Bayh-Dole Act, a contractor receiving government funding is not entitled to reorder the

---

[92] *Id.* at 2192–93.
[93] *Id.*
[94] *Id.* at 2192.
[95] *Id.*
[96] *Id.*
[97] *Id.*
[98] *Id.*
[99] *Id.*
[100] *Id.* at 2193.
[101] *See* Bd. of Trs. of Leland Stanford Junior Univ. v. Roche Molecular Sys., Inc., 487 F. Supp. 2d 1099 (N.D. Cal. 2007).
[102] *See* Bd. of Trs. of Leland Stanford Junior Univ. v. Roche Molecular Sys., 583 F.3d 832, 842 (Fed. Cir. 2009).
[103] Bd. of Trs. of Leland Stanford Junior Univ. v. Roche Molecular Sys., Inc., 563 U.S. 776, 131 S. Ct. 2188, 2182 (2011).

typical priority of rights found in patent law. In other words, the Bayh-Dole Act determines rights between the government and the contractor, but does not directly affect the rights between the contractor and inventors or other third parties. Therefore, contractors should still heed to best practices, obtain proper invention assignments, and understand inventorship rules to avoid costly ownership disputes.

B. *Implications Based on the Type of IP Arising Under the Contract*

FAR and DFARS are the major contractual regulations used today. The information in this discussion is not meant to be a comprehensive primer on what is contained in FAR and DFARS, but rather a discussion of the general concepts and some examples of specific regulations. As repeated throughout this article, always remember to check the regulations carefully and thoroughly. Other supplemental provisions are not discussed in depth, but should be explored before moving forward with any contract. The policies and guidance surrounding patents, data, and copyrights are found under Part 27 of FARS, while the actual clauses are included in Part 52, Solicitation Provisions and Contract Clauses.[104]

1. *Patents*

The patent provisions of FAR closely line up with the Department of Commerce promulgated regulations under Bayh-Dole.[105] Both contain standard clause(s) to be used, the ability of the contractor to choose to only give the government license rights while maintaining title, and the process for the government to "march in" and take title to an invention based on an administrative process.[106]

Under FAR, the contractor who chooses to give title to the government or retain it has the obligation[107] to disclose inventions to

---

[104] *See* 48 C.F.R. §§ 27, 52 (2015).

[105] Diane M. Sidebottom, *Intellectual Property in Federal Government Contracts: The Past, The Present, And One Possible Future*, 33 PUB. CONTRACTS & INTELL. PROP. L.J. 63, 72 (2003).

[106] *Id.*

[107] Under FAR, the contractor who chooses to retain ownership has three basic sets of obligations, laid out in 48 C.F.R. § 52.227-11(c)(1–3). First, the contractor must notify the government within two months after notification from the inventor who was working under the contract. *Id.* The notification must contain enough information to convey a "clear understanding" of the invention and whether or not any manuscripts about the

the government agent in a timely manner, along with any offers for sale, public use, or publication.[108] Other reporting requirements include intent-to-patent inventions, utilization, status of development, and various other general information requests about the use of the invention.[109]

a. *March-In Rights*

If the contractor decides to maintain the title to inventions, under FAR, the government has a right to take title under certain circumstances, such as when the contractor has not and is not expected to take steps to "achieve a practical application" of the invention, as enumerated by the federal regulations promulgated by the Department of Commerce under Bayh-Dole.[110] An agency can force the license or title of an invention under government contract without the consent of the contractor, as long as the agency follows an administrative process that shows why the march-in rights should be exercised and giving the contractor reasonable time to respond.[111]

b. *License Rights*

If the contractor decides to retain title, the contractor must give to the government a "nonexclusive, nontransferable, irrevocable, paid-up license to practice, or have practiced for or on its behalf, the subject invention throughout the world."[112] And if the government retains title, the contractor is "granted a revocable, nonexclusive, paid-up license in each patent application filed in any country on a subject invention and any resulting patent in which the Government obtains

---

invention have been submitted or accepted for publication. *Id.* Second, the contractor has two years from notifying the agency of the invention to notify the agency of whether or not the contractor elects to retain ownership of the invention. *Id.* However, if the one-year statutory patent protection period has been triggered by the sale, publication, or public use of the invention, the agency can shorten the time to any time that is "no more than 60 days prior to the end of the statutory period." *Id.* Third, the contractor must file a provisional or non-provisional application within one year after the election or within the statutory period. *Id.* Finally, 48 C.F.R. § 52-227-11(c)(4) allows for the contractor to file extensions with the agency for any of these requirements.

[108] 48 C.F.R. §§ 52.227-11, 52.227-13 (2015).

[109] 48 C.F.R. §§ 52.227-11, 52.227-13.

[110] 35 U.S.C. § 203 (2012).

[111] 48 C.F.R. § 27.302(f) (2015).

[112] 48 C.F.R. § 52.227-11(d)(2) (2015).

title."[113] Penalties are provided in both cases for not notifying the government of inventions in a timely manner.[114]

License rights can also offer protection for government contractors under 28 U.S.C. § 1498. The government license defense under 28 U.S.C. § 1498 states that the only remedy available to a private party if the government utilizes a privately owned patent is compensation. No injunctive relief is available.[115] This statute applies if the patent infringement is "by or for the United States," covering most government contracts.[116] Therefore, if the contractor is acting with the authorization of the government, then the contractor is able to assert the affirmative government license defense against infringement claims.[117]

One prime example is that of Dr. John M.J. Madey ("Madey"), a scientist at Duke University ("Duke").[118] Madey helped the school get a federal grant, in additional to several grants Duke already had secured.[119] A dispute later arose between Madey and Duke, and Madey resigned from his position at the school.[120] Duke continued to use Madey's lab equipment, which practiced two patents owned solely by Madey.[121] Thereafter, Madey sued Duke for patent infringement.[122] Duke raised the Government License defense, which is based on the Bayh-Dole Act, and argued that it used the patents for the government to conduct research under its grants.[123] In response, Madey contended that Duke's defense was unpersuasive because Duke contributed some of its own funding to the lab equipment.[124]

The court found that Duke had express authorization in some (but fewer than all) of its funding agreements with the government to use the patents for specific programs such that the use was "for the government."[125] Therefore, Duke was entitled to assert the Government

---

[113] 48 C.F.R. § 52.227-13(d)(1) (2015).
[114] 48 C.F.R. §§ 52.227-11, 52.227-13.
[115] 28 U.S.C. § 1498(a) (2012).
[116] Id.
[117] MCEWEN ET AL., supra note 17, § 4.03.
[118] Madey v. Duke Univ., 336 F. Supp. 2d 583, 585 (M.D.N.C. 2004).
[119] Id. at 586.
[120] Id.
[121] Id.
[122] Id. at 587.
[123] Id. at 589.
[124] Id. at 594.
[125] Id. at 595; Madey v. Duke Univ., 307 F.3d 1351, 1359 (Fed. Cir. 2002) (explaining reasoning used in the prior circuit court before remanding to the Middle District of North Carolina).

License defense to some of the alleged infringement claims.[126] However, the court went on to explain that Duke's use of the patented practices pursuant to other funding agreements with the government was not similarly authorized.[127] In sum, the court made it clear that the existence of government funding for a particular research program is alone insufficient to establish authorization and consent under other programs.[128]

To avoid such third-party claims of infringement, contractors should ensure they have express authorization (or implied authorization or consent) from the government to practice a patent, which arises when: (1) the government expressly contracted for work to meet certain specifications, (2) the specification cannot be met without infringing on a patent, and (3) the government had some knowledge of the infringement.[129] Without express authorization, the contractor may be putting itself at risk of a third-party infringement claim.

2. Data

Data drives our lives. It runs our cars, computers, washing machines, web searches, and decides what coupons we will get at Target. The rise of "big data" has not missed government contracting or government contracting regulations. The good news is the government usually only receives a license to the data acquired, not the ownership or other rights.[130]

In 1984, the Department of Defense was mandated to create specific regulations to handle technical data and computer software.[131] DFARS still uses this two-tiered system today.[132] FAR's definitions changed in 2007 in order to mirror DFARS' technical data versus computer software definitions.[133]

Although there are some important differences in the treatment of these two, for the most part the statutorily-based scheme governing technical data is

---

[126] *Madey,* 336 F. Supp. 2d at 595.
[127] *Id.* at 596.
[128] *Id.*
[129] *See* Hughes Aircraft Co. v. United States, 29 Fed. Cl. 197, 223 (1993).
[130] MCEWEN ET AL., *supra* note 17, § 2.05.
[131] H.R. REP. NO. 98-1080, at 4306 (1984).
[132] 48 C.F.R. §§ 227.71, 227.72 (2015).
[133] MCEWEN ET AL., *supra* note 17, § 2.05.

extended by policy to computer software. Thus, it is quite common to refer to these issues using the generic terms data or data rights—which are intended to refer collectively to technical data and computer software and their associated license rights.[134]

The license rights are then determined under one of three methods: (1) standard, Government-unique license categories; (2) contractor's standard license agreement for a commercial technology; or (3) mutually acceptable terms and conditions.[135] When looking at the standard license categories, which is what will be covered in this article, non-commercial technologies are generally licensed in proportion to the amount of government funding used to develop the technology, whereas commercial technologies are presumed to be developed at private expense and so give rise to very limited licenses.[136]

The Court of Federal Claims first discussed issues raised by the Rights in Data–General clause of the FAR in *Ervin and Associates, Inc. v. United States.*[137] The data rights at issue in *Ervin* concerned the rights of U.S. Department of Housing and Urban Development (HUD) vis-à-vis the contractor regarding data stored in a private database compiled in the course of completing a government contract.[138] In 1994, the plaintiff contracted with HUD to analyze approximately 4,800 Annual Financial Statements (AFS) submitted by HUD loan-holders.[139] These statements, at roughly thirty pages apiece, followed no standardized format.[140] A person had to read the AFS documents, identify missing information, and contact the borrowers to gather additional information.[141] Accordingly, the plaintiff read the AFS documents and collected information into a database.

---

[134] *Id.*

[135] *Id.*

[136] *Id.*

[137] Ervin & Assocs., Inc. v. United States, 59 Fed. Cl. 267, 270 (2004) (The court began the judgment by recognizing that "[t]his government contracting case raises an important issue concerning the scope of the Federal Acquisition Regulation ('FAR') 'Rights In Data–General' Clause that neither the United States Court of Federal Claims nor the United States Court of Appeals for the Federal Circuit has had an occasion to consider.").

[138] *Id.* at 289–90.

[139] *Id.* at 270.

[140] *Id.*

[141] *Id.*

In 1995, HUD decided to construct a database of its own and requested from the plaintiff much of the data that it had collected under the contract.[142] The plaintiff begrudgingly supplied the data, while maintaining that it was the rightful owner and trying to limit the government's distribution of the data to third parties.[143] The plaintiff also requested additional compensation from the government for turning over this data.[144] The government refused, and the plaintiff filed suit.[145]

As a threshold matter, despite that the "Rights of Data–General" clause was not explicitly referenced in the contract, the court found that this clause had been included by general reference to several of the FAR clauses which included 48 CFR § 52.227-14.[146] The court summarized the meaning of this clause when it wrote: "As a matter of law, the Government obtains 'unlimited rights' in all data 'first produced' under a government contract, but the contractor may assert that certain data is instead 'limited rights' data."[147] In this case, the court found that the data was first produced in the performance of the contract.[148] The court also explained that to assert that certain data is limited rights data, it must be properly labelled with a "Limited Rights Notice" and exists "only if third parties are not allowed any further use and disclosure."[149] The court continued by stating that if the contractor does not properly label data they believe is entitled to a limited rights designation, they must withhold the data and provide "form, fit, and function" data instead.[150] The court concluded that any exclusive

---

[142] *Id.* at 278.

[143] *Id.* at 280.

[144] *Id.* at 283.

[145] *Id.*

[146] *Id* at 294–95.

[147] *Id.* at 295 (discussing the Rights in Data–General provisions of 48 C.F.R. § 52.227-14(b)(1)(iv), (g) (1987)).

[148] *Id.* (citing 48 C.F.R. 52.227-14(b)(1) (1987)).

[149] *Id.* at 295.

[150] *Id.* at 295–96. The definition of "form, fit, and function" data can be found at FAR 52.227–14(a): "Form, fit, and function data means data relating to items, components, or processes that are sufficient to enable physical and functional interchangeability, and data identifying source, size, configuration, mating and attachment characteristics, functional characteristics, and performance requirements. For computer software it means data identifying source, functional characteristics, and performance requirements but specifically excludes the source code, algorithms, processes, formulas, and flow charts of the software." 48 C.F.R. § 52.227-14(a) (1987) (emphasis added).

ownership rights to the data the plaintiff had in this case, the plaintiff lost when it handed the data over to HUD without proper labeling.[151]

The government obtains strong rights in data first produced under a contract by default. A contractor that desires to maintain control over such data need to take appropriate protective measures. For example, in some circumstances, the data should be withheld in favor of form, fit, and function data. If the data needs to be delivered, the contractor should take great care in properly marking it in accordance with the regulations. Markings such as "Proprietary" without listing whether the data is Limited Rights, Restricted Rights, Government Purpose Rights, etc., are deemed mis-markings and can be ignored (or even removed) by the government if the nonconforming mark is not corrected after the contractor is put on notice of the error.[152]

Furthermore, type of license may play a part in the scope of rights granted. The license types may be better explained by a chart that follows this section. The most restrictive license categories for technical data and computer software are limited rights[153] and restricted rights,[154] respectively. Generally, these are the standard types of licenses for privately funded ventures and "authorize use and disclosure of the data primarily only within the Government, and do not allow release or disclosure outside the Government except in very limited cases that are closely tied to supporting the Government's internal use, or with the express written permission of the contractor."[155]

Under DFARS, these license rights serve as the minimum rights the government can accept when negotiating a special license.[156] FAR, on the other hand, uses these license rights as a standard, but not a floor.[157] Parties are able to negotiate specialized rights, if it meets government need.[158]

The next most restrictive category is found only in DFARS. Government Purpose Rights are specifically used when there is mixed

---

[151] *See Ervin & Assocs.*, 59 Fed. Cl. at 297 ("Even if the Government did not already have unlimited rights and even if Ervin's data and EMFIS were developed at private expense, the Government nonetheless acquired 'unlimited rights' in all technical data and computer software delivered under the terms of the AFS Contract.").

[152] 48 C.F.R. ¶ 52.227-14(e)(1) (2015).

[153] 48 C.F.R. § 252.227-7013(b)(3) (2015).

[154] 48 C.F.R. § 52.227-14(a) (2015).

[155] MCEWEN ET AL., *supra* note 17, § 2.05.

[156] 48 C.F.R. §§ 252.227-7013(b)(4), 252.227-7014(b)(4) (2015).

[157] 48 C.F.R. § 27.404-2(d)(4) (2015).

[158] *Id.*

private and public funding.[159] The license restricts the government use for five years to unlimited use and distribution within the government, but cannot release or distribute.[160] After five years, unless otherwise specified, the license converts to an unlimited license.[161]

Finally, an unlimited rights license applies when a product is developed completely with government funds[162] or where funding status does not matter, such as for computer program manuals.[163] As the name suggests, unlimited rights allow the "[g]overnment to use, disclose, reproduce, prepare derivative works, distribute copies to the public, and perform publicly and display publicly, in any manner and for any purpose, and to have or permit others to do so."[164]

3. Copyrights

a. Works of Government Employees Do Not Give Rise to Copyright

Furthermore, the works of government employees do not give rise to copyright,[165] except in special cases, like the Post Office.[166] Works created specifically with government funding for the public good, as mentioned above in the Segregability Doctrine section, become part of the public domain. The government can, however, obtain and hold copyrights transferred to it by a private actor.[167] For this reason, the licensing scheme in FAR addresses how the government can use, reproduce, modify, prepare derivative works, perform or display publicly, disclose, release, or distribute the licensed work.[168] Keeping somewhat in line with the move to mostly data-based

---

[159] 48 C.F.R. §§ 252.227-7013(b)(2), 7014(b)(2) (2015).

[160] *Id.*

[161] *Id.*

[162] 48 C.F.R. § 252.227-7013(b)(1), 252.227-7014(b)(1) (2015).

[163] 48 C.F.R. §§ 52.227-14(b)(1), 252.227-7013(b)(1), 252.227-7014(b)(1) (2015).

[164] 48 C.F.R. § 52.227-14(a)(2) (2015).

[165] 17 U.S.C. § 105 (2012).

[166] H.R. REP. NO. 94-1476, at 60 (1976), *reprinted in* 1976 U.S.C.C.A.N. 5659, 5674 ("The intent of section 105 is to restrict the prohibition against Government copyright to works written by employees of the United States Government within the scope of their official duties. In accordance with the objectives of the Postal Reorganization Act of 1970, this section does not apply to works created by employees of the United States Postal Service.").

[167] 17 U.S.C. § 105.

[168] 48 C.F.R. § 52.227 (2015).

copyrightable work, the licensing provisions for general copyrightable material is found under "unlimited rights" in the data section of FAR.[169]

b. *Government Does Not Hold March-In Rights to a Contractor's Copyrights, But the Government's Consent to Assert a Copyright May Be Required*

Unlike FAR's patent provisions, there are not provisions that grant the government the right to march-in and take copyrights owned by a government contractor.[170] Instead, FAR requires that a contractor obtains permission from the government before asserting rights in a copyrighted work containing data.[171] 48 C.F.R. § 27.404-3 states that the copyright protection should be granted unless it falls into one of the following categories:

(i) Data consist of a report that represents the official views of the agency or that the agency is required by statute to prepare;
(ii) Data are intended primarily for internal use by the Government;
(iii) Data are of the type that the agency itself distributes to the public under an agency program;
(iv) Government determines that limitation on distribution of the data is in the national interest; or
(v) Government determines that the data should be disseminated without restriction.[172]

The alternative clause IV allows the assertion of copyright without permission, and under FAR this alternative is to be used by colleges and universities for general and applied research or any other contracts that the agency determines "is not necessary" for the contractor to request further permission.[173]

---

[169] *Id.* at 14(a)(2).
[170] If a certain clause is inserted into a contract the contractor must assign the copyright to the Government. 48 C.F.R. § 252.227-7020(c) (2015).
[171] 48 C.F.R. § 27.404-3(a)(1) (2015).
[172] *Id.* at 3(2).
[173] *Id.* at 3(3).

Asserting copyright infringement based on material generated under a government contract can be complex and involve issues beyond those found in typical copyright litigation. For example, in *Innovative Concepts, Inc. v. Symetrics Industries, Inc.*, the court found that "an amendment to the Plaintiff's contract . . . executed after the performance period of the contract was completed [changed] the Government's license from an unlimited rights license to a government purpose license."[174] Based on the conversion, the court declined to charge the defendant for copyright infringement in certain instances because the plaintiff failed to put third parties on notice of the conversion. Further, the court noted, "copyright notice is appropriate, indeed necessary, in addition to the [DFARS] compliant restrictive legends that a contractor may put on its software."[175]

As discussed in the Data section above, marking material produced under a government contract is critically important. This case study highlights the fact that, if the terms of the government contract change, the contracting party needs to update the markings to put third parties on notice of the change or risk forfeiting a copyright infringement claim. Moreover, government markings are not meant to replace other symbols of intellectual property protection. For works copyrighted by a government contractor, the contractor should include (1) ©, the word "Copyright", or the abbreviation "Copr.;" (2) the year of first publication; and (3) the name of the copyright owner, to mitigate the evidentiary weight of a defendant's innocent infringement defense.[176] This puts third parties on notice of the contractor's rights. Further, this case is a reminder that government contracts are not written in stone. Rather, the contracts can be amended post-signing to accommodate different needs.

4. *Trade Secrets*

Trade secrets naturally run into conflict with intellectual property protections requiring registration of information or publication. Patent applicants unwittingly lose the trade secret portion of an invention through disclosures in the patent application.[177] A

---

[174] Innovative Concepts, Inc. v. Symetrics Indus., Inc., Civ. A. No. 02-1040-A, 2003 WL 26082736 (E.D. Va. Apr. 11, 2003).

[175] *Id.* at *2.

[176] 17 U.S.C. § 401 (2012).

[177] 1-2 MCEWEN ET AL., *supra* note 17, § 2.05.

technology license used to combat this issue is a hybrid of a trade secret license for proprietary information and a copyright license.[178] The government regulations under DFARS and FAR follow the same pattern.[179]

Trade secrets can be protected under both sets of regulations by asserting restrictions on licensing. Identification timing is important—identification is required in commercial data or software before contracting,[180] unless it is connected to the ongoing contract performance.[181] For non-commercial data, both FAR[182] and DFARS allow post-contract identification, with DFARS limiting it to cases arising from new information or where the omission would not have "materially affected the source selection decision."[183]

Importantly, regardless of when the restriction is implemented, the restricted data must be marked or the restriction is lost, leaving the government with unlimited rights.[184] Instructions for making are the same under FAR and DFARS, but must be followed before submission of the deliverable or corrected at the expense of the contractor.[185] Even if the product in question was developed with private funding, failure to properly mark the product gives the government unlimited rights.[186]

In *Canadian Commercial Corporation v. Department of Air Force*, the court reversed the decision of the Department of the Air Force (the Government) that Canadian Commercial Corporation (CCC) would be unharmed by the disclosure of its trade secrets and pricing information under the Freedom of Information Act (FOIA) by finding the Government's decision "arbitrary and capricious."[187]

In 2002, the government issued a request for proposal (RFP) for certain aircraft services under a three-year base contract, which included four one-year options.[188] Per federal law, the RFP required

---

[178] *Id.*
[179] *Id.*
[180] See 48 C.F.R. § 12.211, 12.212 (2015) (the actual pre-identification clauses can be found at 48 C.F.R. § 52.227-15 (2015)).
[181] 48 C.F.R. § 27.404-2 (2015).
[182] *Id.*
[183] 48 C.F.R. § 252.227-7013(e)(3).
[184] Xerxe Grp, Inc. v. United States, 278 F.3d 1357, 1360 (Fed. Cir. 2002).
[185] 48 C.F.R. §§ 52.227-14, 52.227-15, FAR 252.227-7013, 252.227-7014.
[186] Ervin & Assocs. v. United States, 59 Fed. Cl. 267, 297 (2004).
[187] Canadian Commercial Corp. v. Dep't of Air Force, 442 F. Supp. 2d 15, 41 (D.D.C. 2006), *aff'd*, 514 F.3d 37 (D.C. Cir. 2008).
[188] *Canadian Commercial Corp.*, 442 F. Supp. 2d at 17.

each bidder to include pricing information in its bid.[189] CCC bid on, and was awarded, the contract.[190] The contract incorporated by reference CCC's pricing information.[191] An unsuccessful bidder, Sabreliner Corporation (Sabreliner), later requested for a copy of the contract between CCC and the government under the Freedom of Information Act (FOIA).[192] The government contacted CCC and requested that it identify trade secret or other sensitive information that it did not want to be released, and asked CCC to explain why the identified language was subject to an exemption from disclosure under the FOIA.[193] CCC responded by seeking exemption for select trade secrets, including its line-item pricing information.[194] The government rejected CCC's response.[195] Thereafter, CCC filed a reverse-FOIA lawsuit in an attempt to enjoin disclosure of its pricing information by the government.[196]

The court found in favor of CCC and enjoined the government from disclosing CCC's trade secrets under the FOIA to Sabreliner.[197] The government contended that CCC would be unharmed by the disclosure because the government was not going to change contractors following the base contract due to the transition costs of changing contractors.[198] The court, however, was unpersuaded by the government and found that a release of CCC's pricing information would cause substantial competitive harm since competitive bidders could use such information to make lower bids for the option-year contracts.[199] The government appealed the decision.[200] On appeal, the Court of Appeals for the District of Columbia Circuit affirmed the lower court's decision.[201]

---

[189] *Id.*

[190] *Id.*

[191] *Id.*

[192] *Id.*

[193] *Id.* at 18.

[194] Canadian Commercial Corp. v. Dep't of Air Force, 442 F. Supp. 2d 15, 18 (D.D.C. 2006), *aff'd*, 514 F.3d 37 (D.C. Cir. 2008).

[195] *Id.* at 21.

[196] *Id.* at 22.

[197] *Id.* at 41.

[198] *Id.* at 38.

[199] *Id.*

[200] Canadian Commercial Corp. v. Dep't of Air Force, 442 F. Supp. 2d 15, 39 (D.D.C. 2006), *aff'd*, 514 F.3d 37 (D.C. Cir. 2008).

[201] *Id.* at 43.

As this case illustrates, it is important to think broadly about what would potentially require trade secret protection. It is not only about the product, but also the pricing, vendors, suppliers, etc. Marking trade secrets is critical. Equally important is not disclosing (or disclosing as little as possible) information from which you derive a competitive advantage. Consider that the information you provide to the government may be subject to disclosure under the FOIA and made available to competitors. This is one of many reasons why you should think twice before bidding on a government contract.

IV. INTROSPECTIVE ANALYSIS OF YOUR ORGANIZATION AND ITS GOALS

For the reasons set forth above, contracting with the federal government comes with a unique set of risks that might not be compatible with every organization for a variety of reasons such as: its stage of life, strategy, or long-term goals. To avoid wasted energy and headaches, a company should have a firm grasp on its organizational identity before submitting a bid. This section offers guidance on how a company can gauge whether it should submit a government contract, and, if so, how to set itself up for success during the procurement process.

A. *What Kind of Organization Are You?*

A company that is contemplating contracting with the federal government needs to know its organization inside and out. A company that does not understand its competitive advantage and core competencies is likely to waste time and money trying to sift through the more than 30,000 opportunities posted on www.fbo.gov. In contrast, a company that knows itself will be able to narrow its searching criteria and target opportunities that match its profile.

Relatedly, a company needs to know and understand itself because the company will be facing stiff competition during the bid process. The company needs to be able to articulate exactly why it should be awarded the contract over its competition. Given these factors, a young company with a weak self-identity might consider putting off a government contract bid until it can better explain its purpose.

A company should also be aware of its size and reputation. Notably, a large company does not necessarily have the advantage typically associated with corporate giants when pursuing a government contract. In fact, the federal government has formal set-asides for companies owned by women, veterans, and other disadvantaged groups.[202] In addition, the government has a goal of engaging small businesses for roughly 25% of its contracts.[203] It is clear that size is not everything, and large and small companies alike need to consider how to address this fact.

Nonetheless, large companies are more likely to have relevant institutional knowledge and established connections on which they can rely. As a means to compete, a small, low-profile company might develop a strategy before randomly submitting bids. For example, a small company could identify two or three agencies that have a need for the organization's goods or services, and make a concerted effort to go to the events and seminars of those agencies. While government forms and databases can seem impersonal, there are opportunities to network with the decision makers and meet large contractors, which will shed light on what the agency is looking for, help establish a name for the company in the space, and increase their likelihood of being awarded a contract.

B. *What Else Do You Have Going On?*

A company considering contracting with the government should first determine whether it will have sufficient human and capital resources in the event it is awarded the contract. In doing so, a company should consider other opportunities that may be on its horizon, as government contracts can conflict the company out of doing business with select third parties. Therefore, a company should conduct a broad survey of its market position and strategy prior to contracting with the government to ensure that it does not thwart other lucrative, private sector opportunities.

On a broader level, if government contracting is not part of a company's long-term success strategy, it might reconsider the value of

---

[202]   *MBDA   Web   Portal,*   MINORITY   BUS.   DEV.   AGENCY, http://www.mbda.gov/main/business-certification (last visited Nov. 30, 2015).
[203]   *The   Small   Business   Agenda,*   SMALL   BUS.   ADMIN., https://www.sba.gov/sites/default/files/aboutsbaarticle/Small%20Business%20Agenda%2 0NEC.pdf (last visited Nov. 30, 2015).

dabbling in the space at all. By way of illustration, a major stumbling for newbies is failing to learn the lingo; it takes a considerable investment to learn more than 57,000 acronyms in government parlance today.[204] A one-time contract is probably not worth the time and money needed to understand the language well enough to secure the contract. Further, understanding the lingo is not just about winning the bid; a failure to understand the language in the contract can lead to non-response and non-performance determinations that can make an unwary company wish that it had not won the bid in the first place. Therefore, a company should take a step back and analyze whether it anticipates making government contracting a part of its ongoing business strategy.

C. *What Risks Are You Willing to Take?*

The risk of losing or diluting intellectual property rights based on a government contract often depends on the type of intellectual property the contract involves: patent or patentable subject matter, data, copyrighted material, or trade secrets. As discussed above, the scope of rights retained by the contractor are governed by a complex mix of legal and regulatory frameworks, and will depend on the subject matter, funding source, and negotiations between the parties. While a company should not rule out government contracting based on a fear of losing its intellectual property rights, a company seeking to do business with the government certainly needs to have a solid understanding of its intellectual property and what is going to be developed or delivered under the contract.

D. *Don't Go it Alone.*

As previously noted, government contracting means big business (i.e., nearly half a trillion dollars!). Unfortunately, the procurement process can also be complicated. Many companies, therefore, seek advice from independent consultants. A cottage industry has developed around providing government contractors with support every step of the way, including registering as a contractor (which is

---

[204] Andy Medici, *Decoding Fed Acronyms for Government Outsiders*, FED. TIMES (Dec. 4,   2012,   01:59   PM) http://archive.federaltimes.com/article/20121204/ACQUISITION03/312040005/Say-what-Website-decodes-fed-acronyms-government-outsiders.

required) and writing proposals. Many companies hire consultants to assist in complying with the government's aggressive auditing system, which can be vital to winning bids.

There are alternatives for companies that do not want to engage a consultant. For example, there are Procurement and Technical Assistance Centers located throughout the country. These centers help businesses market their goods and services for different procurement opportunities. In addition, each agency typically publishes its acquisition forecast on their individual websites, and the federal government has assembled a wealth of resources to help navigate the waters of government contracting. Such resources include:

- GSA's acquisition regulation website at www.acquisition.gov
- Federal Business Opportunities website at www.fbo.gov,
- Federal Procurement Data Base at www.fpds.gov
- GSA schedules website at www.gsaadvantage.gov

In terms of intellectual property, it is essential to engage competent legal counsel.

V. CONCLUSION

Contracting with the government comes with a unique set of risks and rewards. With billions of dollars up for grabs, there are obviously exciting business opportunities. That being said, there are general principles at play that are absent in private contracts, including: sovereign immunity, the actual authority of the contracting agent, the *Christian* doctrine, and the doctrine of segregability. Government contracts also have special rules with respect to intellectual property, including rights and licenses for patents, data, copyrights, and trade secrets. These factors, among many others, are things that a contractor needs to understand before entering a contract with the government. The contractor should conduct an introspective analysis prior to bidding on a contract to determine whether a government contract is in its best interest and how it can best protect its rights though negotiation and performance.

Appendix A

Restriction	Type of License	Regulatory Scheme	Funding	Rights	Standards
MOST Restrictive	Limited Rights	FAR & DFARS	Privately Funded	W/I Government, limited cases supporting internal use, or with permission	DFARS: Minimum required; FAR: Standard but negotiable
MOST Restrictive	Restricted Rights	FAR & DFARS	Privately Funded	W/I Government, limited cases supporting internal use, or with permission	DFARS: Minimum required; FAR: Standard but negotiable
Middle	Government Purpose Rights	DFARS only	Private/Public Mix	5 years limited to only internal government use, then converts to Unlimited	N/A
LEAST Restrictive	Unlimited	FAR & DFARS	Public or categories like computer program manual	As name implies, unlimited rights to use, disclose, reproduce, prepare derivative works, distribute copies to the public, perform publicly, display publicly, and to have or permit others	N/A

PICASSO ON STAFF
EMPLOYEE CLASSIFICATION, COPYRIGHTS,
AND THE CREATIVE PROCESS

SARAH A. HOWES[1]

I.   INTRODUCTION

Pablo Picasso, the Spanish painter who was responsible for 20,000 pieces of art,[2] had a learning style that many of us creatives can

---

[1] Sarah A. Howes, J.D. is a non-union stage actor, and Dramatists Guild of America Associate Member. She is currently a Legal Fellow at the Copyright Alliance in Washington, D.C., and sits on the PAHRTS (Performing Arts Human Resources Toolkit Series) advisory committee with the Minnesota Theater Alliance. Prior to her fellowship, she was the Legal Programs Manager for the Minnesota Lawyers for the Arts program at Springboard for the Arts in St. Paul, Minn. The views expressed are not attributable to the Copyright Alliance, or any of her current or former employers, and was written in the author's personal capacity. The author would like to thank Molly Littman, Editor in Chief, for her intelligent feedback and warm encouragement.
[2] *Pablo   Picasso   (1881–1973)*, METROPOLITAN MUSEUM OF ART, http://www.metmuseum.org/toah/hd/pica/hd_pica.htm ("Even in his eighties and nineties, Picasso produced an enormous number of works and reaped the financial benefits of his success, amassing a personal fortune and a superb collection of his own art, as well as work by other artists.").

relate to. Based on historical accounts, he surely would have been a complicated employee to manage. He regularly abandoned his art school homework for more time to sketch what he wanted.[3] Classical techniques bored him, and he was resentful of teachers who attempted to conform him.[4] It was not until he left art school in Madrid that he actually found a learning environment suitable for his personality.[5] In 1899, he joined a "cluster" of artists in Barcelona at the famous El Quatre Gats café, which "in lieu of an art school environment . . . provided Picasso with an arguably more productive education."[6]

Creative economist John Howkins uses the term "cluster" broadly to describe collaborative environments where he believes "creativity and innovation are sharpened."[7] Today, many products are developed by groups of Picassos, calling on diverse learners and specialties to exchange ideas and provide invaluable criticism.[8] Filmmaker Tiffany Shlain, a "Picasso" herself, believes the creative process involves finding a team of collaborators who are willing to build from one of her many "hunches," and to give her constructive feedback that acknowledges both the good and the bad of her work.[9] This Emmy-nominated filmmaker and Webby Awards founder is perhaps thought of as a solo artist, because she narrates all of her films; but in actuality, she operates in a team environment. Her films are made both through The Moxie Institute and Let it Ripple, her nonprofit film studio her film studio, that employs—not contracts—a creative team of four core team members.[10] She also provides her small creative workforce health and dental benefits.[11]

---

[3] *Pablo Picasso: Painter (1881–1973)*, BIO., http://www.biography.com/people/pablo-picasso-9440021?page=1#early-life-and-education (last visited Oct. 18, 2015).
[4] *Id.*
[5] *Id.*
[6] WILLIAM SCHMEISER, AN INTRODUCTION TO PICASSO loc. 346 (2014) (ebook).
[7] JOHN HOWKINS, THE CREATIVE ECONOMY: HOW PEOPLE MAKE MONEY FROM IDEAS 61 (2d ed. 2013).
[8] *See* Knoll Workplace Research, *Creating Collaborative Spaces that Work: A Performance-based Approach to Successful Planning*, KNOLL, 2–3 (2013), https://www.knoll.com/media/315/283/CollaborativeWorkplace_wp.pdf (noting that companies invest in collaborative workspaces because it encourages innovation, speeds up decision-making, and to cross expertise).
[9] Tiffany Shlain, *The Creative Process in 10 Acts* Farnam Street (Nov. 4, 2015), https://www.farnamstreetblog.com/2015/11/tiffany-shlain-creative-process/.
[10] Email Interview with Tiffany Shlain, Filmmaker, The Moxie Institute, November 29, 2015 ("I have a core team of staff people (employees) and then I always work with other people animators, composers, writers, etc that work for themselves and we are partnering on a project"); The Team, Moxie Institute (last visited December 30, 2015),

I love having people that I have worked creatively
[with] for years. My producer and co-writer Sawyer
Steele and I have made films together for nearly 10
years. Nothing can replace that history and
institutional knowledge. Also, at this point, while
there are many sprints to finish films, this is more of
a long run, so I want everyone to feel they are taken
care of with vacation and health care.[12]

Fewer and fewer employers share Shlain's labor philosophies:
by 2020 a troubling 40% of the U.S. workforce is predicted to be
contractors [13] (or other forms of contingent-status workers). [14]
Employee-status positions often provide workers livable wages,
security, health benefits, [15] and access to many state and federal

---

http://www.moxieinstitute.org/team; Full-Time Event Producer / Director, Let it Ripple,
http://www.letitripple.org/full-
time_event_producer_director?utm_campaign=bat_winter_2015&utm_medium=email&
utm_source=moxieinstitute (last visited December 30, 2015) (advertising a sixth fulltime
position with health benefits).
[11]   Full-time   Event   Producer/Director   (job   posting),   LET   IT   RIPPLE,
http://www.letitripple.org/full-
time_event_producer_director?utm_campaign=bat_winter_2015&utm_medium=email&
utm_source=moxieinstitute.
[12] Email interview with Tiffany Shlain, Filmmaker, The Moxie Institute (Jan. 20, 2016).
[13] There is little data out there to show the full impact on classification in the arts
markets. When organizations invest in studies, it is typically to prove economic growth
with respect to retail sales or the number of jobs without focus on the quality of such
work. We do know that "American artists are highly entrepreneurial, they are 3.5 times
more likely than the total U.S. workforce to be self-employed," which, again, self-
employment is not necessarily a bad thing for those who are well-compensated.
CREATIVE MINNESOTA, THE HEALTH AND IMPACT OF THE NONPROFIT ARTS AND
CULTURE INDUSTRY IN THE STATE OF MINNESOTA 9 (2015), http://creativemn.org/wp-
content/uploads/2015/01/CreativeMN2015Book.pdf.   See   generally   MINNEAPOLIS
CREATIVE   VITALITY   INDEX   (2014),
http://www.ci.minneapolis.mn.us/www/groups/public/@citycoordinator/documents/webc
ontent/wcms1p-135695.pdf.
[14] Intuit 2020 Report: Twenty Trends That Will Shape the Next Decade, INTUIT 21 (Oct.
2010)   http://http-
download.intuit.com/http.intuit/CMO/intuit/futureofsmallbusiness/intuit_2020_report.pdf

[15] ObamaCare Employer Mandate, OBAMACARE FACTS (last visited Dec. 30, 2015),
http://obamacarefacts.com/obamacare-employer-mandate/ ("ObamaCare's 'employer
mandate' is a requirement that all business with 50 or more full-time equivalent
employees provide health insurance to at least 95% of their full-time employees and
dependents up to age 26.").

employment laws that contractors miss out on, such as: unemployment insurance, minimum wage standards, family medical leave protections, workers' compensation, protection from employer sexual harassment, and the ability to collectively bargain under the National Labors Relations Act.[16]

A.   Art as a Business or as a Job

To Picasso, creativity led to great artwork. But creativity is not, nor should it be, reserved for the visual arts. There is true market value in creativity and the creative persons who spin it.[17] There are different theories on what creativity is: is it a method for solving problems,[18] a talent reserved for a select few, or rather a universal channel for how we use our intelligence?[19] Personally, I find comfort in the belief that creativity is how we apply knowledge to new ideas.[20] This non-legal definition honors the creative process by accounting for all manifestations, and is broad enough to suggest that every human possesses creative capacity. But surely not every human is capable of creating great products, and not every industry or community has perfected how to profit from art.

Pablo Picasso is an outlier: he made a large fortune ($50 million net worth at his death)[21] from his artwork. Few artists become millionaires from their craft, as Picasso did. Many artists simply seek livable wages. Springboard for the Arts, a leading economic development organization, teaches artists how to capitalize on their local audiences, and to manage their business affairs so they can make a "living and a life."[22] Laura Zabel, Springboard Executive Director, disagrees with the belief that artists are bad entrepreneurs:

---

[16] Appendix 1: Federal and Minnesota State Employee Classification Chart.

[17] See infra Part II.

[18] See generally Scott G. Isaksen, CPS: Linking Creativity and Problem Solving CREATIVE PROBLEM SOLVING GROUP, http://www.cpsb.com/research/articles/creative-problem-solving/CPS-LinkingCandPS.html.

[19] See infra Part IV.

[20] W. GLENN GRIFFIN & DEBORAH MORRISON, THE CREATIVE PROCESS ILLUSTRATED: HOW BIG IDEAS ARE BORN 8 (2010).

[21] Christi Danner, Artists Who Got Rich Before They Died, COMPLEX, Apr. 17, 2014, http://www.complex.com/style/2014/04/artists-who-got-rich-before-they-died/.

[22] Springboard for the Arts, http://springboardforthearts.org (last visited Dec. 30, 2015).

> I don't think artists are bad at being entrepreneurial. I
> think there are a lot of skills that artists have that lend
> themselves naturally to being entrepreneurial: artists
> already have a DIY ethic about their work, they're
> used to wearing a lot of hats and they understand a lot
> intuitively about engaging clients and audiences,
> about collaboration and iteration. But I also think the
> landscape for artists has changed a lot in the last
> decade. A lot of communities have seen decreased
> funding for arts and culture and the kind of structure
> that used to support artists—patronage structure or
> theater companies where they used to have a resident
> company and now hire everybody freelance, or the
> same thing for visual artists with galleries. So artists,
> more and more, are needing to be their own boss and
> manage all the details and run their careers like a
> business. A lot of training for artists hasn't caught up
> to that yet.[23]

Certainly some artists prefer being entrepreneurs, but others, as Zabel
mentioned, only choose self-employment in response to the loss or lack
of full-time work.[24]

B.   Minnesota and Hollywood Arts Ecosystems

The number of employee-status positions is connected to
overall economic viability of a community and the health of
collaborative art forms.

Arts businesses and the creative people they employ stimulate
innovation, strengthen America's competitiveness in the global

---

[23] Karsten Strauss, *How Entrepreneurship Can Save the Starving Artist*, FORBES, Dec. 18,
2015, http://www.forbes.com/sites/forbestreptalks/2015/12/18/how-entrepreneurship-can-
save-the-starving-artist/ (interviewing Laura Zabel, Executive Director of Springboard
for the Arts).

[24] See generally Elaine L. Edgcomb & Tamra Thetford, *Microenterprise Development as
Job   Creation*,   THE   ASPEN   INSTITUTE,   Feb.   1,   2013,
http://fieldus.org/Publications/JobCreation.pdf; Karsten Strauss, *How Entrepreneurship
Can   Save   the   Starving   Artist*,   FORBES,   Dec.   18,   2015,
http://www.forbes.com/sites/forbestreptalks/2015/12/18/how-entrepreneurship-can-save-
the-starving-artist/ (interviewing Laura Zabel, Executive Director of Springboard for the
Arts).

marketplace, and play an important role in building and sustaining economic vibrancy.[25]

In Minnesota, for example, the nonprofit arts and culture section has a substantial impact on the State: total economic impact is $1.2 billion.[26] What is particularly fascinating about this data is its relationship to employment. 1.5% of the entire Minnesota workforce is artists; whereas the national average sits at a mere 1.1%.[27] This figure is likely due to certain industries and professions supporting more fulltime employment (theater, museums, and most notably book publishing). However, in Minnesota, there are less fulltime positions for independent artists, writers, and performers than the national average.[28]

The U.S. film industry—a drastically different ecosystem than the one found in the Minnesota arts community—is the largest in the world, and supports 302,000 direct workers, paying $47 billion in wages.[29] Even more extraordinary is that while Hollywood is not perfect—with instances of questionable unpaid interns[30] and 79% of freelancers experiencing nonpayment at least once in their careers[31]— its employees bring home salaries 43% higher than the national average.[32] This could be due to the strong labor union system inside of

---

[25] For a general map of how job creation in the arts leads to a healthy society, see the following study: AMERICANS FOR THE ARTS, THE CREATIVE INDUSTRIES IN THE UNITED STATES (2015), http://www.americansforthearts.org/sites/default/files/pdf/2015/by_program/reports_and_data/research_studies_and_publications/creative_industries/2015_United_States.pdf ("702771 Arts-Related Businesses Employ 2,909,382 people").

[26] MINNESOTA CITIZENS FOR THE ARTS, MINNESOTA CREATIVE: THE IMPACT AND HEALTH OF NONPROFIT ARTS AND CULTURE SECTOR 3 (2015), http://www.culturaldata.org/wp-content/uploads/creative-minnesota-impact-health-nonprofit-arts-culture-sector.pdf.

[27] *Id.* at 9.

[28] *Id.*

[29] *Creating Jobs*, MOTION PICTURE ASSOC. AM., Nov. 20, 2015, http://www.mpaa.org/creating-jobs/.

[30] *E.g.* Glatt v. Fox Searchlight Picture, Inc., 791 F. 3d 376 (2d Cir. 2015) (class action lawsuit brought by unpaid interns against the motion picture distribution company).

[31] Laura Murphy, *Glitz, Glamour & Unpaid Bills : The nonpayment problem in film and television*, FREELANCERS UNION, Dec. 22, 2015, https://www.freelancersunion.org/blog/2015/12/22/glitz-glamour-unpaid-bills-nonpayment-problem-film-and-television/.

[32] *The Economic Contribution of the Motion Picture & Television Industry to the United States*, MOTION PICTURE ASSOC. AM., Sept. 2014, http://www.mpaa.org/wp-content/uploads/2014/09/2014-MPAA-Industry-Economic-Contribution-Factsheet.pdf

Hollywood.[33] For example, SAG-AFTRA—the labor union that represents 160,000 actors and other media performers—requires, with exemption, that producers classify SAG members as employees.[34] It is also in Hollywood that we have many full-time positions for writers, another artist traditionally thought of as a contractor. Hollywood has succeeded, arguably more than any other industry, in creating a professional class of artists. Artists who can both invest in their craft and pay their bills.

C.   Freelance Artists and How Little We Know

This is what little we know about the U.S. artist workforce as it relates to this topic:

> American artists are highly entrepreneurial; they are 3.5 times more likely than the total U.S. workforce to be self-employed.
> American artists are generally more educated than other workers. Over half of all artists have received at least a bachelor's degree.
> American artists are less likely than other workers to have full-year or full-time employment, which partly accounts for their annual median incomes being lower than those of workers with similar levels.[35]

I suspect that many employers do not need a staff painter, photographer, writer, or actor because any need might be sporadic or

---

[33] *E.g.*, White House Summit on Worker Voice, October 7, 2015 (interview of President Barack Obama), *available at* https://www.whitehouse.gov/campaign/worker-voice ("I am big believer of ... collective bargaining and unions as a tool to empower workers ... unions made sure ... there were direct negotiations, and the workers were at the table ... provided muscle and lift to get [legislation] passed.").

[34] *See* SCREEN ACTORS GUILD – AM. FED'N OF TELEVISION AND RADIO ARTISTS, 2005 SAG   BASIC   AGREEMENT   3, http://www.sagaftra.org/files/sag/2005TheatricalAgreement.pdf. One reason for this phenomenon is that labor laws only have jurisdiction over "employees." *See* 29 U.S.C. § 152(3) (2015). Union contracts thus require hiring parties to classify labor union members as employees, regardless of duration.

[35] MINNESOTA CITIZENS FOR THE ARTS, MINNESOTA CREATIVE: THE IMPACT AND HEALTH OF NONPROFIT ARTS AND CULTURE SECTOR 9 (2015) (citing National Endowment for the *Arts, Artists and Arts Workers in the United States: Findings from the American Community Survey (2005-2009)* and the *Quarterly Census of Employment and Wages (2010)*).

limited. Other reasons why so many employers hire artists as freelancers might be small operating costs, or simply the incorrect view that creative labor is not labor under the law. There is no survey, at least not one that I can find, to say why it is that employers choose to classify artists as contractors, or even how many artists out there are employees, contractors, or misclassified. But, we do know that contractor-status is one explanation for why artists make such little money.[36]

There is no denying that hiring employees over contractors is more expensive.[37] "At face value, building a workforce this way seems like a no-brainer for many startups, which save about 30% on the cost of labor by paying workers as independent contractors."[38]

But what impact will this way of doing business have on finished products or services? Hiring an employee means you, the employer, have no restrictions in terms of collaboration, direction, or how you decide to power the creative process.[39] There are limitations under the law to how you can manage and collaborate with a contractor that many managers would seemingly like to avoid. Furthermore, will the growing use of contractors to perform creative functions increase the administration of termination rights, effectively shortening companies' copyright interests to thirty-five years? We are seeing the courts respond by reminding companies of the legal consequences of misclassifying workers,[40] but the underlying concern might not be legal at all, but rather one of leadership. With the expansion of gig-economy type companies growing in popularity, there seems to be less focus on the worker, but a belief that good products will come about regardless.

This essay will introduce additional considerations to determining a creative worker's classification. Much of the current discussions on this topic have either been from a business or employment law lens, disregarding the impact on copyright interests

---

[36] *Id.*

[37] Hyam Singer, *Don't Be Fooled: Calculate the Real Cost of Employees and Consultants*, TOPTAL DEVELOPERS, http://www.toptal.com/freelance/don-t-be-fooled-the-real-cost-of-employees-and-consultants (last visited Oct. 6, 2015) (According this this calculation, a contractor will cost less than an employee even when the contractor makes $70 an hour and the employee makes $46 an hour).

[38] Sarah Kessler, *In A Backlash to the Gig Economy, Hiring Employees is Cool Again in Silicon Valley*, FAST COMPANY (June 10, 2015, 6:06 AM), http://www.fastcompany.com/3047105/a-backlash-to-the-gig-economy-hiring-employees-to-do-work-is-cool-in-silicon-valley-again.

[39] *See infra* note 147 and accompanying text.

[40] *See* O'Connor v. Uber Techs., Inc., 82 F. Supp. 3d 1133 (N.D. Cal. 2015).

and the creative process.[41] The needs of a position ought to define the classification, not the 1099 discount.[42] Under the existing legal framework, companies and creative workers can organize in a mutually beneficial way. My goal for this essay is to persuade companies to re-think how they approach employee classification and utilize the current law for such mutual benefit.

Part I provides a discussion of how our society is asking for more and more creative products and some of the challenges of managing creative workers. Part II gives an overview of how employees are legally classified, and provides some misclassification cases brought by Uber drivers and performing artists. Finally, part III analyzes how employee classification impacts intellectual property rights and plays into the application of the termination right.

II.   CREATIVITY IS ON THE RISE

According to Americans for the Arts,[43] "the value of the creative is on the rise" as blue-collar positions decline.[44] That is, the need for creative positions is increasing in our entertainment-focused society. For example, the average U.S. adult will watch five hours and thirty-one minutes of video each day.[45] Music consumption is growing as well, as paid streaming subscriptions made up thirty-three percent of total industry revenues from 2014 to 2015, up from 26 percent in

---

[41] *E.g.*, Julien M. Mundale, Note: *Not Everything That Glitters is Gold, Misclassification of Employees: The Blurred Line Between Independent Contractors and Employees Under the Major Classification Tests*, 20 SUFFOLK J. TRIAL & APP. ADVOC. 253 (2015) (identifying the current legal climate as lacking the incentive for employers to properly classify their workers).

[42] For a quick primer on employment taxes, see ABA Section of Taxation, *Employment Tax Primer for Small Businesses: I'm Ready to Hire My First Employee. What Should I Know About Taxes?*, presented at the 2015 Joint Fall CLE Meeting (Sept. 18, 2015).

[43] Americans for the Arts serves, advances, and leads the network of organizations and individuals who cultivate, promote, sustain, and support the arts in America. Founded in 1960, Americans for the Arts is the nation's leading nonprofit organization for advancing the arts and arts education.

[44] Felipe Buitrago Restrepo, *Arts & the Workforce*, AM. FOR ARTS, 75 (2015), http://www.americansforthearts.org/sites/default/files/Arts%26America_Workforce.pdf.

[45] *US Adults Spend 5.5 Hours with Video Content Each Day*, EMARKETER, Apr. 16, 2015, http://www.emarketer.com/Article/US-Adults-Spend-55-Hours-with-Video-Content-Each-Day/1012362.

2013.[46] More than ever, Americans are tuning in, logging in, or clicking through media produced by creative professionals.

"In 2013, the value added by the core copyright industries to U.S. GDP reached more than $1.1 trillion dollars."[47] This creative economy, as measured by the core copyright industries, supports 5.5 million jobs.[48] These workers sometimes work in isolation, and other times in collaborative environments with thoughtful direction.[49] And all of these companies have at least one Pablo Picasso on staff, often many more.[50] These people possess impeccable judgment and skill when it comes to design, the senses, and communication.[51]

One such Picasso is comedy writer and performer Tina Fey. After leaving college with a degree in drama, she went on to train at Second City, the school of improvisation in Chicago.[52] While there, she learned to embrace a more collaborative creative process than her traditional Stanislavski acting training provided.[53] Improvisational acting or sketch comedy writing requires equal part talent, equal part

---

[46] Joshua P. Friedlander, *News and Notes on 2015 RIAA Music Industry Shipment and Revenue Statistics*, RIAA, https://www.riaa.com/wp-content/uploads/2015/09/2015_RIAAMidYear_ShipmentData.pdf (last visited Jan. 9, 2016).

[47] Stephen E. Siwek, *Copyright Industries in the U.S. Economy*, INT'L INTELL. PROP. ALLIANCE, 2 (2014), http://www.iipa.com/pdf/2014CpyrtRptFull.PDF ("The "core" copyright industries are those industries whose primary purpose is to create, produce, distribute or exhibit copyright materials.").

[48] Stephen E. Siwek, *Copyright Industries in the U.S. Economy*, INT'L INTELL. PROP. ALLIANCE, 2 (2014), http://www.iipa.com/pdf/2014CpyrtRptFull.PDF. These numbers are based on the core copyright industries—those "whose primary purpose is to create, produce, distribute, or exhibit copyrighted material." I'd wish to account for a broader net of workers who engage in the creative process— not all creative products are protected by U.S. copyright law—but that data is not available.

[49] These skills are what many believe can make artists a most-valuable employee. *See, e.g.*, Lisa Phillips, *The Top 10 Skills Children Learn From the Arts*, AM. FOR ARTS, Nov. 26, 2012, http://blog.americansforthearts.org/2012/11/26/the-top-10-skills-children-learn-from-the-arts.

[50] Artists bring something valuable to the workforce, which is why companies like Another Limited Rebellion attempt to expand an artist skill set to other types of workers. Leah Lamb, *Why You Should Hire an Artist as Your Next Business Consultant*, FAST COMPANY (Sept. 18, 2015, 5:12 AM), http://www.fastcompany.com/3051224/hit-the-ground-running/why-you-should-hire-an-artist-as-your-next-business-consultant.

[51] *Id.*

[52] *Tina Fey: "Bossypants,"* GOOGLE, Apr. 21, 2011, https://www.youtube.com/watch?v=M8Mkufm3ncc.

[53] *Id.*

process, and equal part teamwork.[54] She brought this training to the *30 Rock* writing room, which is what arguably made the show's dialogue so brilliant. Kay Cannon, *30 Rock* staff writer and *Pitch Perfect* screenwriter, remembers:

> The first eight weeks [of writing for *30 Rock*], everything was so new, and in preproduction you are sitting in a room full of people and you are just talking, and talking about your life, and coming up with ideas and pitching ideas and it's much more casual and laidback. And because I was new to this, I was like 'Oh, is this what this is? Cuz [sic] this is easy. I can do this all day!' and then of course you get into the writing of it and you're like 'Ok, this is hard." . . . . Every day you've gotta bring it.[55]

One can assume, that the staff writer position gave her both the capacity to participate in a team writing environment, and the time for those slower, incubation periods that are key to the creative process.[56]

Creativity's market value is not lost on executives. After research connected daydreaming to better ideas, many tech companies adopted "laziness" policies.[57] Google, for example, lets workers dedicate some of their workday to goofing off.[58] Daydreaming lets

---

[54] *See generally* KELLY LEONARD & TOM YORTON, YES, AND: HOW IMPROVISATION REVERSES "NO, BUT" THINKING AND IMPROVES CREATIVITY AND COLLABORATION— LESSONS FROM THE SECOND CITY (Harper Business 2015).

[55] Rachel Mason, *Inside the Writer's Room: Behind the Scenes at 30 Rock with Writer/Producer Kay Cannon*, SPLITSIDER, Oct. 14, 2010, http://splitsider.com/2010/10/inside-the-30-rock-writers-room-with-writerproducer-kay-cannon/. Cannon, a Picasso and Writers Guildof America Award Winner, was an employee of NBC Universal. *Id.*

[56] In *The Art of Thought*, political scientist Graham Wallas broke the creative process into four stages: 1) preparation, 2) incubation, 3) illumination, and 4) verification. W. GLENN GRIFFIN & DEBORAH MORRISON, THE CREATIVE PROCESS ILLUSTRATED: HOW ADVERTISING'S BIG IDEAS ARE BORN 6–7 (2010) (citing GRAHAM WALLAS, THE ART OF THOUGHT (Harcourt Brace 1926)).

[57] Jonan Lehrer, *The Virtues of Daydreaming*, NEW YORKER, June 5, 2012, http://www.newyorker.com/tech/frontal-cortex/the-virtues-of-daydreaming.

[58] *See* Jillian D'Onfro, *The Truth About Google's Famous '20% Time' Policy*, BUS. INSIDER, Apr. 17, 2015, http://www.businessinsider.com/google-20-percent-time-policy-2015-4. While the Google 20% policy is now said to be dead, some of its workers still claim to take advantage of it. *Id.*

workers stimulate the senses, "think uncensored thoughts," make novel connections, and "tap into the most complex regions of [their] brain."[59] In *Creativity, Inc.,* Pixar President Edwin Catmull shares an anecdote of how he threw away a table and its place cards when it became apparent that only executives were speaking up at meetings.[60] When it comes to something as creative as making animated films, Catmull feels everyone needs to throw ideas into the hat.[61] In his book, Catmull communicates his distaste for hierarchical work environments as being unsuitable for good storytelling.[62] As Catmull details, he worked to design an environment conducive with the creative process.[63]

Creative geniuses are rare, and creativity is tricky to manage:

> Managing creative employees can be challenging: It's a constant balancing act. On the one hand, you need to maintain an environment that encourages exploration, experimentation, and risk-taking. On the other hand, you need to push people forward to produce work on time and on budget that meets the needs of the business.[64]

Companies in the business of producing creative products need to prioritize the establishment of workplaces that are conducive to the creative process. Many Picasso-like thinkers contribute to our rich creative economy, and many of these thinkers benefit from the financial stability and collaborative environments afforded to them by employee-classified positions.

Inspiring creativity in teams is no easy feat; it requires discipline, training, and company policies flexible enough to adapt to any creative environment or worker.[65] As such, companies should

---

[59] Amy Fries, *Sparking Creativity in the Workplace: Work and Daydreaming Really Do Go Together . . . Honest!,* PSYCHOLOGY TODAY, Feb. 9, 2010, https://www.psychologytoday.com/blog/the-power-daydreaming/201002/sparking-creativity-in-the-workplace.

[60] ED CATMULL, CREATIVITY, INC. loc. 160–67 (2014).

[61] *Id.* at loc. 166.

[62] *See id* at loc. 144.

[63] *Id.*

[64] Nelson Rodriguez, *5 Keys to Successfully Manage Creative Employees,* ENTREPRENEUR, Jan. 28, 2015, http://www.entrepreneur.com/article/242229.

[65] Richard Florida & Jim Goodnight, *Managing For Creativity,* HARV. BUS. REV., July–Aug. 2005, https://hbr.org/2005/07/managing-for-creativity ("Though all people chafe under what they see as bureaucratic obstructionism, creative people actively hate it,

know that under employment laws, labeling someone a proper contractor actually takes the company out of the creative process.[66] And for most creative works out there, it also grants the creator the right to take the copyright back decades later.[67]

III.   Employee Classification

A.   Overview of Employee Classification

In response to a growing number of misclassification complaints across the country,[68] the U.S. Department of Labor (DOL) recently released an Administrator's Interpretation to provide workers clarity on what makes a worker an employee under the Fair Labor Standards Act (FLSA).[69] Clarity is difficult when employee classification is tested differently across state and federal laws. Each area of law maintains its own independent body of case law to guide it.[70]

In *Chaves v. King Arthur's Lounge* an exotic dancer in Massachusetts was ruled to be an employee of the establishment because she performed her service in the lounge, the service was not customary in independently established business of the same nature,

---

viewing it not just as an impediment but as the enemy of good work. Do what you can to keep them intellectually engaged and clear petty obstacles out of their way, and they'll shine for you.").

[66] *See infra* Part IX.

[67] *See infra* Part X.

[68] Some predict that the government is growing more concerned with employee classification because of the 2008 recession's effect on unemployment insurance and the passage of the Affordable Care Act. Once reclassified, employers owe back pay, fines, and damages. Jeff Saviano & Debera Salam, *Why are Tax Audits Increasingly Focused on Incorrect Classification of Workers as Independent Contractors?*, J. OF MULTISTATE TAX'N & INCENTIVES, July 2015, at 32, 33.

[69] DAVID WEIL, WAGE & HOUR DIV., U.S. DEP'T OF LABOR, ADMINISTRATOR'S INTERPRETATION   NO.   2015-1   at   1,   July   15,   2015, http://www.dol.gov/whd/workers/Misclassification/AI-2015_1.pdf.

[70] *See* Robert Sprague, *Worker (Mis)Classification in the Sharing Economy: Square Pegs Trying to Fit in Round Holes*, 31 ABA J. LABOR & EMPLOYMENT (forthcoming 2015), http://works.bepress.com/cgi/viewcontent.cgi?article=1054&context=robert_sprague; Jack E. Karns, *Current Federal and State Conflicts in the Independent Contractor Versus Employee Classification Controversy*, 22 CAMPBELL L. REV. 105 (1999). *See e.g.*, Gryga v. Ganzman, 991 F. Supp. 105, 109 (E.D.N.Y. 1998) ("Since the cases cited [, *e.g.*, Cmty. for Creative Non–Violence v. Reid, 490 U.S. 730 (1989),] by defendant address a somewhat different issue—whether an individual is an 'employee' or an 'independent contractor' within the meaning of various federal statutes—they are not dispositive of the present motion.").

and the lounge asserted direct control over her. In other states, if the
same facts applied, the outcome would have differed, it may have also
differed if the dancer's classification as made under the tax statutes or
under the Fair Labor Standards Act.[71]

The common law agency test is the historical underpinning for
employee classification analysis. It is applied in actions under the
National Labor Relations Act,[72] in many state employment laws,[73]
and—relevant to this discussion—copyright laws.[74] Factors include:

1.   The hiring party's right to control the manner
     and means by which the product is
     accomplished;
2.   The skill required;
3.   The source of the instrumentalities and tools;
4.   The location of the work;
5.   The duration of the relationship between the
     parties;
6.   Whether the hiring party has the right to assign
     additional projects to the hired party;
7.   The extent of the hired party's discretion over
     when and how long to work;
8.   The method of payment;
9.   The hired party's role in hiring and paying
     assistants;
10. Whether the work is part of the regular business
     of the hiring party;
11. Whether the hiring party is in business;
12. The provision of employee benefits; and
13. The tax treatment of the hired party.[75]

---

[71] Julien M. Mundele, Note, *Not Everything that Glitters is Gold, Misclassification of
Employees: The Blurred Line Between Independent Contractors and Employees Under
the Major Classification Tests*, 20 SUFFOLK J. TRIAL & APP. ADVOC. 253, 254 (2015)
(citing Chaves v. King Arthur's Lounge, No. 07-2505, 2009 Mass. Super. LEXIS 298
(Mass. Super. Ct. July 30, 2009)) (citations omitted).
[72] *E.g.*, Lancaster Symphony Orchestra and the Greater Lancaster Fed'n of Musicians,
357 N.L.R.B. No. 152, at *4 (2011).
[73]   *Classification   Tests,*   WORKERSCLASSIFICATION.COM,
http://www.workerclassification.com/Classification-Tests (last visited Oct. 14, 2015).
[74] *See* Cmty. for Creative Non-Violence v. Reid, 490 U.S. 730, 751–52 (1989).
[75] *Id.* (citing RESTATEMENT (SECOND) OF AGENCY § 220 (1958)); *see also* Charles J.
Muhl, *What is an employee? The answer depends on the Federal law*, MONTHLY LAB.
REV., Jan. 2002, at 3, 7–8, http://www.bls.gov/opub/mlr/2002/01/art1full.pdf.

The FLSA—the federal law that sets minimum wage and overtime conditions—defines "employee" under the "economic realities" test.[76] This test, also applied to Title VII of the Civil Rights Act,[77] inquires as to whether "[a] worker is economically dependent upon the alleged employer or is instead in business for himself."[78] Factors include:

1. The extent to which the work performed is an integral[79] part of the employer's business;
2. The worker's opportunity for profit or loss depending on his or her managerial skills;
3. The extent of the relative investments[80] of the employer and the worker;
4. Whether the work performed requires special skills and initiative[81];
5. The permanency[82] of the relationship; and
6. The degree of control exercised or retained by the employer. [83]

---

[76] Weil, *supra* note 69, at 2.

[77] 42 U.S.C. § 2000e, *et seq.* (2012). *See* Susan N. Houseman, *9.1 Who Is an Employee? Determining Independent Contractor Status, in* U.S. DEP'T OF LABOR, A REPORT ON TEMPORARY HELP, ON-CALL, DIRECT-HIRE TEMPORARY, LEASED, CONTRACT COMPANY, AND INDEPENDENT CONTRACTOR EMPLOYMENT IN THE UNITED STATES (1999), http://www.dol.gov/dol/aboutdol/history/herman/reports/futurework/conference/staffing/ 9.1_contractors.htm (stating that the economic realities test "is often applied by courts in determining independent contractor status . . .").

[78] Hopkins v. Cornerstone Am., 545 F.3d 338, 343 (5th Cir. 2008); *see generally* Nancy E. Dowd, *The Test of Employee Status: Economic Realities and Title VII*, 26 WM. & MARY L. REV. 75 (1984) (detailing the economic realities test and arguing that the test thwarts the purpose of the law by being too narrow).

[79] Weil, *supra* note 69, at 7 ("For a construction company that frames residential homes, carpenters are integral to the employer's business because the company is in business to frame homes, and carpentry is an integral part of providing that service.").

[80] *Id.* at 9 ("The worker's investment must be significant in nature and magnitude relative to the employer's investment in its overall business to indicate that the worker is an independent businessperson.").

[81] *Id.* at 10 ("A worker's business skills, judgment, and initiative, not his or her technical skill, will aid in determining whether the worker is economically independent.").

[82] *Id.* at 12 ("The key is whether the lack of permanence or indefiniteness is due to 'operational characteristics intrinsic to the industry' (for example, employers who hire part-time workers or use staffing agencies) or the worker's 'own business initiative.') (citing Brock v. Superior Care, 840 F.2d 1054,1060 (2d Cir. 1988)).

While no one factor is determinative, the FLSA strives to "provide broad coverage for workers."[84] To the DOL, "the correct classification of workers as employees or independent contractors has critical implications for the legal protections that workers receive, particularly when misclassification occurs in industries employing low wage workers."[85]

The Internal Revenue Service also has its own spin on the common law factors, grouping them into three categories: 1) behavioral control;[86] 2) financial control;[87] and 3) the relationship of the parties.[88] Again, this body of regulations looks to know who had control or paid for expenses, and whether the work was a permanent and integral part of business operations.[89]

It seems employee classification differs among the various laws mostly in the underlying policies. As mentioned, the DOL has a policy to classify most workers as employees, whereas in copyright law—where employee classification deprives a worker of his or her copyright interests—the courts are hesitant to label a worker an employee.[90]

It is estimated that between ten and twenty percent of employers are misclassifying their employees under these tests.[91] One

---

[83] *Id.* at 13. ("The worker's control over meaningful aspects of the work must be more than theoretical—the worker must actually exercise it.") (citing Dole v. Snell, 875 F.2d 802, 808 (10th Cir. 1989)).

[84] *Id.* at 4.

[85] *Id.* at 15.

[86] IRS TAX TOPICS 762, http://www.irs.gov/taxtopics/tc762.html; BEHAVIORAL CONTROLS, IRS, http://www.irs.gov/Businesses/Small-Businesses-&-Self-Employed/Behavioral-Control.

[87] IRS TAX TOPICS 762, http://www.irs.gov/taxtopics/tc762.html; FINANCIAL CONTROL, IRS, http://www.irs.gov/Businesses/Small-Businesses-&-Self-Employed/Financial-Control.

[88] IRS TAX TOPICS 762, http://www.irs.gov/taxtopics/tc762.html; TYPE OF RELATIONSHIP, IRS, http://www.irs.gov/Businesses/Small-Businesses-&-Self-Employed/Type-of-Relationship.

[89] *See Employer's Supplemental Tax Guide, Publication 15-A*, DEP'T OF THE TREASURY: INTERNAL REVENUE SERVICE, 8 (2015), https://www.irs.gov/pub/irs-pdf/p15a.pdf.

[90] *Compare* Weil, *supra* note 69, at 5, *with* Jessica Litman, *Copyright, Compromise, and Legislative History,* 72 CORNELL L. REV. 857, 890 (1987) ("[Pre-legislative dialogue of the 1976 Copyright Act] indicate that by using the term 'employee' the parties meant to limit works made for hire under this branch of the definition to works created by a salaried worker in a long-term position.").

[91] Francois Carre, *(In)dependent Contractor Misclassification,* ECON. POL'Y INST., June 8, 2015, http://www.epi.org/publication/independent-contractor-misclassification/.

thing is certain, misclassification is a growing concern, even if its impacts are yet to be fully understood or felt.

B. Misclassification in the Arts: Ballerinas & Opera Singers

In the Second Circuit, a prima ballerina[92] was classified an employee under the Federal Tort Claims Act when she was injured at the Kennedy Center for Performing Arts.[93] Per her employment contract,[94] New York law applied: "the typical test of whether one is an independent contractor lies in the control exercised by the employer, and in who has the right to direct what will be done and when and how it will be done."[95] The ballerina met this test because she was hired to attend scheduled rehearsals and performances for "a specific part in a specific musical," wear particular clothes, and style her hair and makeup in a particular way.[96]

This opinion was consistent with New York law, where performers are typically found to be employees.[97] All that is required is a showing that the employer has control "over such aspects of the workers' employment as the dates and times of performances and the work to be performed."[98]

Interestingly, these same facts in other states would have resulted in an opposite result. In Minnesota, for example, a group of performers hired for short-term engagements by a small non-profit

---

[92] It should be stated that this ballerina was an Equity Actor. Her contract requires she be treated like an employee, but this relationship did not go into the court's analysis. Makarova v. U.S., 201 F.3d 110, 112 (2d Cir. 2000).

[93] In this unique scenario, the ballerina was disadvantaged in being an employee, as it made her ineligible to sue the government. Id. at 115.

[94] The court continued to analyze the contract under D.C. law, and found the same result. It found her to be "in the service of" the Kennedy Center. Id.

[95] Id. at 114.

[96] Id.

[97] Id.

[98] Id. at 115 (citing Challis v. Nat'l Producing Co., 275 A.D. 877, 88 N.Y.S.2d 731, 732 (3d Dept. 1949). See also Jack Hammer Assocs. v. Delmy Prods., 118 A.D.2d 441, 499, N.Y.S.2d 418, 419–20 (1st Dept. 1986).

opera company[99] were narrowly found to be contractors by the Minnesota Court of Appeals.[100]

In finding the performers to be contractors,[101] the court disregarded any control inherent in the rehearsal process itself: "Artists who perform . . . necessarily attend scheduled rehearsals and take directions from a director. If this type of control, without more, were enough to establish employee status, it is difficult to conceive of a circumstance in which an [artist] hired by a theater would not be an employee."[102] As opposed to New York law, the Minnesota Court of Appeals felt the performers were the ones in control: they prepared for roles in their own time, and were free to pursue other work.[103] Although, it seems the court was mostly persuaded by the brevity of the performance schedules.[104]

Still, this was a close call for Minnesota—the decision itself cannot be cited in future cases.[105] The court was clear, stating:

> Our decision today is a narrow one. We merely hold, on the specific facts presented in this case . . . our decision should not be construed to extend to all persons hired by operas, orchestras, or theaters. As we noted above, "[i]n employment-status cases, there is no general rule that covers all situations, and each case will depend in large part upon its own particular facts."[106]

---

[99] The Skylark Opera Company is one of many small nonprofit performing arts organizations in Minnesota.[99] The company hosts four performances each year, and employs only one permanent employee, its Artistic Director. Skylark Opera v. Dep't of Employment & Econ. Dev., 2014 WL 4672360, at *1 (Minn. Ct. App. Sept. 22, 2014)

[100] *Id.* (analyzing why orchestra and technical staff were also contractors).

[101] *Id.* at *4 ("Traditionally, five factors are used to determine whether a worker is an employee or an independent contractor: '(1) The right to control the means and manner of performance; (2) the mode of payment; (3) the furnishing of material or tools; (4) the control of the premises where the work is done; and (5) the right of the employer to discharge.'").

[102] *Skylark Opera*, 2014 WL 4672360, at *4.

[103] *Id.* at *1–2.

[104] *Id.* at 5.

[105] *Id.* ("Notice: This opinion is designated as unpublished and may not be cited except as provided by Minn. St. Sec. 480A.08(3).").

[106] *Id.* at *6 (citing St. Croix Sensory Inc. v. Dep't of Emp't & Econ. Dev., 785 N.W.2d 796, 800 (Minn.App.2010)).

Depending on the jurisdiction or law, a manager's flexibility in directing contractors differs greatly, which has an enormous impact on the creative process. Even though creativity is thought to be fleeting and unconfined, in practice, it typically involves bringing teams together at scheduled meetings. In these meetings there is a leader, someone acting much like a stage director, who shepherds an idea to its fruition.[107]

C. Uber Case Sparks New Policy Debates About How We Classify Employees

Uber is the $50 billion mobile transportation company that poses as a technology company.[108] Uber drivers (160,000 and growing)[109] transport customers in their personal cars, and use the company's application (installed on a provided iPhone) to make transactions.[110] This past June, the Labor Commissioner of the California Department of Labor told Uber that it had misclassified one of its drivers as an independent contractor because a proper independent contractor, unlike an employee, is actually someone who operates an independent business, hired on for a specific project with a definite duration.[111]

The company argued it was simply operating an app that provides independent drivers access to its customer base.[112] The California Labor Commission disagreed, finding, instead, that the drivers are an integral part of the well-orchestrated Uber operation.[113] From requiring background checks to imposing restrictions on eligible vehicles and setting payments at a non-negotiable rate, Uber acted like an employer to its employee drivers.[114]

---

[107] *E.g.*, CATMULL, *supra* note 60, at loc. 166–97.

[108] Mike Isaac & Natasha Singer, *California Says Uber Driver is Employee, Not a Contractor*, N.Y. TIMES, Jun. 17, 2015, http://www.nytimes.com/2015/06/18/business/uber-contests-california-labor-ruling-that-says-drivers-should-be-employees.html?_r=0.

[109] Noam Scheiber, *Growth in the 'Gig Economy' Fuels Work Force Anxieties*, N.Y. TIMES, July 12, 2015, http://www.nytimes.com/2015/07/13/business/rising-economic-insecurity-tied-to-decades-long-trend-in-employment-practices.html?_r=0.

[110] *Berwick v. Uber*, No. 11-46739, 2015 WL 4153765, at *3, 8 (CA. Dep't of Indus. Relations June 3, 2015).

[111] *See id.* at *5.

[112] *Id.* at *6.

[113] *Id.*

[114] *Id.*

As it happens . . . Uber is not so much a labor-market innovation as the culmination of a generation-long trend. Even before the founding of the company in 2009, the United States economy was rapidly becoming an Uber economy writ large, with tens of millions of Americans involved in some form of freelancing, contracting, temping or outsourcing.[115]

Reading the facts of *Berwick v. Uber*, it is apparent that the company spent a great deal of money designing the position to favor a finding of independent contractor.[116] Even the company's recruiting language illustrates its deliberate attempt to avoid employee classification: "Uber needs partners like you. Drive with Uber and earn great money as an independent contractor. Get paid weekly just for helping our community of riders get rides around town. Be your own boss and get paid in fares for driving on your own schedule."[117] From the consumer's perspective, ordering an Uber is a bit of a roll of the dice.[118] Without trainings or company cars and uniforms, the company settled for a lesser quality product in exchange for a higher profit margin.[119] Like Uber's improper employee classification, such misclassification can create life-changing results for creatives.

---

[115] Noam Scheiber, *Growth in the 'Gig Economy' Fuels Work Force Anxieties*, N.Y. TIMES, July 12, 2015, http://www.nytimes.com/2015/07/13/business/rising-economic-insecurity-tied-to-decades-long-trend-in-employment-practices.html?_r=0.

[116] *See* Berwick v. Uber Techs., Inc., No. 11-46739 EK, 2015 WL 4153765, at *1–4 (Cal. Dep't of Indus. Rel. June 3, 2015).

[117] *Sign up to Drive*, Uber, https://get.uber.com/cl/?city_name=washington-DC&utm_source=Bing_Brand&utm_campaign=search%7Cdesktop%7Cdrivers%7Cwashington-DC%7Ccountry-1%7Ccity-8%7Ckeyword_uber%20driver%7Cmatchtype_e%7Cad_9673883932%7Ccampaign_brand%7Cgroup_uberdriver%3Eexact&utm_medium=kenid_06ef919f-24e1-3808-6afa-000002c2775a (last visited Oct. 13, 2015).

[118] *See* Mike Isaac, *Uber Flunks the Better Business Bureau Test*, BITS (Oct. 9, 2014, 3:57 PM), http://bits.blogs.nytimes.com/2014/10/09/uber-flunks-the-better-business-bureau-test/?_r=1 (stating that Uber has received more than ninety customer complaints filed with the Bureau and with most of them centered on Uber's surge pricing, which is based on driver demand); *see also* Kessler, *supra* note 38 (quoting Caleb Merkl, the CEO of Maple, a New York delivery-only restaurant) ("'It's easy to add up the cost savings from having independent contractors—you know exactly how much you are saving per employee by not paying for workers' compensation—but it's much harder to quantify all of the benefits of having full-time employees that, in our view, offset many (if not all) of the 1099 savings . . . . If you look at our delivery team, they are essentially our only point of human contact with our customers, so it's a case where who's doing the job and how they are doing it is incredibly important to our success.'").

[119] *See* Isaac, *supra* note 118; *Cf.* Kessler, *supra* note 38 (citing interview with Caleb Merkl, the CEO of Maple, a New York delivery-only restaurant) (explaining how training

IV.   INTELLECTUAL PROPERTY CONCERNS

Sure intellectual property rights are not relevant for an Uber driver—whose contributions are the labor of driving and a personal car—but employee classification makes or breaks a creative worker's rights to his or her intellectual property. Copyright law does not protect ideas, only expressions. [120] This federal law protects qualifying "original works of authorship fixed in any tangible medium of expression."[121] Just about anything fixed on film, print, or the Internet is copyrightable. In fact, it is easier to give examples of what is not copyrightable than try to summarize the wide net of content that is. A list of names or facts is not copyrightable,[122] nor is a fashion design,[123] or a dramatic performance.[124] But this essay is copyrightable, as is a magazine cover,[125] and even a broadcast of your favorite football team.[126]

A.   Contractors Own Copyrights

Once content falls within the scope of protection, copyright holders may license or assign their work to others.[127] But the current statutory scheme places limits on hiring parties who claim authorship. Authorship is presumed to be in the creator, but under the work made

---

is necessary to ensure deliveries and customer interactions abide by the company's values).

[120] Herbert Rosenthal Jewelry Corp. v. Kalpakian (Bee Pin Case), 446 F.2d 738, 742 (providing guidance on applying the idea/expression dichotomy) ("The critical distinction between "idea" and "expression" is difficult to draw. . . . What is basically at stake is the extent of the copyright owner's monopoly—from how large an area of activity did Congress intend to allow the copyright owner to exclude others? We think the production of jeweled bee pins is a larger private preserve than Congress intended to be set aside in the public market without a patent.").

[121] 17 U.S.C. § 102(a) (2012).

[122] Feist Publ'ns, Inc. v. Rural Tel. Serv. Co., 499 U.S. 340, 361 (1991).

[123] MELVILLE B. NIMMER & DAVID NIMMER, 1-2 NIMMER ON COPYRIGHT § 2.08[H][3] (2015).

[124] Garcia v. Google Inc., 766 F.3d 929, 941 (9th Cir. 2014), aff'd en banc, 786 F.3d 733,742 (9th Cir. 2015).

[125] Rosebud Entm't, LLC v. Prof. Laminating LLC, 958 F. Supp. 2d 600, 604–05 (D. Md. 2013).

[126] See generally Nat'l Football League v. PrimeTime 24 Joint Venture, 211 F.3d 10 (2d Cir. 2000).

[127] 17 U.S.C. § 204 (2012).

for hire doctrine, it instead vests in the employer.[128] This classification is anything but trivial; it dictates the term duration, and affects a creator's ability to terminate or to bring a Visual Artists Rights Act claim.[129] "The contours of the work for hire doctrine therefore carry profound significance for freelance creators—including, artists, writers, photographers, designers, composers, and computer programmers—and for publishing, advertising, music, and other industries which commission their works."[130]

Tucked in the definitions section of the Copyright Act is the "work made for hire" doctrine:

> (1) a work prepared by an employee within the scope of his or her employment; or
> (2) a work specially ordered or commissioned for use as a contribution to a collective work, as a part of a motion picture or other audiovisual work, as a translation, as a supplementary work, as a compilation, as an instructional text, as answer material for a test, or an atlas, if the parties expressly agree in a written instrument signed by them that the work shall be considered a work made for hire.[131]

Under § 101(2), Congress enumerated nine works that provide hiring parties authorship regardless of whether the creator was an employee or not.[132] Still even for these works, a work made for hire agreement needs to be signed *before the work begins*.[133] From a practical standpoint, § 101(2) is straightforward. If, for example, a screenwriter signs a work made for hire agreement before he starts writing, the film's producer is the rightful owner of the script.

---

[128] 17 U.S.C. § 101 (2012).

[129] *Cmty. for Creative Non-Violence v. Reid*, 490 U.S. 730 (1989). See Shannon M. Nolley, *The Work for Hire Doctrine and the Second Circuit's Decision in Carter v. Helmsley* for further background on the doctrine, and specifically how it relates to the Visual Artists Rights Act. 7 DEPAUL-LCA J. ART & ENTM'T L. 103, 127 (1996) ("The Second Circuit's refusal [in *Carter v. Helmsley*] to consider the artists' retention of copyright in the work as a 'plus factor' brings to light the fundamental conflict in U.S. law between its long-held notion of copyright ownership, and the more recently recognized international concept of moral rights.").

[130] *Reid*, 490 U.S. at 737.

[131] 17 U.S.C. § 101(2) (2012).

[132] *Id. See also* NIMMER, *supra* note 123, § 5.03(2)(a)(i).

[133] *Id.* at § 5.03.

Conversely, when it comes to non § 101(2) works, agreements are basically irrelevant—an agreement cannot just label a contractor's work as "work made for hire" if it is not. The employer-employee relationship only manifests after a judge applies the agency law common law test from *Community for Creative Non-Violence v. Reid*[134] to the specific working conditions involved.[135]

1.   Post-1978 Employer-Employee Test

Under § 101(1), a court applies the general principles of agency law—now called the *Reid* or *CCNV* test—to the circumstances leading up to the finished product.[136] In *Community for Creative Non-Violence v. Reid*, a sculpture artist was classified an independent contractor under the 1976 Copyright Act by the Supreme Court.[137] The sculpture artist in *Reid* was approached by a nonprofit to construct a sculpture depicting homelessness.[138] In exchange, he was paid a lump sum without benefits or taxes withheld.[139] He also worked in his own studio, and received little oversight from the nonprofit.[140]

In practice, the test can be thought of as an inquiry into whether the hiring party participated in the creative process, and whether the worker was treated like a conventional salaried employee. In contrast to other laws, copyright law actually places less weight on the exercise of control.[141] Every case of this type certainly digs into the creative process—the process by which the idea was transformed into the final product—but not without first finding what resembles "the conventional relation[ship] of employer and employ[ee]."[142]

---

[134] *Reid*, 490 U.S. at 751–52.
[135] NIMMER, *supra* note 123, § 5.03.
[136] *Reid*, 490 U.S. at 750–51.
[137] *Id.* at 752.
[138] *Id.* at 733.
[139] *Id.* at 753.
[140] *Id.* at 752–53.
[141] Aymes v. Bonelli, 980 F.2d 857, 861 (2d Cir. 1992) ("Some factors, therefore, will often have little or no significance in determining whether a party is an independent contractor or an employee. In contrast, there are some factors that will be significant in virtually every situation. These include: (1) the hiring party's right to control the manner and means of creation; (2) the skill required; (3) the provision of employee benefits; (4) the tax treatment of the hired party; and (5) whether the hiring party has the right to assign additional projects to the hired party. These factors will almost always be relevant and should be given more weight in the analysis, because they will usually be highly probative of the true nature of the employment relationship.").
[142] *Reid*, 490 U.S. at 740.

Central to the creative process is the delegation of artistic control. Similarly, "control is [usually] the principal guidepost"[143] for traditional employee classification because agency law defines a servant to mean one who is "subject to the other's control or right to control."[144] However, in copyright law, even when the hiring party controls the work, if the other factors weigh heavily in favor of contractor status, this factor will actually be disregarded.[145] In other words, because hiring parties are not supposed to collaborate with contractors, it will not be rewarded with copyright ownership when it disobeys this principal. Unless a worker is treated like a traditional salaried employee with-benefits, courts are cautious to classify a work as "made for hire."[146]

In *Marco v. Accent Publishing,* the Third Circuit vacated a misapplication of the *Reid* test, and found a freelance photographer to be a contractor despite there being enough creative control by his employer.[147] Marco was hired to shoot a series of images that were used in six consecutive issues of a costume jewelry trade journal.[148] For the most part, the photos were shot in the photographer's home studio.[149] The hiring party gave opinions on how the models and jewelry looked, but left the technical matters like color balance and light to the photographer.[150] The hiring party also provided jewelry, models, and props to be photographed, and sketches to guide the photo's composition.[151] At some points, an art director also attended some of the sessions to "[direct him] on the composition of a photograph . . . the mood of the lighting, the emotion within a given scenario."[152] This was enough for the court to accept a finding of

---

[143] Clackamas Gastroenterology Assocs., P. C. v. Wells, 538 U.S. 440, 448 (2003).
[144] *Id.* (citing Restatement (Second) of Agency § 220(1) (1958)) (defining "employee" under the American Disability Act).
[145] *See Reid,* 490 U.S. at 751–52 (1989).
[146] Aymes v. Bonelli, 980 F.2d 857, 862–63 (2d Cir. 1992); *see, e.g.* Jessica Litman, *Copyright, Compromise, and Legislative History,* 72 CORNELL L. REV. 857, 890 (1987) ("[E]very case since *Reid* that has applied the test has found the hired party to be an independent contractor where the hiring party failed to extend benefits or pay social security taxes").
[147] Marco v. Accent Pub. Co., Inc., 969 F.2d 1547, 1553 (3rd Cir. 1992).
[148] *Id.* at 1548.
[149] *Id.* at 1549.
[150] *Id.*
[151] *Id.* at 1548–49.
[152] *Id.* at 1552.

control.[153] But it was not enough to find that Marco was an actual employee.[154]

Even though the hiring party participated in the actual creative process, it did not act like an employer in other ways. For example, pay-roll taxes were not withheld, nor were benefits provided.[155] The court was also persuaded by how limited the hiring party's engagement was: "The record does not suggest that [the hiring party] could assign any more than one issue's worth of photographs . . . during any particular period. [It] could not, for example, require [the photographer] to photograph its employee of the month."[156] He also did not hold regular hours with the company, even during the six-month period in question.[157] Thus, this photographer was a contractor, and as a result, the copyrights to the photos were his.[158]

2.   Pre-1978 Employer-Employee Test

Prior to the 1976 Copyright Act, it was much easier for a contractor's work to be "made for hire," as the courts applied the basic "Instance and Expense Test," instead of the Agency common law test. In 2013, the Second Circuit reinstated this test in *Marvel v. Kirby*, but only for pre-1978 works.[159]

The comic artist Jack Kirby is responsible for many of the characters that fill our screens and toy boxes.[160] While working as a freelance artist in the sixties, he created—along with Stan Lee—entire teams of superheroes like the X-Men, the Fantastic Four, and the Avengers.[161] Under the "Marvel Method," Stan Lee and a comic artist would talk ideas, then the artist would draw what they wished at

---

[153] *Id.* ("The only significant difference between this case and CCNV is that here the hiring party is in the business of regularly publishing photographs in connection with advertisements and articles. This distinction does not give rise to an employment relationship.").
[154] *See id.* at 1552.
[155] *Id.* at 1549; *see also* SHL Imaging, Inc. v. Artisan House, Inc., 117 F. Supp. 2d 301 (S.D.N.Y. 2000) (finding contractor status when there was little control, taxes were not withheld, and benefits were not given).
[156] *Id.* at 1551.
[157] *Id.*
[158] *Id.* at 1553.
[159] Marvel Characters, Inc. v. Kirby, 726 F.3d 119, 137 (2d Cir. 2013).
[160] *Id.* at 124.
[161] *Id.* at 125.

home.[162] He purchased all of the supplies necessary to draw the pages.[163] If Lee approved the art then a writer would "put in all the dialogue and the captions."[164] Kirby was paid on a per-page rate, without any consideration for his future.[165] He did not hold a staffed position, nor did he receive vacation time, health benefits, a pension, or a cut in any of his character's success.[166] To give an example of how valuable his work is today, the 2012 *Avengers* release alone brought in $1.5 billion in worldwide box office proceeds.[167] Kirby himself made a mere $35,000 for every year he worked as a freelancer for Marvel.[168]

When the heirs of his estate sought to terminate the original deal in 2010, the court found all his works to be "made for hire" property of the company.[169] Because the works were created prior to the 1978 effective date of the 1976 Copyright Act, the court applied the now abolished "Instance and Expense" test.[170] The instance prong merely requires that the hiring party provide the "impetus for" or participate in the work, or have "the power to supervise."[171] The expense prong looks to see who bore the financial risk of the work.[172] Even absent a showing of "instance," the test is still met if there is "a particularly strong showing that the work was made at its expense."[173] Ultimately, the court sided with Marvel.[174] To the court, while both parties bore some risk in the work, Marvel was the one on the hook for

---

[162] *Id.* at 126.
[163] *Id.*
[164] *Id.*
[165] *Id.*
[166] *See id.* at 125–126.
[167] *Marvel's The Avengers (2012)*, BOX OFFICE MOJO, http://www.boxofficemojo.com/movies/?id=avengers11.htm (last updated Oct. 4, 2015, 7:11 PM).
[168] *Jack Kirby*, https://en.wikipedia.org/wiki/Jack_Kirby#cite_ref-98 (last updated Sept. 28, 2015, 8:40 PM); *see also* Saul Braun, *Shazam! Here Comes Captain Relevant*, NY TIMES (May 2,1971), *available at* http://timesmachine.nytimes.com/timesmachine/1971/05/02/170499242.html?pageNumber=402.
[169] *Marvel*, 726 F.3d at 124.
[170] *Id.* at 137.
[171] *Id.* at 139 (citing Shapiro Berstein & Co. v. Jerry Vogal Music Co., 221 F.2d 569, 570 (2d Cir. 1955)). The court notes that when a work already exists before the hiring party gets involved, the mere requesting of revisions is insufficient.
[172] *Marvel*, 726 F.3d at 140–43. The Second Circuit struggled with the expense prong, feeling both parties bore risk, but sided with Marvel because it paid a flat rate to Kirby, and provided "creative and production value."
[173] *Id.* at 139 (citing Scherr v. Universal Match Corp., 417 F.2d 497, 501 (2d Cir. 1969)).
[174] *Id.* at 143.

how successful a work would become.[175] Furthermore, Kirby was technically paid for accepted pages.[176] However, Kirby was not paid for the countless pages that were rejected.[177]

There is little doubt that if the court had applied the modern "employer-employee" test, the Kirby estate would have won because the court would have recognized Kirby as a true contractor.[178] Even the Second Circuit admits this fact: "it is undisputed that Kirby was a freelancer." [179] As well articulated by the American Society of Architectural Illustrators, Kirby would have had a different outcome after 1978:

> When reaching its decision, the Second Circuit ignored the conventional employer/employee relationship defined under the common law of agency, ignored Kirby's authorial rights under the 1909 Act and the 1976 Act, ignored the teachings of the Supreme Court precedent of [*Reid*] whereby the Court defined the seminal conditions necessary for work-for-hire regarding freelance authors, and nullified Congress's clear objectives in enacting copyright termination provisions for authors. Instead, the court relied on an erroneous, simplistic and controversial judicial test. Called the "instance and expense" test, it redefines nearly any business

---

[175] *Id.* at 140.

[176] *Marvel*, 726 F.3d at 142.

[177] *Id.* at 125–26; *Making Music: IP & the Creative Process*, GEO. MASON UNIV.: CENTER FOR THE PROTECTION OF INTELL. PROP. (Sept. 30–Oct. 1, 2015), http://cpip.gmu.edu/conferences/. (Marc Beeson, a panelist at the CPIP George Mason 2015 conference in the session Making Music: IP & the Creative Process, remarks that fans do not realize that for every hit song produced, a songwriter spends thousands of hours spent on unknown songs that were never selected. Not to mention the other thousands of hours spent on mastering the skills necessary to be a professional songwriter).

[178] *See* Joseph Cornelius Johnson, *My Hero?: The Work for Hire Doctrine and Termination Rights in Marvel Characters, Inc. v. Kirby*, 14-18, *available at* http://scholarship.shu.edu/cgi/viewcontent.cgi?article=1498&context=student_scholarshi p; *see, e.g.,* Wayne M. Cox, *The Fantastic Failure: How Current Copyright Law Stacks the Deck Against the Original Authors of Justice*, 55 IDEA 361, 379 (2015).

[179] *Marvel*, 726 F.3d at 125.

transaction between an independent creator and a commissioning party as work-for-hire.[180]

B.   Contractors Can Terminate

The work made for hire doctrine puzzles many, even experts of copyright law. Employment contracts regularly include "work made for hire" language, so the phrase is thrown around to describe what is actually an assignment, a license, or nothing at all. As a result, wise practitioners cover their bases by including both work made for hire and assignment language in their contracts.[181] An assignment is the legal transfer of all exclusive rights (in writing) of a copyright.[182] With this transfer, companies can freely use the copyright just like an owner, but with significant artist rights limitations.[183] In the case of fine art, a company is limited in how it labels, manipulates, or handles a physical piece of art.[184] And, most importantly, all assigned copyrights are subject to the filing of a termination notice.[185] A work made for hire is a work in which the legal author is not the creator but is a hiring party.[186] Because the creator never authored the work to begin with, he or she cannot claim any of the author rights provided by law.

---

[180] Cynthia Turner & Dena Matthews, *Understanding the* Kirby *Case: ASAI joins Amicus Brief for* Kirby v. Marvel Comics, *Disney, American Society of Architectural Illustrators*, (June   26,   2014), https://americansocietyofarchitecturalillustrators.wordpress.com/2014/06/26/understanding-the-kirby-case-asai-joins-amicus-brief-for-kirby-v-marvel-comics-disney/. Prior to the Kirby settlement, Bruce Lehman, former Director of the U.S. Patent and Trademark Office, and Ralph Oman, former U.S. Register of Copyrights, wrote an amicus brief to the Supreme Court on behalf of freelancers. The Turner article provides an excellent summary and outline of their legal argument. *Id.*

[181] Email interview with Joel Leviton, Partner, Stinson, Leonard, Street (Jan. 8, 2016) ("Contracts often refer to the works that are to be created as 'work for hire.' However, not all copyrightable works qualify to be a work for hire. If a work does not qualify as a work made for hire, to transfer ownership the copyrights must be assigned. There are benefits, for the owning party, for a work to be considered a work made for hire. For example, no termination rights. As such,, in the first instance, the party who will own the copyright likely will want the work to be considered a work made for hire if possible. But, in the event a work does not qualify as a work made for hire, the party seeking to own the work will want to assure it obtains an assignment in the alternative.").

[182] 17 U.S.C. § 1320 (2012).

[183] NIMMER, *supra* note 123, at § 5.03.

[184] Visual Artists Rights Act, 17 U.S.C. § 106(A) (2012).

[185] 17 U.S.C. § 1305 (2012).

[186] NIMMER, *supra* note 123, at § 5.03.

While not always packaged as an inalienable[187] author right, the termination right dates back to the Statute of Anne.[188] Today copyrights enjoy lengthy terms, but authors once had to renew registrations to extend their term duration.[189] As a result of this system, assignments entered into during the first term ended with the beginning of a renewal term. When it came time to craft the 1976 Copyright Act, Congress chose to abandon the unpopular renewal requirement, and replaced it with a codified termination right.[190] Congress recognized that freelancers were too often taken advantage of in the marketplace, particularly when just starting out. An inalienable termination right would grant authors of successful work a second chance at profits.[191]

Works under the 1976 Copyright Act are governed by the statutory scheme laid out in section 203.[192] Between twenty-five and thirty-three years after an assignment, a creator may file a termination notice with the U.S. Copyright Office. The right will then terminate (aka return to the original creator) within a five-year window thereafter. As a result of the work made for hire exception and the inalienability of the right, much litigation has spurred, and will continue to come,

---

[187] Fred Fisher Music Co. v. M. Witmark & Sons, 318 U.S. 643, 656 (1943), *superseded by statute*, Copyright Act of 1976, Pub. L. No. 94-553, 90 Stat. 2541.

[188] Statute of Anne, 1710, 8 Anne, c. 19, *reprinted in* COPYRIGHT LAW VOLUME I: THE SCOPE AND HISTORICAL CONTEXT 189 (Benedict A. C. Atkinson & Brian F. Fitzgerald eds. 2011).

[189] Copyright Act of 1909, ch. 320, 35 Stat. 1075 (1909) (duration, renewal and extension). ("[T]he proprietor of such copyright shall be entitled to a renewal and extension of the copyright in such work for the further term of twenty-eight years . . .").

[190] H.R. REP. NO. 94-1476, at 134 (1976), *reprinted in* 17 U.S.C. § 304 at 1152 (2012) ("One of the worst features of the present copyright law is the present copyright law is the provision for renewal of copyright. A substantial burden an expense, this unclear and highly technical ... is the cause of inadvertent and unjust loss of copyright.").

[191] *See* Stewart v. Abend, 495 U.S. 207, 230 (1990) (the reversion right was intended to be inalienable); Peter S. Menell, *Pooh-Poohing Copyright Law's Inalienable Termination Rights* 57 J. COPYRIGHT SOC'Y 799, 806 (citing DISCUSSION & COMMENTS ON THE REPORT OF THE REGISTER OF COPYRIGHTS ON THE GENERAL REVISION OF THE U.S. COPYRIGHT LAW 93 (Gov't Printing Off. 1963) (rejected language included "limiting all copyright assignments to twenty years with automatic reversions thereafter; permitting termination of assignments deemed to be unfair to authors; and granting termination of assignment rights to who authors who were paid only a lump sum upfront.").

[192] 17 U.S.C. § 203 (2012). ("In the case of any work other than a work made for hire, the exclusive or nonexclusive grant of a transfer or license of copyright or of any right under a copyright, executed by the author on or after January 1, 1978, otherwise than by will, is subject to termination . . .").

between hiring parties and freelancers in regards to employee-status, and other technical matters.[193]

The easiest way to avoid this risk is to hire employees instead of freelancers, and to provide workers with employee benefits.

V.   CONCLUSION

Perhaps no creative industry has felt the affects of this changing workforce more than the newspaper industry. Once a copyright industry giant,[194] newspapers now struggle to stay profitable in the digital marketplace.[195] And "labor is still the biggest cost," said Paul Godfrey, President of Postmedia Network.[196] In 2000, there were 25,593 staff reporters and writers hired by newspapers; in 2013, just 17,422 and declining.[197] That's a 32% drop, which is still less than the 43% drop felt by staff photographers.[198]

---

[193] *See, e.g.* Milne v. Stephen Slesinger, Inc., 430 F.3d 1036, 1040 (9th Cir. 2005) (Winnie the Pooh); Penguin Group, Inc. v. Steinbeck, 573 F.3d 193 (2d Cir. 2008); Larson v. Warner Bros Entm't (Superman), 213 U.S. Dist. LEXIS 55949 (C.D. Cal. 2013). For commentary on the YMCA case, see Eriq Gardner, *Village People's Victor Wills Wins Huge Rights Reversion Case Over 'YMCA'*, BILLBOARD, May 8, 2012, http://www.billboard.com/biz/articles/news/1097011/village-peoples-victor-willis-wins-huge-rights-reversion-case-over-ymca.

[194] *Size of the Copyright Industries*, COPYRIGHT LAW REVISION, STUDIES PREPARED FOR THE SUBCOMMITTEE ON PATENTS, TRADEMARKS, AND COPYRIGHTS, 28 tbl. II (1960), http://copyright.gov/history/studies/study2.pdf (Newspaper publishing's national income was over $1.5 billion, while the movie industry brought in only $917 million).

[195] Monica Anderson, *At newspaper, photographers feel the brunt of job cuts*, Nov. 11, 2013, http://www.pewresearch.org/fact-tank/2013/11/11/at-newspapers-photographers-feel-the-brunt-of-job-cuts/ ("Shrinking newsroom budgets play a significant part, but so does the explosion of mobile technology and social media, making it easier for citizens and non-professionals to capture and share images. When it laid off several photographers in 2011, CNN cited the 'impact of user-generated content and social media . . . in breaking news,' as a key reason.").

[196] Sarah A. Howes, Newspaper is Made from Megabtyes, COPYRIGHT ALLIANCE, Oct. 13,   2015, https://copyrightalliance.org/2015/10/newspaper_made_megabytes#.VoRYMotSb8E (coverage of the Center for the Protection of Intellectual Property event Future of the News).

[197] Anderson, *supra* note 195. However, there appears to be an increase in the number of newsroom jobs at either very big or very small newspapers. Ken Doctor, *Newsonomics: The halving of America's daily newsroom*, NIEMAN LAB, July 28, 2015, http://www.niemanlab.org/2015/07/newsonomics-the-halving-of-americas-daily-newsrooms/.

[198] Anderson, *supra* note 195.

An email exchange between journalist Nate Thayer and the Global Editor of the Atlantic, Thayer details how the magazine—now only offering $100 to re-post his articles—once offered him $125,000 to write six articles a year as a staff journalist.[199] This new era may require new ways of delivering the news, but quality still demands well-compensated journalists who have the funding to investigate matters of public importance, and the capacity to master their craft.[200]

Creativity is best served when collaborators are fairly compensated, and when managers have total discretion to give as much freedom as they see fit. More and more employers are choosing the contractor model, which only adds to the frustrations felt by our workforce and sacrifices the quality of the creative products entering our marketplace.

Companies of all sizes should perform internal audits of contractor relationships to evaluate whether roles should be clarified or re-classified.[201] This audit should take into consideration the company's creative process and the worker's role in producing copyrightable content. Additionally, workers should look to organizing groups for advocacy support, such as a union, trade association, or to Sara Horowitz's Freelancers Union. Finally, organizations dedicated to bettering the lives of American artists ought to survey employee classification in their communities to provide policymakers a clearer picture of revenue streams and misclassification in the arts.

It may be that new lines may need to be drawn on employee classification—that this legal framework has not been poked enough—but in the meantime, the decision to hire contractors involves much more than pinching pennies. Especially when you have a Picasso on staff.

---

[199] Nate Thayer, *A Day in the Life of a Freelance Journalist* (2013), https://natethayer.wordpress.com/2013/03/04/a-day-in-the-life-of-a-freelance-journalist-2013/.

[200] The general consensus of the panelists—made up of news industry representatives—was that cutting labor costs was a poor long-term solution, as it would sacrifice quality. Howes, *supra* note 196.

[201] Peter C. Godfrey, *The Employee or Independent Contractor Dilemma: Practical Advice to Minimize Misclassification-Related Risks and Exposure*, ASPATORE 6–9 (2014).

APPENDIX

FEDERAL AND MINNESOTA STATE
EMPLOYEE CLASSIFICATION
EMPLOYEE V. INDEPENDENT CONTRACTOR

This chart is only meant to serve as a guide to the various laws affected by employee classification. Every situation is evaluated on a case-by-case basis. Laws are subject to change, and up to interpretation by the judiciary. Chart updated by Sarah A. Howes, J.D. in October 2015.

Law	Description	Relevant Statutes and Case Law	Test
DEED: Unemployment Insurance	"The Minnesota Unemployment Insurance (UI) Program provides a temporary partial wage replacement to those Minnesota workers who become unemployed through no fault of their own." Employers are only required to pay UI taxes for employees.	Statute: Minn. Stat. § 268. Cases: Guhlke v. Roberts Truck Lines, 128 N.W.2d 324 (1964) ("the most important factor considered in light of the nature of the work is the right of the employer to control the means and manner of the performance"); St. Croxi Sensory, Inc., v. DEED, 785 N.W.2d 796 (Minn. Ct. App. 2010).	(1) The right to control the means and manner of performance; (2) the mode of payment; (3) the furnishing of material or tools; (4) the control of the premises where the work is done; and (5) the right of the employer to discharge.

DLS: Minnesota Fair Labor Standards Act	Employees, whether part-time or full-time, must receive a minimum wage and overtime pay that is set by law. www.dli.mn.gov/LS/Pdf/minwage_er-rates.pdf	Statue: The law exempts certain workers. *See* Minn. Stat. § 177.23, subd. 7.	Adopts the same test as DEED
DLS: Workers' Compensation	Employees receive benefits for injuries or illnesses caused or made worse by the workplace, regardless of fault by either the employer or employee.	Statute: Minn. Stat. § 176.011, subd. 9. Case: Iverson v. Independent School District, 257 N.W.2d 573 (1977) (finding an independent contractor)	Adopts the same test as DEED

MDOR: State Income Tax	Employers must "withhold and deposit income taxes, Social Security taxes and Medicare taxes." Contractors are permitted to file Schedule C forms to deduct business expenses.	Statute: Minn. Stat. § 290.92, subd. 1(3). Agency Doc: Withholding Fact Sheet 8 ("If you are generally in control of (or have the right to control) these factors, the worker is most likely your employee.") Case: Hetland v. Comm'n of Revenue, 2011 WL 1045457 (Minn. Tax Regular Div. 2011) (finding employees)	(1) Behavior Control; (2) Financial Control; and (3) Relationship of the Parties
EEOC: Title VII	Title VII of the Civil Rights Act of 1964 protects against many offenses, including sexual harassment. It applies to both government agencies and private businesses who employ more than 15 employees. The law prohibits	Statute: 42 U.S.C. § 2000e(f) (Title VII) Cases: Farlow v. Wachovia Bk. of North Carolina, 259 F.3d 309, 313 (4th Cir. 2001) (finding a contractor) ("We place greater weight on: 1) the financial relationship	Restatement (Second) of Agency § 220 (1958). (1) The hiring party's right to control the manner and means by which the product is accomplished; (2) the skill required; (3) the source of the instrumentalities and tools; (4) the

	against unwelcome sexual advances that interfere with work performance, one's employment, or that creates a hostile work environment. Note for contractors: Despite claims under Title VII require employee classification, EEO counselors are instructed to facilitate a resolution between a worker and a government agency. *See* Workbook: Independent Contractor v. Employee (2012).	between the parties in which she was paid not a salary but only in response to her bills, for services actually rendered; 2) the financial relationship between the parties in which Wachovia did not withhold or pay any taxes that are incident to an employment relationship; 3) the financial relationship between the parties in which Farlow did not receive employee benefits such as medical and life insurance; 4) Farlow's filing of income tax returns under a self-employed status; 5) the express intent of the parties as indicated in the contract Farlow signed labeling her as an independent contractor; 6) that Farlow did not work exclusively for Wachovia during her working	location of the work; (5) the duration of the relationship between the parties; (6) whether the hiring party has the right to assign additional projects to the hired party; (7) the extent of the hired party's discretion over when and how long to work; (8) the method of payment; (9) the hired party's role in hiring and paying assistants; (10) whether the work is part of the regular business of the hiring party; (11) whether the hiring party is in business; (12) the provision of employee benefits; and (13)the tax treatment of the hired party. Note: No one factor will prevail alone.

		relationship with it; and (7) that Wachovia exercised no control over the manner of her work.")	
DOL: FLSA - Federal Minimum Wage Law	This law applies to government agencies, schools, and companies that engage in interstate commerce (typically $500,000 in annual volume). Non-exempt employees must be provided a minimum wage (currently $7.25) and be provided overtime pay.	Statute: Fair Labor Standards Act, 29 U.S.C. § 203 (e)(1) Cases: See, e.g., Hopkins v. Cornerstone Am., 545 F.3d 338, 343 (5th Cir. 2008) ("To determine if a worker qualifies as an employee, we focus on whether, as a matter of economic reality, the worker is economically dependent upon the alleged employer or is instead in business for himself.") See DOL, Administrator's Interpretation No. 2015-1 (2015).	Economic Realities Factors typically include: A) The extent to which the work performed is an integral part of the employer's business; B) the worker's opportunity for sharing or loss depending on his or her managerial skills; (C) the extent of the relative investments of the employer and the worker; (D) whether the work performed requires special skills and initiative; (E) the permanency of the relationship; and (F) the degree of control exercised or retained by the employer. Note: Some courts have considered other factors.

DOL: Federal Family and Medical Leave Act	This law entitles a worker to unpaid, job-protected leave for certain family and medical reasons. A worker's health insurance may not be canceled during the leave. Applies to employees whose employer employs fifty or more employees within 75 miles of the worksite.	Statute: 29 U.S.C. § 2611(3) Cases: Bonnetts v. Arctic Express, Inc., 7 F. Supp. 2d 977 (S.D. Ohio 1998).	Adopts the same test as FLSA
IRS: Federal Income Tax	Both the federal government and your state government is allowed to tax income.	Agency Doc: Topic 762 – Independent Contractor v. Employee Cases: Robert Patrick Day v. Comm', 80 T.C.M. 834 (2000); Gierek v. Commissioner, 66 T.C.M. 1866 (1993) (finding employee) ("doubtful questions should be resolved in favor of employment in order to accomplish the remedial purposes of the legislation involved).	(1) Behavior Control; (2) Financial Control; and (3) Relationship of the Parties

| NLRA: Federal Labor Laws | The NLRB is the government authority that regulates collective bargaining and the formation of labor unions.

All workers are afforded certain collective bargaining rights, including section 7 rights to engage in concerted activity, but only employees are afforded the full protections of this law. | Statute: 29 U.S.C. § 152(3)

Cases: *FedEx Home Delivery v. NLRB*, 563 F.3d 492, 496 (D.C. Cir. 2009)

See generally Micah Prieb Stolzfus Jost, Note, *Independent Contractors, Employees, and Entrepreneurialism Under the National Relations Act: A Worker-by-Worker Approach* 68 Wash. & Lee L. Rev 311 (2011) (providing a history and illustrating various attempts to address misclassification, including Pres. Obama's 2011 proposed budget to increase the DOL staff to identify employers who misclassify employees). | Restatement (Second) of Agency § 220 (1958). |
| Federal: U.S. Copyright Act | Under the work made for hire doctrine, the copyrighted products of an | Statute: 17 U.S.C. § 101(1),(2)

Cases: Community for Creative Non- | All Agency Law Factors (above) for post-1978 works, but these are considered in most |

	employee are owned by his or her employer. Note: certain non-employees (aka statutory employees) may also be subject to this doctrine if their work is one of the enumerated works and an agreement is signed.	Violence v. Reid v. Reid, 490 U.S. 730 (1989) (post-1978 works) (Agency Law Test); Marvel v. Kirby 726 F.3d 119 (2d Cir. 2013) (pre-1978 works) ("Instance and Expense Test").	circumstances: (1) the hiring party's right to control the manner and means of creation; (2) the skill required; (3) the provision of employee benefits; (4) the tax treatment of the hired party; and (5) whether the hiring party has the right to assign additional projects to the hired party. Aymes v. Bonelli, 980 F.2d 857 (2d Cir. 1992) (noting that at the time "every case since Reid that has applied the test has found the hired party to be an independent contractor where the hiring party failed to extend benefits or pay social security taxes.)

Early Works by Pablo Picasso

The Old Guitarist (1903)   Sabartès Seated (1900)

www.ingramcontent.com/pod-product-compliance
Lightning Source LLC
Chambersburg PA
CBHW030935180526
45163CB00002B/568